Putting On The Grits

presented by

THE

JUNIOR

LEAGUE

OF

COLUMBIA

SOUTH CAROLINA

The purpose of the Junior League is exclusively educational and charitable and is to promote voluntarism, to develop the potential of its members for voluntary participation in community affairs, and to demonstrate the effectiveness of trained volunteers. Proceeds from the sale of **Putting On The Grits** will be used to support Junior League projects in the community.

First Edition

First Printing: 10,000 copies, March 1985
Second Printing: 10,000 copies, October 1985
Third Printing: 5,000 copies, October 1989
Fourth Printing: 5,000 copies, September 1990
Fifth Printing: 5,000 copies, March 1993

Additional copies may be obtained by addressing:

Putting On The Grits
The Junior League of Columbia, Inc.
3612 Landmark Drive, Suite A
Columbia, South Carolina 29204

Library of Congress Catalog Card Number: 84-23356

ISBN 0-9613561-0-3

Printed in the United States of America
by
State Printing Company
Columbia, South Carolina

Introduction

The slow, gracious Southern way of life still exists and flourishes in South Carolina. Opportunities abound to celebrate with friends, family and good food. A wealth of bounty from the coastal waters and inland farms ensure never-ending temptations to the cook. Plentiful game in the region means enticing kitchen aromas from a day's hunt. To many, a gastronomic trip through Southern cooking would not be complete without an array of sideboard sweets.

All this and more awaits you in **Putting On The Grits**. Our book attempts to bring you the best selection of our regional favorites; some time-honored, some new.

The Cookbook Committee

Ellen Dozier
Lucy Little

Jean Humphrey
Janet Timmerman

Nancy Schulhoff
Plum Hammond

Committee Members

Kathy Armato	Bit Howell	Elizabeth D. Powers
Susie Ashley	Sue Lacy	Barbara Ransford
Nan Bracy	Susalee Lamb	Sally Shelnut
Kathy Bristow	Alice Lashley	Johnie Smith
Frannie Bryan	Cindy Macdonald	Jill Tobias
Carole Clark	Louise Martin	Amelia Usry
Elizabeth Clark	Jane McCutcheon	Ann Waites
Nancy Dukes	Pat McKay	Suzanne Warthen
Mary Grimball	Beth McMaster	Margaret Webb
Edith Hines	Elizabeth Moore	Elmira Weston

The recipes in **Putting On The Grits** were tested for quality by Active, Provisional and Sustaining members of The Junior League of Columbia and their family and friends.

Cover art and divider pages were created by Martha-Elizabeth Ferguson, a free-lance artist and illustrator for commission as well as gallery exhibition. Her first major exhibition was during the 1984 Spoleto Festival, U.S.A., in Charleston, South Carolina. An alumnus of the North Carolina School of Arts and the University of South Carolina, Martha-Elizabeth has her work displayed in national galleries and private collections.

Table of Contents

Entertaining

Entertaining brings to mind a spotless house, best table linens, beautifully prepared food from your favorite recipes, and relaxed and genial hosts. The Southern approach recalls wafting strains of soft music, scents of jasmine or wisteria floating in the wind and unobtrusive servants passing silver trays of centuries-old family receipts.

This region, as in all other areas of our country, has been affected by the hustle and bustle of contemporary living, and all forms of entertaining are acceptable in today's South. Our best formula for a successful gathering is to let the entertainment reflect your own style and personality. Do what is comfortable for you, and your guests will naturally enjoy themselves. From the most casual of beach parties to the elegance of a gourmet dinner, your personal choice of serving pieces, food, flowers and music will set the mood you wish to create and which is distinctly you.

As a general rule of thumb to follow for large groups, we offer this guideline of quantities needed.

FOR 50 PEOPLE

Bar Needs

Glasses:	36 highball 36 wine 36 old-fashioned
Liquor:	½ case mixed: Scotch, bourbon, vodka plus 1 bottle rum and 1 bottle gin
Beer:	3-4 6 packs
White wine:	1 gallon
Mixer:	1½ cases mixed: club soda, gingerale, cola, tonic, Perrier water
Ice:	1 pound per person
Non-Alcoholic:	Sparkling cider (available at wine shops)
Bar fruit:	3 limes, 3 lemons, cherries

Food Items

Beef:	2 tenderloins (approximately 10-14 pounds)
Turkey:	1 20 pound
Seafood:	10 pounds
Pâté :	2 pounds
Cheese:	8-inch round Brie, 3-inch wedge Cheddar, 3-inch wedge blue, 1 cheeseball
Crackers:	4 1-pound boxes
Sandwiches:	25, cut into fourths
Bread:	4 loaves, thin-sliced
Mayonnaise:	4 cups
Mustard:	3 small jars

Vegetables for Dips and Marinades

Vegetables	Amount	Marinade
Artichoke hearts	3 14-ounce cans	1 cup
Broccoli	4 heads	2 cups
Carrots	4 pounds, blanched	1 cup
Cauliflower	3 heads, blanched	1½ cups
Cherry tomatoes	3 pints	1½ cups
Cucumbers	6	1 cup
Mushrooms	3 pounds	2 cups
Squash, yellow	10	1½ cups
Zucchini	6	1 cup

Dip for vegetables: 3 cups (Choose 5 vegetables from preceding list)

Fruits

Strawberries	4 pints
Grapes	2 pounds
Melons	2 ripe, each type

1 1-pound box powdered sugar, sifted, for fruit

Sweets

1 serving per person

Menus

Many tempting combinations are possible for you in **Putting On The Grits**. Some of our favorites follow, but we encourage you to explore and experiment.

CAROLINA CUP STEEPLECHASE PICNIC

Sweet Potato Biscuits with Country Ham

Marinated Shrimp   *Fried Chicken*

Sea Shell Party Salad

Dilly Dip for Fresh Vegetables

Better Than Brownies   *Raspberry Squares*

FOOTBALL TAILGATE

Bloody Marys   *Mexican Quiche*

Broccoli Cornbread

Marinated Cucumber Salad

Rice Salad   *Fresh Apple Cake*

Menus

COCKTAILS FOR FIFTY

Brie Quiche   Cozy's Artichokes

Company Tenderloin with Spicy Beef Spread

Coastal Crab Mold   Pumpernickel Bread

Bollin Party Sandwiches

Hot Broccoli Dip   Sherried Cheese Ball

Sugared Peanuts

COKE-TAILS FOR TEENS

Soft Drinks

Hot Mini-Reubens   Mayfest Meatballs

Tex-Mex Dip   Harvest Popcorn

Chocolate Heaven   Pecan Sandies

Menus

DEBUTANTE BRUNCH

Plantation Cooler

Mushroom Canapés   Caviar Egg Mold

Cold Crabmeat Omelets with Tomato Mayonnaise Sauce

Cinnamon Pecan Rolls

Summer Fruit Salad with Poppy Seed Dressing

SPRING AZALEA BREAKFAST

Raspberry Fizzlet

Stewed Shrimp with Grits

or

Overnight French Toast

Greenwood Sherried Fruit   Poppy Seed Coffee Cake

BRIDAL SHOWER LUNCHEON

Melon Ball and Shrimp Salad

Stuffed Chicken Breasts with Avocado Curry Sauce   Ice Box Rolls

Carrots Consommé   Jenny's Strawberry Torte

Menus

BEACH HOUSE WEEKEND

Mushrooms à la Grecque

Tossed Salad with White Wine Vinegar

Beaufort Stew   Herbed Pita Toast

Best Fudge Cake

GET-TO-KNOW-YOUR NEIGHBORS PARTY

Vichyssoise   or   Gazpacho

Cheese Straws   Waccamaw Crab Quiche

Smoked Turkey   Tarragon Dill Slaw

Frozen Tomato Salad with Horseradish Dressing

Apricot Florentine Cookies   Amaretto Cheesecake

JUST FAMILY SUNDAY SUPPER

Sherman's Spaghetti

Spinach and Orange Salad with Honey-Caraway Dressing

English Muffin Bread   Sophie's Bar Cookies

Menus

SOUTHERN CLASSIC SUPPER

Southern Iced Tea

Buttermilk Biscuits   Dingle Shrimp Sauté

Chicken Bog

Fried Green Tomatoes   Southern Green Beans

Artichoke Pickle

Swamp Fox Peach Pie

GOURMET DINNER FOR SIX

Bermuda Rum Swizzle

Avocado Velvet Soup

Christening Day Seafood Appetizer

Elegant Stuffed Veal Loin with Duxelles

Green Beans with Dill   Wild Rice with Pecans

Popovers

Italian Meringue Cake

Menus

HUNT BOARD REPAST

Fresh Tomato Soup

Cream Cheese Biscuits with Amaretto Peach Preserves

Hot Spinach Molds on Tomato Rings

Sweet Potato Casserole

Sherried Quail Palmetto Bluff Lodge

Grilled Venison Loin

Mahogany Cake

CHRISTMAS EVE BUFFET

Party Champagne Punch   *Eggnog*

Avocado with Caviar

Crab and Artichoke Casserole

Marinated Tenderloin   *Herbed Cheese Bread*

Broccoli - Stuffed Tomatoes   *Garlic Rice*

Baked Mushrooms

Lemon Charlotte surrounded by Pots de Crème

Appetizers

Appetizers

*Other Appetizer recipes may be found in **Southern Classics.***

Appetizers

Asparagus Sandwiches

1   15-ounce can asparagus
1   8-ounce package cream
     cheese, softened
½   cup mayonnaise
3-4 dashes Tabasco sauce
     Salt to taste

1   3-ounce package slivered
     almonds or chopped pecans
1   small onion, grated
1   16-ounce loaf thinly sliced
     whole wheat bread

Drain and mash asparagus, blotting any juice with paper towel. Mix asparagus and remaining ingredients with electric mixer until well blended. Refrigerate until ready to use. To serve, spread generously on bread slices, top with another slice and cut in quarters, trimming crust if desired. Yields 15 whole sandwiches, 5 dozen quarters.

Bollin Party Sandwiches

1   8-ounce package cream
     cheese
1   4½-ounce can pitted black
     olives, drained and sliced
6-7 slices crisp bacon, crumbled
1   cup finely chopped toasted
     pecans

1   cup chopped fresh parsley
1   small onion, grated
2   teaspoons lemon juice
     Salt and pepper to taste
     Mayonnaise for desired
      consistency
     Sandwich bread

Soften cheese and add other ingredients. Mix well. Spread filling generously to make sandwiches. Trim crusts and cut into triangles. Yields 7 dozen small sandwiches.

Appetizers

Special Ham Rolls

1	cup butter	1	teaspoon Worcestershire sauce
3	tablespoons prepared mustard	3	7½-ounce packages party rolls
3	tablespoons poppy seed	½	pound boiled ham, chopped
1	medium onion, finely chopped	⅓	pound Swiss cheese, grated

In a small skillet, melt butter and add mustard, poppy seed, onion and Worcestershire. Cook over low heat until onions are transparent. Without separating into individual rolls, slice and open party rolls. Spread both sides evenly with sauce. Fill with ham and cheese. Return rolls to container and wrap each package in foil. Refrigerate until ready to use. Bake at 400 degrees for 10 to 20 minutes. Serves 10 to 12.

Excellent to prepare ahead and freeze. Good for picnics, football games or bridge. Country ham may be substituted for boiled ham for a special touch.

Asparagus Rolls

20	slices white bread, crust removed	1	egg, beaten
1	3-ounce package blue cheese	1	14-ounce can asparagus spears, drained
1	8-ounce package cream cheese, softened	1	cup butter, melted

Flatten bread with rolling pin. Mix cheeses together. Brush each slice of bread with egg; then spread with cheese mixture. Roll bread slice around 1 asparagus spear. Brush with melted butter. Freeze on a tray and transfer to freezer bags. When ready to use, thaw slightly and cut each roll into 3 or 4 pieces. Bake on ungreased baking sheet for 15 minutes at 375 degrees and serve warm. Yields 60 small rolls.

Appetizers

Herbed Pita Toast

¾ cup butter, softened
2 tablespoons finely chopped
   parsley
1 tablespoon chopped chives
1 tablespoon lemon juice
1 large clove garlic, finely
   chopped
   Salt and pepper to taste
6 pita loaves

Combine all ingredients except pita loaves; mix well and let stand covered at least 1 hour. Preheat oven to 450 degrees. Halve pita loaves horizontally and separate. Spread each half with mixture. Bake on ungreased baking sheet in top third of oven for about 10 minutes or until brown and crisp. Drain and cool. Break into bite-size pieces. Serves 12.

Hot Mini-Reubens

24 slices party rye bread
¼   cup Thousand Island salad
    dressing
¼   pound corned beef, thinly
    sliced
1   16-ounce can sauerkraut,
    well drained and chopped
4   ounces Swiss cheese, sliced

Spread each slice of bread with dressing. Layer a slice of corned beef and 1 tablespoon sauerkraut. Top with cheese cut to fit the bread. Bake on an ungreased baking sheet at 400 degrees for 10 minutes. Serve warm. Yields 24.

Variation: For a Reuben Dip, combine the following ingredients in top of a double boiler:

2 12-ounce cans corned beef,
   flaked
1 16-ounce can sauerkraut,
   drained and chopped
1 pound Swiss cheese, grated
6 tablespoons mayonnaise
2 tablespoons prepared
   mustard
2 tablespoons prepared
   horseradish, drained

Heat until cheese melts; transfer into chafing dish and serve with crackers or melba toast.

Appetizers

Hot Shrimp and Asparagus Rounds

½ cup mayonnaise
⅓ cup chopped water
    chestnuts
1 10½-ounce can asparagus
    tips, drained

¼ teaspoon curry powder
1 4½-ounce can tiny shrimp,
    drained
    Melba toast rounds
    Toasted sesame seed

Gently combine all ingredients except melba rounds and sesame seed. Spread about 1 teaspoon mixture on each round. Sprinkle with sesame seed and bake on an ungreased baking sheet at 350 degrees for 10 to 12 minutes. Serve hot. Yields approximately 40.

Spinach Cheese Squares

4 tablespoons butter
3 eggs
1 cup flour
1 cup milk
1 teaspoon salt
1 teaspoon baking powder

1 pound Monterey Jack
    cheese, grated
2 10-ounce packages frozen
    chopped spinach, thawed
    and well drained

Preheat oven to 350 degrees. Melt butter in oven in a 9 x 13-inch pan. Beat eggs in a large bowl. Add flour, milk, salt and baking powder. Mix well. By hand, fold in cheese and spinach. Pour into pan of melted butter. Bake 35 minutes at 350 degrees. Cool for 30 minutes. Cut into bite-size squares. Serves 10 to 12.

May be frozen and reheated in foil.

Appetizers

Cheesy Artichoke Squares

4   eggs, slightly beaten
½   pound Cheddar cheese, grated
¼   cup dry bread crumbs
1   14-ounce can artichoke hearts, drained and chopped
½   teaspoon salt
½   teaspoon dried oregano
½   teaspoon garlic powder
½   teaspoon dried basil
1-2   dashes Tabasco sauce
1   tablespoon finely chopped onion

Combine ingredients and mix well. Pour into a greased 8½ x 11-inch pan. Bake 30 minutes at 325 degrees. To serve, cut in squares and serve hot or cold. Yields 60 small squares.

Also excellent on crackers such as water wafers or in larger squares as a filling for pita bread. If desired, 1 cup each chopped green pepper and sliced mushrooms may be sautéed in butter and substituted for artichokes.

Stuffed Mushrooms

1½   pounds fresh mushrooms
⅓   cup grated Parmesan cheese
½   cup dry bread crumbs
½   cup grated onion
2   cloves garlic, finely chopped
2   tablespoons chopped parsley
1½   teaspoons salt
¼   teaspoon pepper
½   teaspoon dried oregano
¼-½ cup butter
    Fresh parsley or pimiento strips for garnish

Rinse and dry mushrooms. Remove and chop stems; reserve caps. Mix chopped stems with remaining ingredients except butter and garnish. Stuff mushroom caps with mixture and arrange in a lightly buttered shallow baking dish. Top each mushroom with a small amount of butter and bake at 350 degrees for 25 minutes. Serve warm, topping each with a small sprig of fresh parsley or slice of pimiento. Serves 10 to 15.

Appetizers

Mushroom Canapés

Cream cheese pastry:

3   3-ounce packages cream
     cheese, softened

½   cup butter
1½   cups sifted flour

Mushroom filling:

1   small onion, finely chopped
2   tablespoons butter
¼   pound fresh mushrooms,
     finely chopped
⅛   teaspoon dried thyme

¼   teaspoon salt
⅛   teaspoon pepper
1½   tablespoons flour
½   cup sour cream

Pastry: Combine cream cheese and butter. Add flour and work with hands to mix well and form a flattened ball. Wrap in waxed paper and chill at least 1 hour.

Mushroom filling: Sauté onion in butter until lightly browned. Add mushrooms, thyme, salt and pepper and cook about 5 minutes, stirring frequently. Sprinkle with flour and stir. Reduce heat and stir in sour cream. Cook, stirring constantly, until thickened. Cool, then chill.

To assemble: Roll out pastry to ⅛-inch thickness. Cut into 1½-inch rounds. Place ½ teaspoon of filling on each round and place on ungreased baking sheet. To serve, bake at 450 degrees for 15 minutes. Serve warm. Yields approximately 4 dozen.

Pastry and filling may be prepared several days ahead and frozen separately. Canapés may be assembled ahead of time, refrigerated and baked prior to serving.

Hot Bacon Bits

1½   cups brown sugar
1½   teaspoons dry mustard

2   pounds thick sliced bacon

Combine brown sugar and mustard. Place bacon slices in single layer in a shallow baking pan. Sprinkle with sugar mixture. Bake 1 hour at 250 degrees or until crisp. When completed, drain and cut into bite-size pieces. May be frozen and reheated. Serves 20.

Appetizers

Spicy Chicken Tidbits

1	8-ounce package cream cheese, softened	3	tablespoons chopped chutney
4	tablespoons mayonnaise	1	teaspoon salt
1½	cups chopped almonds	2	teaspoons curry powder
1	tablespoon butter	1	cup grated coconut
2	cups chopped cooked chicken		

Blend together cream cheese and mayonnaise. Sauté almonds in butter until lightly browned. Add almonds, chicken, chutney, salt, and curry powder to cheese mixture. Shape into 1-inch balls and roll in coconut. Chill until ready to serve. Yields 6 dozen.

May be frozen.

Chicken Nuggets

6	chicken breast halves, boned and skinned	¼	cup grated Parmesan cheese
½	cup butter	2	teaspoons MSG (optional)
½	cup unseasoned bread crumbs	1	teaspoon salt
		1	teaspoon dried thyme
		1	teaspoon dried basil

Cut breasts into bite-size pieces. Melt butter. Make mixture of remaining ingredients. Dip chicken in butter and then into bread crumb mixture. Place in a single layer on foil-lined baking sheet. Bake at 400 degrees for 20 minutes. Yields 40 to 50 pieces.

Appetizers

Spinach Balls

2   10-ounce packages frozen
      chopped spinach
¼   cup finely chopped onion
2   cups herb seasoned stuffing
1   cup grated Parmesan cheese
6   eggs, beaten

¾   cup butter, softened
    Dash garlic salt
    Dash onion juice
    Dash cayenne pepper
    Salt to taste

Cook spinach according to package directions and drain well. Combine all ingredients, mixing well. Form into ½-inch balls. Freeze on baking sheet; then place in freezer bag. Without thawing, bake 15 minutes at 350 degrees. Serve with a curry, mustard or cocktail sauce. Serves 8.

Chutney Cheese Canapés

2   8-ounce packages cream
      cheese, softened
½   cup chutney
½   teaspoon dry mustard

2   teaspoons curry powder
1   large pineapple
    Toasted almonds for garnish

Blend cream cheese, chutney, dry mustard and curry. Let stand for 4 hours. Cut pineapple in half and scoop out meat and reserve for other use. Fill with cheese mixture. Sprinkle with almonds. Serve with crackers. Serves 24.

To make cheese ball: Form cheese mixture into a ball and roll in chopped pecans. Refrigerate until firm. Serve with crackers.

Appetizers

Cocktail Crêpe Stack

12	crêpes (recipe follows)	¼	cup finely chopped green pepper
2	8-ounce packages cream cheese, softened	2	tablespoons finely chopped onion
1	8½-ounce can crushed pineapple, drained	1	tablespoon seasoned salt
2	cups finely chopped pecans, divided	1	3-ounce package cream cheese, softened, for garnish

Prepare crêpes; set aside. Combine all ingredients except 1 cup pecans and 3-ounce package cream cheese. Mix well. Alternate layers of crêpes and filling, ending with filling. Garnish top with cream cheese piped around edge and remaining pecans sprinkled over the center. Loosely cover and refrigerate several hours. To serve, cut into small wedges. Serves 20.

The cheese filling may also be made into a ball, rolled in chopped pecans and served with crackers. Other cheese balls or spreads may be substituted as filling for a crêpe stack.

Basic Crêpe Recipe

1	cup cold water	½	teaspoon salt
1	cup cold milk	2	cups sifted flour
4	eggs	4	tablespoons butter, melted

Place the liquids, eggs and salt in a blender. Add flour and butter. Cover and blend at high speed for 1 minute. Strain batter and refrigerate at least 2 hours. Cook crêpes in a skillet or commercial crêpe pan. Stack between pieces of waxed paper. Yields 12 crêpes.

Freeze crêpes between sheets of waxed paper in a plastic bag and remove as needed.

Appetizers

Christening Day Seafood Appetizer

Ingredients:

1	pound fresh scallops	1	13-ounce can pitted black olives, sliced and drained
2	tablespoons butter		
1	pound cooked cleaned shrimp	½	head raw cauliflower, broken into flowerets
2	8-ounce cans sliced water chestnuts, drained	2	cups cherry tomatoes, halved

Sauce:

2	cups mayonnaise	2	teaspoons hot dry mustard
½	cup prepared horseradish, drained	2	teaspoons lemon juice
½	teaspoon MSG (optional)	½	teaspoon salt

In a skillet, gently sauté scallops in butter until they are white, about 3 minutes. Do not overcook. Combine seafood and vegetables and set aside. To prepare sauce, combine all ingredients, mixing well. Add sauce to seafood mixture and toss. Refrigerate overnight to marinate. Serve in a bowl resting in crushed ice and provide individual plates.

For a richer appetizer, double the sauce recipe.

Scotch Eggs

6	hard-cooked eggs, peeled Salt and pepper to taste	1	tablespoon finely chopped onion
3	ounces herb seasoned stuffing	⅛	teaspoon ground nutmeg
½	pound mild bulk sausage	1	egg, beaten
½	pound hot bulk sausage		Additional herb seasoned stuffing
½	teaspoon grated lemon rind		

Sprinkle eggs with salt and pepper. Finely crush stuffing in blender or food processor and combine with sausage, lemon rind, onion and nutmeg to make a paste. Mold the paste ¼-inch thick around each individual egg, covering completely. Dip in beaten egg and roll in additional crushed stuffing. Fry in deep fat at 375 degrees for 5 minutes. To serve, cut in halves or quarters and serve with spicy mustard. Yields 6 eggs.

May be prepared ahead and frozen. Reheat in oven.

Appetizers

Miniature Mushroom Cups

1   pound fresh mushrooms, chopped
2   tablespoons chopped parsley
2   tablespoons finely chopped onion
2   tablespoons butter
½   cup pork sausage
2   tablespoons white wine

1   tablespoon ketchup
½   teaspoon salt
½   teaspoon celery salt
   Pepper to taste
4   tablespoons bread crumbs
9-10 slices very thin white bread
   Melted butter
   Grated Parmesan cheese

Sauté mushrooms, parsley and onion in butter and set aside. In a skillet, cook sausage and drain well. Blend sausage, wine and ketchup. Add salt, celery salt, pepper and bread crumbs. Set aside. Trim crusts from bread slices. Quarter each slice and mold into miniature muffin tins. Brush lightly with melted butter and bake at 350 degrees until lightly browned. Fill each bread cup with mushroom mixture. Sprinkle with Parmesan cheese. Bake 10 to 15 minutes at 350 degrees. Serve immediately. Yields approximately 3 dozen.

Individual Sausage Quiches

2   10-ounce packages refrigerated biscuits
1   pound bulk sausage, cooked and drained
10   eggs

5   cups cottage cheese
5   tablespoons chopped chives
   Pepper to taste
1¼   cups grated Parmesan cheese

Line 3-inch muffin tins with thin layer of biscuit dough. Place sausage on top of biscuits. Beat eggs and combine with cottage cheese, chives, pepper and cheese. Drop mixture from teaspoon over sausage. Bake at 350 degrees for 20 minutes. Yields 36 individual quiches.

May be frozen after baking; thaw and warm thoroughly before serving.

Appetizers

Brie Quiche

8	ounces Brie cheese, softened and rind removed	4	eggs, beaten
1	8-ounce package cream cheese, softened	4	dashes Tabasco sauce
¼	cup butter, softened	1	tablespoon chopped chives
6	tablespoons whipping cream	1	9-inch pie shell, partially baked

Mix Brie, cream cheese, butter and cream. Add eggs and blend until smooth. Add Tabasco and chives. Pour into pie shell and set in upper third of oven. Bake at 375 degrees for 25 to 30 minutes until puffed and brown. Serves 12.

May also be cut into bite-size pieces and served with toothpicks.

Marinated Fresh Artichokes

Ingredients:

8	fresh artichokes	½	lemon, sliced
½	teaspoon salt	2	tablespoons olive oil

Marinade:

½	cup vegetable oil	¼	teaspoon chopped parsley
½	cup olive oil	1½	teaspoons salt
4	tablespoons lemon juice	1½	teaspoons freshly ground pepper
2	tablespoons chopped chives		
¾	teaspoon dry mustard		

Wash artichokes, drain and cut off stems. Snip tips with scissors. Place in a large pan and cover with cold water; add salt, lemon and oil. Cook covered 30 to 45 minutes until leaves pull away. Drain and cool. Mix all marinade ingredients, pour over upright artichokes and refrigerate several hours or overnight. Serves 8.

Appetizers

Mushrooms à la Grecque

1½	pounds small whole mushrooms	1	bay leaf
			Pinch coriander
2	cups water	½	teaspoon dried thyme
1	tablespoon lemon juice	4	peppercorns
⅓	cup tarragon vinegar	1	teaspoon salt
¾	cup olive oil	3	tablespoons finely chopped
1	clove garlic, chopped		fresh parsley

Trim ends of mushroom stems. Put all ingredients except parsley in a saucepan. Bring to a boil and simmer for 5 minutes. Chill mixture overnight. To serve, drain and sprinkle mushrooms with parsley. Yields 30 to 36 mushrooms.

These keep for weeks and improve with age. Liquid may be saved and used again.

Marinated Shrimp

1	tablespoon sugar	1	green pepper, finely chopped
	Salt and pepper to taste		
2	tablespoons dry mustard	1	medium onion, finely chopped
1	cup vinegar		
1	cup ketchup	1	clove garlic, finely chopped
½	cup vegetable oil	1	teaspoon celery seed
1	teaspoon Worcestershire sauce	3	bay leaves
1	teaspoon Tabasco sauce	2-3	pounds raw shrimp, cooked and cleaned

Mix sugar, salt, pepper and dry mustard with vinegar and stir until smooth. Add remaining ingredients, except shrimp, and blend well. Pour over shrimp, cover and chill at least 24 hours. Keeps for two weeks in refrigerator. Serve undrained with toothpicks on the side. Serves 15 to 20.

Appetizers

Hot Broccoli Dip

1	10-ounce package frozen chopped broccoli	¼	teaspoon pepper
2	small onions, chopped	1	teaspoon Worcestershire sauce
2	tablespoons butter	¼	teaspoon Tabasco sauce
1	10¾-ounce can cream of mushroom soup	1	4-ounce can chopped or sliced mushrooms, drained
8	ounces garlic cheese	¾	cup slivered almonds

Cook broccoli and drain. Sauté onion in butter. Add soup, cheese and seasonings. Heat slowly until cheese melts. Add drained broccoli and cook 1 minute. Add mushrooms and almonds. Serve in a chafing dish with crackers or chips.

Mayfest Meatballs

2	pounds ground chuck	⅓	cup ketchup
1	cup cereal crumbs (corn flakes or bran)	¼	cup finely chopped onion
¼	cup parsley flakes	1	16-ounce can jellied cranberry sauce
2	eggs, beaten	1	12-ounce bottle chili sauce
2	tablespoons soy sauce	2	tablespoons brown sugar
¼	teaspoon pepper	1	tablespoon lemon juice
½	teaspoon garlic powder		

Combine ground chuck, cereal, parsley, eggs, soy sauce, pepper, garlic powder, ketchup and onion. Mold into 1-inch meatballs. Place in shallow baking dish. Blend cranberry sauce, chili sauce, brown sugar and lemon juice. Pour sauce over meatballs and bake uncovered for 20 to 30 minutes at 350 degrees. Serve in chafing dish with toothpicks on the side.

 To make perfectly round meatballs, bring a large saucepan of beef broth to a boil. Drop uncooked meatballs into broth. When they rise to the top, they are done and can be drained and placed in sauce. Shorten baking time if precooked.

Cozy's Artichoke Hearts

3	14-ounce cans artichoke hearts, drained and quartered	2	4-ounce packages blue cheese, crumbled
		1	cup butter, melted

Combine artichoke hearts and crumbled cheese. Place in a 1½-quart baking dish. Top with butter. Heat covered for 10 to 15 minutes at 350 degrees. Stir gently and spoon into a chafing dish. Serve on party crackers.

Seafood Fondue

5	8-ounce packages cream cheese	5	dashes Tabasco sauce
1	tablespoon prepared mustard	¼	cup dry Vermouth
2½	tablespoons mayonnaise	1	pound cooked cleaned shrimp, chopped
2	tablespoons garlic powder	1	pound crabmeat

Melt cream cheese and add all other ingredients except seafood. Remove from heat. Stir in shrimp and crabmeat. Refrigerate 24 hours. Reheat and serve in a fondue pot or chafing dish with French bread or crackers.

Must be prepared ahead.

Appetizers

Hilton Head Shrimp and Artichokes

4	tablespoons olive oil	½	teaspoon salt
2	cloves garlic, finely chopped		Dash freshly ground pepper
1	pound raw shrimp, cleaned	½	teaspoon dried oregano,
¼	pound small whole		crumbled
	mushrooms	2	tablespoons lemon juice
2	14-ounce cans artichoke	2	tablespoons chopped
	hearts, drained and		parsley
	quartered		

In a skillet, heat olive oil and sauté garlic. Add shrimp and mushrooms, stirring until shrimp turn pink. Add artichokes, salt, pepper and oregano. Heat thoroughly. Sprinkle with lemon juice and parsley. Stir to blend flavors. Serve in a chafing dish with toothpicks. Serves 20 to 25.

Elegant!

Caviar Egg Mold

1	teaspoon unflavored gelatin	1	cup mayonnaise
2	tablespoons dry sherry	1	teaspoon Worcestershire
2	tablespoons fresh lemon		sauce
	juice	1	2½-ounce jar lumpfish
6	hard-cooked eggs		caviar

Generously grease 2-cup mold. Soften gelatin in sherry and lemon juice in a small saucepan over very low heat until gelatin is dissolved, stirring several times. Chop eggs in food processor or blender. Transfer to mixing bowl. Stir in gelatin, mayonnaise and Worcestershire and mix thoroughly. Turn into mold. Cover and refrigerate until firm. Unmold and layer top with caviar. Serve with crackers or thin slices of black bread. Serves 12 to 15.

Appetizers

Coastal Crab Mold

1	pound fresh backfin crabmeat	1	teaspoon Worcestershire sauce
1	cup finely chopped celery	2	teaspoons chopped chives
3	hard-cooked eggs, chopped	1	teaspoon salt
2	tablespoons lemon juice		Onion juice to taste
1	cup mayonnaise		Pepper and cayenne pepper to taste
1	envelope unflavored gelatin		
2	cubes beef bouillon		Parsley for garnish
⅓	cup warm water		Olive for garnish
4	dashes Tabasco sauce		

Combine first 5 ingredients. In smaller bowl, dissolve gelatin and bouillon cubes in water. When completely dissolved, add to first mixture. Add remaining seasonings. Pour into lightly oiled 4-cup fish mold. Chill until firm. To serve, unmold and garnish with an olive for the eye and parsley around sides. Serve with crackers. Serves 20.

Shrimp and Clam Mold

1	envelope unflavored gelatin	½	cup chopped onions
¼	cup water	2	4½-ounce cans shrimp, drained, rinsed and chopped
1	6½-ounce can clams, finely chopped		
1	8-ounce package cream cheese	2	teaspoons lemon juice
			Tabasco sauce to taste
1	cup mayonnaise		Salt and pepper to taste
1	cup chopped celery		Parsley for garnish

Soften gelatin in water. Drain clams, reserving juice. Heat clam juice and add to gelatin, stirring until dissolved. Set aside.

Soften cream cheese. Mix with mayonnaise. Add remaining ingredients and mix well. Pour into lightly oiled 1-quart mold. Refrigerate until firm. Unmold and garnish with parsley. Serve with crackers.

Appetizers

Chicken Liver Pâté

6	tablespoons butter	1	pound chicken livers
½	cup finely chopped yellow onion	2	tablespoons cognac
		½	teaspoon salt
2	cloves garlic, chopped (optional)		Pepper to taste
		½	teaspoon ground allspice
1	teaspoon dried thyme	5	teaspoons water-packed green peppercorns, drained and divided
2	bay leaves		
10	black peppercorns		
½	cup celery tops	¼	cup whipping cream
6	cups water		

Melt butter in skillet. Add onion, garlic and thyme. Cook covered until onion is tender. Place bay leaves, black peppercorns and celery tops in a large saucepan with water. Bring to a boil, reduce heat and simmer for 10 minutes. Add chicken livers to water and simmer for 10 minutes. Drain livers and discard celery tops, bay leaves and peppercorns. Place livers and onion mixture in a food processor. Add cognac, salt, pepper, allspice and 4 teaspoons of green peppercorns. Process until smooth. Pour in cream and process again. Stir in by hand the remaining teaspoon of green peppercorns. Scrape mixture into a 2-cup serving container. Cover and refrigerate 4 hours. Let stand at room temperature for 30 minutes before serving. Yields 2 cups.

Dilly Dip for Fresh Vegetables

1	cup sour cream	2	tablespoons parsley flakes
1	cup mayonnaise	¼	cup finely chopped onion
2	tablespoons dried dill weed	2-3	teaspoons seasoned salt

Combine ingredients and mix well. Refrigerate several hours before serving. Yields 2 cups.

Appetizers

Marshland Crab Dip

1½   cups mayonnaise
1¾   cups fresh crabmeat
½   cup grated sharp Cheddar
     cheese

1   tablespoon prepared
     horseradish, drained
1   tablespoon Worcestershire
     sauce
1   tablespoon French dressing

Mix all ingredients together and chill about 2 hours. Serve with crackers. Serves 20 people.

Spinach Dip

2   cups sour cream
1   cup mayonnaise
1   2-ounce package Knorr's
     onion soup mix
1   10-ounce package frozen
     chopped spinach, thawed
     and drained

1   8-ounce can sliced water
     chestnuts, drained and
     chopped
½   cup chopped green onions
½   cup chopped parsley
1   teaspoon salad seasoning
     Dash garlic powder

Combine all ingredients. Refrigerate several hours. Serve with chips or crackers. Serves 20 generously.

Appetizers

Tex-Mex Dip

2   10½-ounce cans jalapeño bean dip
3   medium avocados, peeled and mashed
2   tablespoons lemon juice
½   teaspoon salt
¼   teaspoon pepper
1   cup sour cream
½   cup mayonnaise

1   1¼-ounce package taco seasoning
6-8 green onions, chopped
2   medium tomatoes, cored and chopped
1   7-ounce can pitted black olives, drained and chopped
1   cup grated sharp Cheddar cheese

Spread bean dip in bottom of a 12-inch plate with a rim or a 9 x 13-inch casserole. In a food processor, blend avocados, lemon juice, salt and pepper until smooth. Spread mixture on top of bean dip layer. Mix together sour cream, mayonnaise and taco seasoning and spread over avocado layer. Continue layering with chopped onion, tomatoes and black olives; top with cheese. If refrigerated, allow to reach room temperature before serving. Serve with crispy tortilla chips. Serves 20 to 25.

As eye-catching as it is delicious!

Sarah's Olive and Pecan Spread

1   3-ounce package cream cheese with chives, softened
1   cup sour cream
1   tablespoon finely chopped onion
½   teaspoon Tabasco sauce
½   teaspoon Beau Monde seasoning

1½ cups chopped black olives
1   cup chopped salted pecans
    Pepper to taste
    Melba toast rounds
    Paprika and chopped fresh parsley for garnish

In a bowl, beat together cream cheese and sour cream. Stir in onion, Tabasco, Beau Monde, olives, pecans and pepper. Cover and chill overnight. To serve, spread the mixture on toast rounds and garnish lightly with paprika and parsley. Yields approximately 3 cups.

Appetizers

Amaretto Cheese Spread

1   8-ounce package cream
      cheese
¼   cup Amaretto liqueur

1   2½-ounce package slivered
      almonds, sautéed in butter

Soften cream cheese and blend in Amaretto. Form a ball and chill until firm. Before serving, cover with almonds and allow to reach room temperature. Serve with thinly sliced apples and pears which have been soaked in pineapple juice to prevent browning.

This also may be served as after-dinner fruit and cheese.

Beer Cheese

1   pound sharp Cheddar
      cheese, grated
1   6-ounce jar Olde English-
      style cheese spread
¼   pound blue cheese
1   teaspoon dry mustard
2   teaspoons butter, softened

1   teaspoon Worcestershire
      sauce
2   teaspoons grated onion
1   cup beer
2   3-5 pound round loaves rye
      bread
     Paprika

Soften cheeses. In a medium-size bowl, combine all ingredients except beer, bread and paprika. Add beer slowly and beat until smooth and fluffy. Remove the center from one of the rounds of bread, forming a bowl. Do not cut through bottom of bread. Fill bread loaf with cheese mixture and garnish with paprika. Tear remaining bread and second loaf into bite-size pieces. Place around filled bread. Bread pieces are used to dip into cheese mixture.

Appetizers

Boursin Cheese

2	8-ounce packages cream cheese, softened	¼	teaspoon dried basil
		¼	teaspoon dried marjoram
1	8-ounce carton whipped butter	2	cloves garlic, finely chopped
		¼	teaspoon salt
1	teaspoon dried oregano	¼	teaspoon freshly ground pepper
¼	teaspoon dried dill weed		
¼	teaspoon dried thyme	½	teaspoon paprika

Mix all ingredients with an electric mixer. Place in an airtight container and store in refrigerator 3 to 4 days. Serve with crackers. Serves 10 to 15.

Brie and Bacon Spread

1	9-inch wheel Brie cheese	1	pound lean bacon, cooked and crumbled
1	9-ounce jar chutney		

Remove top rind of Brie, leaving ½-inch border, and place in 9-inch pie or quiche pan. Spread chutney on top. Sprinkle bacon on top of chutney. Bake at 325 degrees for 20 to 30 minutes. Serve spread, still in baking dish, with crackers. Serves 20.

Brown sugar and pecans may be substituted for chutney and bacon.

Sherried Cheese Ball

8	ounces Cheddar cheese, grated	3	tablespoons sherry
			Salt to taste
1	8-ounce package cream cheese, softened		Tabasco sauce to taste
		1	9-ounce jar chutney
1½	teaspoons chopped onion	4-6	green onions, chopped
1	teaspoon curry powder		

Combine cheeses, onion, curry, sherry, salt and Tabasco. Shape into ball. Pour chutney over ball and sprinkle with onions. Serve with crackers.

Appetizers

Hot Mushroom Spread

2	medium onions, chopped	1	pound mushrooms, chopped
½	cup butter	½	teaspoon Worcestershire
1	8-ounce package cream		sauce
	cheese, softened		Salt and pepper to taste
1	clove garlic, finely chopped		Melba toast rounds

Sauté onions in butter. Combine onions with remaining ingredients and blend well. Fold into small ungreased baking dish and bake uncovered for 20 minutes at 375 degrees. Serve on melba toast rounds.

Lowcountry Crab Spread

1	8-ounce package cream	½	teaspoon prepared
	cheese, softened		horseradish, drained
1	6½-ounce can crabmeat,	¼	teaspoon salt
	drained		Dash pepper
2	tablespoons finely chopped		Dash lemon juice
	onion	⅓	cup slivered almonds,
1	tablespoon milk		toasted (optional)

Combine all ingredients except almonds until well blended. Spoon into 8-inch square casserole, sprinkle with almonds and bake at 375 degrees for 15 to 20 minutes. Serve hot with crackers or melba toast rounds. Serves 6 to 8.

 Store prepared horseradish sauce upside down in jar in refrigerator to retain freshness.

Appetizers

Carolina Cup Shrimp Spread

½	cup butter, softened	2	teaspoons lemon juice
1	8-ounce package cream cheese, softened	2	tablespoons finely chopped onion
2	teaspoons mayonnaise	4	stalks celery, finely chopped
	Dash pepper	2	4½-ounce cans small shrimp, drained
⅛	teaspoon Worcestershire sauce		

Cream first 6 ingredients, mixing well. Add onion, celery and shrimp. Place in airtight container and refrigerate several hours or overnight. Serve with crackers. Yields 2 cups.

Flavor is improved if prepared the day before serving. An excellent filling for tiny cream puffs.

Sugared Peanuts

1	cup sugar	2	cups raw shelled peanuts
1	cup water		

Dissolve sugar in water in large saucepan over medium heat. Add peanuts and cook, stirring frequently until peanuts are completely sugared, with no liquid remaining. Spread peanuts on ungreased baking sheet, separating peanuts with fork. Bake 10 minutes at 350 degrees. Serves 4 to 6.

An excellent bridge party snack.

Beverages

Beverages

*Other Beverage recipes may be found in **Southern Classics.***

Beverages

Lemon Delight Punch

12	lemons	3	cups pineapple juice
5	cups sugar	4	cups ginger ale
2	cups water	1	gallon water

Squeeze lemons, reserving juice and rinds. In a saucepan, combine sugar and water and bring to a boil. Pour boiling syrup over lemon rinds and let stand for 24 hours. To serve, discard lemon rinds and mix lemon juice, syrup, pineapple juice, ginger ale and water in a punch bowl. Garnish with an ice mold. Serves 50.

Wonderful to serve for club meetings and teas.

Perkie Cranberry Punch

2	quarts cranberry juice	⅔	cup brown sugar
2	quarts unsweetened pineapple juice	1	tablespoon whole cloves
		1	tablespoon whole allspice
1	quart water	4	cinnamon sticks
2	lemons, quartered and seeded		

Combine liquids and lemons in bottom of 30-cup electric percolator. Place remaining ingredients in basket of percolator. Perk 30 minutes. Serves 25.

Brunch Punch

1	46-ounce can pineapple-grapefruit juice	1	46-ounce can apple juice
		2	quarts ginger ale, chilled
1	46-ounce can grapefruit juice		Red food coloring (optional)

In a large plastic container, mix together the juices. Freeze. Remove from freezer 4 to 5 hours before serving. Place in a large punch bowl and add ginger ale. Yields 1½ gallons.

Children and adults love this! For a small punch bowl, freeze the mixed juices in two plastic containers.

Beverages

Presbyterian Punch

1	quart boiling water	1	12-ounce can frozen
2	family-size tea bags		lemonade, thawed
1¼	cups sugar	1	46-ounce can pineapple
1	12-ounce can frozen orange		juice
	juice, thawed		Mint for garnish (optional)

Steep tea in boiling water for 30 minutes. Remove tea bags and add sugar while still hot. Add enough water to dilute tea to 1 gallon. Add orange juice and lemonade and the amount of water recommended on the cans. Add pineapple juice. Refrigerate. Serve over ice. Yields 2¼ gallons.

A perfect refresher to keep on hand on a hot summer day at the lake or beach.

Plantation Cooler

3	12-ounce cans frozen	3	quarts ginger ale, chilled
	lemonade	2	quarts club soda, chilled
3	12-ounce cans frozen	1	quart tonic water, chilled
	orange juice	1	gallon ice water
3	46-ounce cans pineapple	1-2	ice ring molds
	juice		

In a large punch bowl, mix together the liquids. Float ice molds on top. Serves 50.

Variations: Add 1 fifth vodka. Substitute 1 fifth champagne for ginger ale. Add cranberry juice to taste. Add fresh strawberry halves to taste.

Wedding Punch

1	quart orange juice	2	quarts vanilla ice cream
1	tablespoon honey	1	quart ginger ale
2	tablespoons lemon juice		

In a punch bowl, combine orange juice, honey and lemon juice. Add ice cream and let soften a few minutes. Pour ginger ale over ice cream and serve. Serves 25.

Also excellent for afternoon tea.

Beverages

Mulled Cider

8	quarts apple cider	48	whole allspice
1	cup sugar	48	whole cloves
48	cinnamon sticks	1	teaspoon salt

Combine all ingredients in a large pot. Bring to a boil. Cover and simmer for 15 minutes. Pour into a large jar or crock. Allow to stand for 12 hours. Strain and reheat to serve. Yields 2 gallons.

Hot Spiced Tea

2	cups sugar	1	46-ounce can pineapple juice
1	gallon water, divided	2	6-ounce cans frozen orange
2-4	whole cinnamon sticks		juice
22	whole cloves	8	small tea bags

Combine sugar, 8 cups water, cinnamon sticks and cloves in a large pot and boil for 10 minutes. Add fruit juices and simmer. In another pot, boil 8 cups water with tea bags for 10 minutes. Remove tea bags. Combine the two mixtures and simmer for at least 30 minutes. Serve warm. Yields 7 quarts.

Keeps beautifully in refrigerator for up to 10 days. May be reheated in a pot or individually heated in a mug in the microwave.

Robin's French Hot Chocolate

4	1-ounce squares semi-sweet chocolate	4	cups milk
¼	cup light corn syrup	1	cup whipping cream, whipped
½	teaspoon vanilla	8	peppermint sticks

Melt chocolate with corn syrup in a double-boiler. Cover and refrigerate for 30 minutes. Stir in vanilla. Heat milk in a saucepan until bubbles form around the edges. Add chocolate and stir. Divide the whipped cream equally among 8 mugs. Pour chocolate mixture over top. Garnish with peppermint sticks. Serves 8.

Beverages

Eggnog

12	eggs, separated	2½	quarts half and half
1	pound sugar	2	cups whipping cream
2-4	cups bourbon		Grated nutmeg, as needed
1	cup Jamaican rum		

At least 24 hours before serving, use mixer to blend egg yolks, sugar, bourbon and rum. Add half and half. Refrigerate overnight. When ready to serve, beat egg whites until stiff. In a separate bowl, whip cream until stiff. Fold both gently into bourbon mixture. Pour into a punch bowl and sprinkle with nutmeg. Yields approximately 1 gallon.

Party Champagne Punch

2	fifths pink champagne	4	cups orange juice
2	fifths Sauterne wine	2	oranges, sliced
6½	cups ginger ale	1	6-ounce bottle maraschino
1	fifth vodka		cherries, drained
1	cup orange curaçao liqueur		

Refrigerate champagne, wine, ginger ale, vodka and curaçao for at least 24 hours, then combine. To make ice mold, pour orange juice into 6-cup ring mold, freeze partially and add orange slices and cherries. Cover with plastic wrap and freeze. To serve, unmold orange juice mold and place in a punch bowl; add punch mixture. Yield 1½ gallons.

Elegant served in crystal water glasses, each garnished with an orange slice and cherry on a toothpick.

"Midnight Goodnight"

1	quart vanilla ice cream, slightly softened	½	cup Kahlúa
		⅛	cup Grand Marnier

Place ingredients in a blender, half at a time, and blend at highest speed until consistency of milk shake. Add a little milk if needed for desired thickness. Serves 6 to 8.

Beverages

Margarita

3	ounces tequila	1	ounce bartender's lime juice
1	ounce Triple Sec	1	lime, cut
2	ounces bottled whiskey sour mix		Margarita salt

Mix tequila, Triple Sec, whiskey sour mix and lime juice in blender. Blend a few seconds. Rub rim of glasses with cut lime; then dip glass rim in salt. Pour drink over ice cubes. Serves 2.

Great with a Mexican dinner or on a hot summer night.

Banana Daiquiri

4	ripe bananas, cut in pieces	6	tablespoons fresh lime juice
¾	cup light rum	6	ice cubes or more
½	cup simple syrup (recipe follows)	6	lime slices
		6	mint sprigs

Place bananas, rum, simple syrup ar d lime juice in blender. Blend well. (May be prepared ahead to this point.) When ready to serve, add the ice and blend. Serve in chilled wine glasses with a lime slice and mint sprig. Serves 6.

Basic Simple Syrup:

1	cup sugar	1	cup water

Combine sugar and water in saucepan. Stir over medium heat about 1 minute to dissolve sugar. Store in refrigerator indefinitely. Yields 1½ cups.

Peach or Strawberry Daiquiri

1	6-ounce can frozen limeade, lemonade or pink lemonade	3-4	ripe peaches, pitted and unpeeled or 1½ cups fresh or 1 10-ounce package frozen strawberries
¾	cup vodka or light rum		
6	ice cubes or more		

Place all ingredients in blender and blend on high speed 2 to 3 minutes. Place in freezer until ready to use. To serve, thaw slightly and pour or spoon into glasses. Yields 6 5-ounce drinks.

Beverages

Bloody Mary

2   cups canned V-8 juice
2   cups tomato juice
2   tablespoons lemon juice
1   cup vodka

2   tablespoons Worcestershire
    sauce
1   tablespoon seasoned salt
    Celery sticks

Combine all ingredients except celery. Stir and chill. Pour into ice-filled glasses. Garnish each with celery stick. Serves 6.

Bermuda Rum Swizzle

1   cup orange juice
1   cup grapefruit juice
1   cup pineapple juice
2   tablespoons lime juice
4   teaspoons simple sugar
    syrup (optional, see Banana
    Daiquiri for recipe)
¼   cup apricot brandy

½   cup light rum
½   cup dark rum
½   cup Bermuda Black Seal
    Rum (optional)
¼   teaspoon Angostura Bitters
    Orange slices for garnish
    Maraschino cherries for
    garnish

Mix liquids together. May prepare in advance, adding rum just before serving. Pour into ice-filled glasses. Garnish with orange slices and a cherry. Serves 4.

Watch out!

Raspberry Fizzlett

1   10-ounce package frozen
    raspberries in syrup,
    puréed and strained
1   cup fresh orange juice
¾   cup ginger ale

¾   cup whipping cream
¼   cup fresh lemon juice
3   eggs
4   teaspoons sugar
10 ice cubes

Combine all ingredients except ice cubes in a blender and process. Pour half of mixture into another container until ready to serve. Add 5 ice cubes to mixture in blender and process. Repeat with remaining ingredients. Serves 6.

If desired, add ½ to ¾ cup vodka and serve in chilled champagne glasses.

Beverages

Gin or Vodka Slush

2	cups sugar	2	cups gin or vodka
9	cups water	1	liter 7-Up
1	12-ounce can frozen orange juice, thawed		Maraschino cherries for garnish
1½	cups lemon juice		

In a medium-size saucepan, bring sugar and water to a boil. Reduce heat and simmer 15 minutes. Cool. Add juices along with gin or vodka. Place in a container, cover and freeze. To serve, spoon slush into glasses and fill ⅔ full. Fill glasses with 7-Up and garnish with cherries. Serves 16.

Ideal for patio, pool or ladies' luncheon, this will keep indefinitely in the freezer.

Hot Spiced Kir

2	cups Beaujolais wine	4	whole allspice
½	cup crème de cassis liqueur	2	3-inch pieces cinnamon stick
4	strips lemon peel	4	lemon slices

In a stainless steel saucepan, combine wine, crème de cassis, lemon peel, allspice and cinnamon sticks. Simmer for 10 minutes. Serve in mugs and garnish with lemon slices. Serves 4.

Brandied Tangerine Tea

¼	cup frozen tangerine juice concentrate	2	tablespoons sugar
1	cup California brandy	2	cups hot tea
2	tablespoons lemon juice		Orange slices
2	tablespoons water		Cinnamon sticks

In a saucepan, combine tangerine juice, brandy, lemon juice, water and sugar. Warm over low heat; do not boil. Combine with tea and pour into warm mugs. Garnish with orange slices or cinnamon sticks. Serves 6.

Undiluted frozen orange juice may be substituted for tangerine juice.

Beverages

Hot Scotch

1	teaspoon honey	2	ounces boiling water
1	slice lemon	2	ounces Scotch, warmed
1	cinnamon stick		Ground nutmeg

Put honey, lemon and cinnamon in a large old-fashioned glass. Add water and stir. Add Scotch. Dust with nutmeg. Yields 1 drink.

Amaretto

4	quarts water	5	ounces almond extract
7	cups sugar	¼	cup vanilla
1	cup dark corn syrup	1	fifth vodka

In a large pot, combine water and sugar. Boil 25 to 30 minutes. Stir in corn syrup. Cool. Add almond extract, vanilla and vodka. Pour into clean, used wine bottles and cover or seal. Age 2 to 3 months. Yields 2 to 3 quarts.

Kahlúa

2	cups water	1	quart vodka
¼	cup instant coffee granules	½	vanilla bean, slit
3	cups sugar		

Bring water to a boil in a saucepan. Stir in coffee and sugar. Let mixture cool to room temperature. Check periodically to make sure all sugar is dissolved. Pour contents into a large, dark bottle (preferably a 1-gallon wine bottle with cap). Add vodka and vanilla bean and store in cool, dark place for a minimum of 6 weeks. Yields approximately ½ gallon.

Soups

Soups

*Other Soup recipes may be found in **Southern Classics.**

Soups

Holly Kirby's Mountain People's Brunswick Stew

Paprika
1 teaspoon salt
2 pounds chicken pieces
¼ cup butter
2 medium onions, sliced
1 medium green pepper, chopped
2 cups water
2 16-ounce cans tomatoes, undrained
2 tablespoons chopped parsley
¼ teaspoon Worcestershire sauce
½ teaspoon Tabasco sauce
2 teaspoons salt
2 cups canned corn
1 10-ounce package frozen lima beans
3 tablespoons flour

Sprinkle paprika and 1 teaspoon salt on chicken. Melt butter in a large saucepan; brown chicken. Add onion and green pepper and cook until onion is transparent. Add water, tomatoes, parsley, Worcestershire, Tabasco and 2 teaspoons salt. Bring to a boil and simmer 30 minutes. If desired, remove chicken pieces; bone and return meat to pan. Add corn and lima beans, return to boiling and simmer 20 minutes. Blend flour with enough water to make a paste. Add to mixture and simmer 10 minutes, stirring occasionally. Serves 6 to 8.

 Herbs and spices may lose flavor by extended cooking and should be added the last 45 minutes.

To substitute various forms of herbs, use the following:
*¼ teaspoon ground or powdered herbs **or** ¾ to 1 teaspoon dried herbs **or** 2 teaspoons fresh herbs*

Soups

Turkey Gumbo

Rich Turkey Stock:

1 turkey carcass, neck and giblets	1 carrot, unpeeled and quartered
1 onion, unpeeled and quartered	3 chicken bouillon cubes
1 stalk celery, leaves included	Salt to taste

Place all stock ingredients in a large pot, cover with water and simmer covered, one hour or more. Cool and strain, reserving stock. Remove meat from bones of turkey and reserve.

Soup:

1½ quarts rich turkey stock	1 cup thinly sliced celery, leaves included
2 cups chopped cooked turkey	
1 16-ounce can tomatoes, undrained and chopped	1 medium onion, peeled, sliced and separated into rings
1½ cups sliced fresh okra or 1 10-ounce package frozen sliced okra	¼ cup uncooked rice
	2 chicken bouillon cubes
	Salt and pepper to taste

In a large soup kettle, bring turkey stock to a boil. Add remaining ingredients and simmer covered 20 to 25 minutes, or until rice is done. Adjust salt and pepper. Serves 10 to 12.

Soups

Hot and Sour Soup

4	large black dried mushrooms	½-1	teaspoon pepper
⅓	cup dried fungus	3-6	tablespoons vinegar
4	cups boiling water	2	tablespoons cornstarch,
1-2	lean pork chops		dissolved in ¼ cup water
⅔	cup bamboo shoots	1	cup thinly sliced fresh bean
½	teaspoon salt		curd (TOFU)
1	teaspoon cornstarch	2	eggs, beaten
2	tablespoons vegetable oil	1	teaspoon sesame seed oil
6	cups chicken broth	1	green onion, top included
2	tablespoons soy sauce		

Put mushrooms and fungus in separate bowls and cover with boiling water. Soak for at least 3 hours or overnight and drain. Remove stems of mushrooms and any hard parts of fungus. Cut mushrooms, fungus, pork, and bamboo shoots into julienne strips. Mix salt and cornstarch with pork. Stir-fry pork in oil until no longer pink. In a soup kettle, bring broth to a boil and add mushrooms, fungus, pork and bamboo shoots. Mix well. Add soy sauce. Add pepper and vinegar to taste. Thicken soup with dissolved cornstarch, stirring constantly. Add bean curd. Bring to a boil. Remove from heat and slowly add eggs while stirring constantly. Stir in sesame seed oil. Serve in individual bowls, garnished with green onion sliced in 1-inch lengths. Serves 6.

This soup may be prepared ahead of time and frozen before bean curd is added. The ingredients for this soup are readily available at Oriental grocery stores.

Mushroom and Barley Soup

1	pound fresh mushrooms, sliced	1	cup barley
2	tablespoons butter	1	tablespoon lemon juice
1	onion, finely chopped	1	cup whipping cream
¼	cup bacon drippings	3	egg yolks
4	cups beef broth		Salt and pepper to taste

Sauté mushrooms in butter. Set aside. In a medium-size saucepan, sauté onions in bacon drippings. Stir in beef broth and barley. Cook covered about 45 minutes or until barley is tender. Add mushrooms and lemon juice. Cook covered for 15 minutes on low heat. Combine cream and egg yolks and stir slowly into soup. Season with salt and pepper. Continue heating but do not boil. Serve hot. Serves 10.

Soups

French Onion Soup

4	large onions, thinly sliced	2	cups dry white wine
5	tablespoons unsalted butter		Salt and pepper to taste
2	heaping teaspoons flour		French bread, sliced
4	cups beef broth		Grated Swiss cheese

Sauté onion in butter until golden. Stir in flour. Add broth and wine. Simmer slowly 1 to 1½ hours, stirring often. Add salt and pepper if needed. To serve, fill individual bowls ¾ full with soup. Place a slice of bread in each bowl and cover with a generous amount of cheese. Put bowls on a baking sheet and place under broiler until cheese bubbles and browns slightly. Serves 4 to 6.

Served with a Bibb lettuce salad and fruit, this soup is ideal for a light supper or lunch.

Retta's Fish Chowder

2	pounds fresh or frozen fish filets	¼	teaspoon pepper
5	slices bacon	2	cups milk
½	cup chopped onion	2	tablespoons flour
6	medium potatoes, peeled and cubed	1	13-ounce can evaporated milk
2	cups water		Parsley (optional)
2	teaspoons salt, or more to taste		Garlic powder (optional)

Thaw fish if frozen. In large saucepan, fry bacon until crisp. Set aside bacon and drain all but 1 to 2 tablespoons bacon drippings. Add onion and cook until tender. Add potatoes, water, fish, salt and pepper. Bring to a boil, reduce heat, cover and cook 15 to 20 minutes or until fish flakes and potatoes are tender. Break fish into bite-size pieces. In a separate bowl, combine milk, flour and evaporated milk. Blend well and add to fish mixture. Cook over low heat until heated but do not boil. Adjust salt and pepper to taste, adding parsley and garlic powder if desired. Flavor is best if prepared the day before serving. If reheated, do not boil. Serves 8.

Soups

New England Clam Chowder

¼ pound lean salt pork, finely chopped
1 cup chopped onions
3 cups peeled, cubed raw potatoes
3 10½-ounce cans clams, liquid reserved, chopped

2 cups half and half
2 cups milk
Dash Tabasco sauce
Salt and pepper to taste

In a large kettle, fry pork until golden. Remove pork and reserve. Drain off all but ¼ cup of fat. Add onions and sauté for 5 minutes. Add potatoes and clam liquid. (Add clam broth or water to reserved clam liquid to make 4 cups.) Simmer until potatoes are tender. Add clams, salt pork and remaining ingredients. Heat and serve. Serves 10 to 12.

This chowder is best when made a day ahead. Salt pork may be removed before serving, if desired.

Better Than Boston Bean Soup

1 cup dry Great Northern beans
1 cup dry navy beans
½ cup large dried lima beans
3 quarts water
1 medium onion, finely chopped

1 teaspoon celery salt
1 pound fresh pork, ham or smoked sausage
½ teaspoon dry mustard
Salt and pepper to taste
1 tablespoon finely chopped parsley

Soak beans in water overnight. Drain. Add 3 quarts water, onion, celery salt and pork. Cook until beans are very soft. Remove bones from pork. Add mustard, salt and pepper. Put two-thirds of the soup in blender. Blend; then combine with remainder. Garnish with parsley. Serves 8 to 10.

Good with garlic bread.

Soups

Cuban Black Bean Soup

1	pound dried black beans	3	tablespoons olive oil
1	tablespoon vinegar	2	tablespoons Worcestershire
5	cloves garlic, finely chopped		sauce
2	large onions, finely chopped	4	bay leaves
1	green pepper, finely chopped	½	teaspoon ground cumin
			Salt to taste

Rinse beans well. Cover with water and soak overnight in a large pot. Drain and cover with fresh water. Add vinegar and simmer until tender, about 2 hours. Sauté garlic, onions and green pepper in olive oil and add to beans. Add remaining ingredients and simmer covered 2 to 3 more hours on very low heat, adding water if needed. Serves 6 to 8.

Serve over steamed rice and garnish with chopped onion.

Mulligatawny Soup

1	cup finely chopped onion	1	8-ounce can tomatoes, drained and chopped
1	cup finely chopped celery		
1	cup finely chopped carrots	2	bay leaves
¼	cup butter	⅛	teaspoon dried thyme
2	teaspoons curry powder	½	cup chopped cooked chicken
¼	cup rice, uncooked		
6	cups chicken broth		Salt and pepper to taste

In a large saucepan, sauté onion, celery and carrots in butter until tender, about 5 minutes. Add curry and rice. Cook 1 minute, stirring constantly. Stir in chicken broth, tomatoes, bay leaves and thyme. Heat to boiling; cover and simmer over low heat 25 minutes. Stir in chicken. Salt and pepper to taste. Warm thoroughly. Serves 8.

Soups

Cream of Artichoke Soup

1	14-ounce can artichoke hearts	3	egg yolks	
2	tablespoons chopped onion	½	cup whipping cream	
4	tablespoons butter	1	teaspoon lemon juice	
2	tablespoons flour	¼	teaspoon ground nutmeg (optional)	
½	cup cold milk		Salt and pepper to taste	
1	14½-ounce can chicken broth			

Drain and chop artichokes, reserving liquid. Sauté onions in butter until transparent. With wire whisk, stir in flour, then milk. Add reserved artichoke liquid and chicken broth. Bring to a boil. Remove from heat, stir in egg yolks and cream. Blend well. Return to medium heat, add lemon juice, nutmeg and artichokes. Season with salt and pepper. Simmer 10 minutes. Serves 4.

This is good as a first course, or add bite-size pieces of cooked chicken or turkey and serve over white rice as an entrée.

Claudia's Chicken Vegetable Soup

1	2-3 pound chicken	1	17-ounce can corn, drained
1	cup chopped carrots	1	8-ounce package frozen butter peas
1	cup chopped onions	½	teaspoon Tabasco sauce
1	cup chopped potatoes	1-2	teaspoons Worcestershire sauce
1	cup chopped celery		Salt and pepper to taste
2	cups chopped cabbage		
2	16-ounce cans stewed tomatoes		

In a large pot, barely cover chicken with water and stew. Remove chicken from broth and bone, reserving liquid. Cook carrots, onions, potatoes, celery and cabbage in chicken broth until tender. Add chicken, tomatoes, corn, butter peas, Tabasco, Worcestershire, salt and pepper. Simmer for 3 to 4 hours. Serves 12.

Flavor is improved if refrigerated and reheated the following day.

Soups

Canadian Cheese Soup

½ cup butter
½ cup chopped carrots
½ cup chopped onion
½ cup chopped celery
⅓ cup flour
4 cups hot chicken broth
2 cups hot milk

3 cups grated Cheddar cheese, firmly packed
Salt to taste
Freshly ground pepper to taste
¼ cup dry sherry
Chopped fresh parsley

In a large saucepan, melt butter and sauté carrots, onion and celery. Using a whisk, mix in flour and cook 2 minutes, stirring constantly. Add hot broth gradually, beating vigorously to prevent lumping. Add milk, stirring over medium heat until soup has thickened. Add cheese. Reduce heat and simmer until cheese is melted, stirring to blend. Adjust seasonings. Before serving, blend in sherry. Serve in warm soup bowls and garnish with parsley. To reheat, use a double boiler. Serves 8.

With warm French bread or cornbread and a tossed salad, this soup makes a meal.

Cream of Broccoli Soup

1 10-ounce package frozen chopped broccoli
2 14½-ounce cans chicken broth
½ onion, chopped
3 tablespoons butter
3 tablespoons flour

2 cups half and half
Dash ground nutmeg
Dash ground cardamon
Salt to taste
¼ teaspoon white pepper
½ cup whipping cream
2 egg yolks

Cook broccoli, using one can of chicken broth as cooking liquid; drain, reserving liquid. Purée broccoli in food processor with 3 to 4 tablespoons broth. In a large saucepan, sauté onion in butter; add flour and cook 2 to 3 minutes over medium heat. Remove from heat and add reserved liquid, second can of broth and half and half. Mix until smooth. Return to heat, bring to a boil and reduce heat. Add puréed broccoli and seasonings. (May be made up to 3 days ahead and refrigerated at this point.)

Before serving: (Reheat soup if refrigerated.) Mix cream and egg yolks. Add 3 to 4 tablespoons warm soup to cream-egg mixture and then add to soup. Heat, do not boil, until slightly thickened and serve in warmed soup bowls. Serves 6.

Soups

Fresh Vegetable Soup

1½   pounds stew beef, cut into
     bite-size pieces or 2
     pounds beef shank (with
     bone)
3   quarts water
1   large onion, chopped
1   tablespoon salt
½   teaspoon dried thyme,
     crumbled
½   cup dried split peas
5   medium carrots, sliced
2   cups sliced celery
3   medium tomatoes, peeled,
     seeded and coarsely
     chopped

1½   cups fresh corn
1   large potato, peeled and
     chopped
1   large green pepper, chopped
1   cup fresh green peas
1   cup shelled fresh
     butterbeans
1   cup fresh green beans,
     broken in small pieces
1   cup chopped fresh spinach
1   cup ketchup
2   tablespoons chopped fresh
     parsley
     Salt and freshly ground
     pepper to taste

Cover beef with water in a large stockpot. Add onion, salt and thyme and bring to a boil. Skim fat from surface. Add split peas. Cover and simmer 4 hours. Discard any bones, cutting meat into bite-size pieces. Add all remaining ingredients. Cover and simmer for 1 hour or until vegetables are tender. Season with salt and freshly ground pepper. Flavor is best if prepared ahead, refrigerated (removing fat from surface when chilled) and reheated the next day. Yields 6 quarts.

To prepare in the winter when fresh vegetables are not available, use canned tomatoes and frozen vegetables.

Cream of Spinach Soup

2   tablespoons butter
3   tablespoons finely chopped
     onion
1   tablespoon flour
1½-2 cups cooked chopped
     spinach, frozen or fresh

2   cups chicken broth
½   cup chopped celery leaves
4   sprigs parsley, stems removed
1   cup milk
     Salt and pepper to taste
     Swiss cheese, grated

In a saucepan, melt butter, add onion and brown slightly. Stir in flour. Place onion mixture, spinach, broth, celery and parsley in blender or food processor. Blend until smooth. Return mixture to saucepan and bring to a boil; add milk gradually and stir constantly. Add salt and pepper. Serve hot, topped with grated Swiss cheese. Serves 4 to 6.

Soups

Fresh Tomato Soup

1	large onion, thinly sliced	3	tablespoons uncooked rice
⅓	cup finely chopped celery	½	teaspoon salt
3	tablespoons sliced carrots	½	teaspoon dried thyme
3	tablespoons unsalted butter		Freshly ground pepper to
8	large tomatoes, peeled,		taste
	seeded and chopped	⅓	cup finely chopped fresh
8	cups chicken broth		parsley

In a saucepan, sauté onion, celery and carrots in butter until soft but not brown. Add tomatoes and a small amount of chicken broth. Simmer 20 minutes. In a soup kettle, combine sautéed vegetables, remaining chicken broth and rice. Season with salt, thyme and pepper. Simmer 20 to 30 minutes. Serve garnished with parsley. Serves 8 to 10.

Delicious with tossed salad and bread, this soup may be prepared ahead of time and freezes well.

Cold Tomato Soup

3	cups tomato juice	½	teaspoon grated lemon rind
2	tablespoons tomato paste	2	tablespoons lemon juice
4	green onions, finely		Salt and pepper to taste
	chopped		Sugar to taste
	Dash thyme	1	cup sour cream
½	teaspoon curry powder		Chopped parsley

Mix all ingredients except sour cream and parsley. Chill. Before serving, blend in sour cream and top with chopped parsley. Serves 6.

Avocado Velvet Soup

2	avocados	¼	teaspoon onion salt
1	cup chicken broth		Dash white pepper
1	cup half and half	1	teaspoon lemon or lime
1	teaspoon salt		juice

Peel avocados and remove seeds. Blend avocados and chicken broth in blender until smooth. Combine with remaining ingredients except lemon or lime juice. Chill thoroughly; stir in lemon or lime juice. Garnish with grated lemon rind, lemon slices, watercress, a spoonful of sour cream or a combination of garnishes. Serves 6.

Soups

Summer Soup

3	carrots	3	tablespoons mayonnaise
1	medium onion		Salt and pepper to taste
1	medium cucumber		Milk (optional)
1	8-ounce package cream cheese, softened		Fresh mint, parsley or chopped chives, for garnish
1	cup sour cream		

Peel and finely grate vegetables. Blend together cream cheese, sour cream and mayonnaise. Add vegetables and blend well. Add salt and pepper to taste. Stir in milk if needed for desired consistency. Chill and serve cold in demitasse cups or crystal punch cups. Serves 8.

Gazpacho

6	cups tomato juice	2	tablespoons cider vinegar
1	onion, finely chopped	1	teaspoon dried tarragon
6	tomatoes, chopped	1	teaspoon dried basil
1	green pepper, chopped	1	teaspoon ground cumin
1	cucumber, chopped	1	teaspoon cayenne pepper
2	green onions, chopped	3	tablespoons olive oil
¼	cup chopped fresh parsley	1	tablespoon honey
¼	cup lemon juice		Salt and pepper to taste

Combine all ingredients and chill thoroughly before serving. Serves 8 to 10.

This soup may be puréed in blender, if desired.

Soups

Vichyssoise

1	pound leeks, chopped	½	teaspoon white pepper
½	cup chopped onion	2	14½-ounce cans chicken
¼	cup butter		broth
3	medium potatoes, peeled	2	cups milk
	and cubed	1	cup whipping cream, chilled
½	teaspoon salt		Chopped chives

In a large saucepan, sauté leeks and onion in butter until transparent. Add potatoes, salt, pepper and broth. Simmer 45 minutes, covered. Put mixture, 2 cups at a time, in blender or food processor and blend on low until smooth. In a small saucepan, scald milk and add to mixture, blending with wire whisk. Refrigerate, covered, for 6 hours or longer. Before serving, fold in cream. Pour into cups and top with chives. Serves 8.

Add 1 teaspoon curry powder for a different version.

Chilled Cucumber Soup

1	chicken bouillon cube	1	teaspoon salt
1	cup hot water	2	tablespoons flour
2	cups peeled, sliced	3	tablespoons butter
	cucumbers	1	cup half and half
¼	cup chopped chives	½	cup finely chopped
¼	cup celery leaves		cucumber
3	tablespoons chopped parsley	3	tablespoons sour cream

In a saucepan, dissolve bouillon cube in hot water. Stir in sliced cucumbers, chives, celery leaves, parsley and salt. Transfer to a blender and process until smooth. In top of a double boiler, mix flour and butter. Add mixture from blender and heat thoroughly. Blend in half and half and chill. Before serving, stir in chopped cucumbers and sour cream. Serves 4.

Refreshing on a hot summer day!

Salads

Salads

*Other Salad recipes may be found in **Southern Classics.***

Salads

Shrimp Louis

2	pounds shrimp, cooked and cleaned	4	hard-cooked eggs, sliced
1	14-ounce can artichoke hearts, drained and sliced	4	tomatoes, peeled and quartered
		1	head Boston lettuce

Dressing:

½	cup mayonnaise or whipping cream	½	cup bottled French dressing
		½	cup chili sauce

Arrange shrimp, artichoke hearts, eggs and tomatoes on lettuce. Mix dressing ingredients and pour over salad. Serves 4.

Grecian Salad

4	cups Boston lettuce	1	cup halved pitted black olives
2	cups unpeeled, cooked, sliced red potatoes	¼	cup peanut oil
2	cups cherry tomatoes	2	tablespoons white vinegar
1	cup sliced radishes	¼	teaspoon dried oregano, crushed
¼	cup coarsely chopped fresh parsley	½	teaspoon salt
½	cup crumbled feta cheese	¼	teaspoon pepper

In a large salad bowl, arrange lettuce leaves on bottom and layer potatoes, tomatoes, radishes and parsley over lettuce. Top with cheese in center. Arrange olives around the cheese. Combine the remaining ingredients to make a dressing and pour over salad just before serving. Serves 6 to 8.

Salads

Spinach and Orange Salad with Honey-Caraway Dressing

Salad:

10 ounces fresh spinach
1 medium head iceberg
    lettuce
2 tablespoons chopped onion
1 small cucumber, sliced

2 tablespoons chopped green
    pepper
2 large oranges, peeled,
    seeded and chopped

Rinse and drain spinach and lettuce; refrigerate. About 30 minutes before serving, tear spinach and lettuce into bite-size pieces. Mix with remaining ingredients in large salad bowl. Before serving, toss with Honey-Caraway Dressing to coat ingredients. Serves 8 to 10.

Honey-Caraway Dressing:

¾ cup mayonnaise
2 tablespoons honey

1 tablespoon lemon juice
1 tablespoon caraway seed

In a small bowl, stir all ingredients together with fork or whisk until blended. Yields 1 cup.

Salad may also be served with Celery Seed Dressing.

Fresh Spinach Salad

8 cups (2 bunches) fresh
    young spinach
1 pound bacon, fried and
    drained

2 hard-cooked eggs, chopped
1 cup sliced mushrooms

Wash spinach and tear into pieces, removing stems. Crumble bacon. Add bacon, eggs and mushrooms to spinach. Before serving, pour on dressing and toss lightly. Serves 10 to 12.

Excellent with White Wine Vinegar Dressing. Sliced red onions, mandarin orange sections or sliced water chestnuts may be added, if desired.

Salads

Marinated Asparagus

1½-2 pounds fresh asparagus
1   green pepper, chopped
4-5 whole green onions, chopped
1   stalk celery, finely chopped
¾   cup vegetable oil

½   cup red wine vinegar
½   cup sugar
½   clove garlic, finely chopped
¼   teaspoon paprika
    Pimiento strips for garnish

Steam asparagus 5 minutes. Drain. Place asparagus in a 9 x 13-inch baking dish. Combine remaining ingredients except pimiento; mix well and pour over asparagus. Cover and chill 4 hours or overnight. Before serving, drain marinade and garnish with pimiento strips. Serves 6 to 8.

If fresh asparagus is not available, substitute 2 15-ounce cans asparagus spears, drained.

Broccoli Salad

2   10-ounce packages frozen broccoli spears
1   7-ounce jar pimiento-stuffed olives, drained
½   cup chopped onion

3   hard-cooked eggs, peeled and chopped
1   cup chopped celery
1   cup mayonnaise

Cook broccoli slightly (should remain crisp). Drain and cool. Cut into 1-inch pieces and combine with remaining ingredients. Chill. Serves 6 to 8.

Marinated Cucumber Salad

2   medium cucumbers, thinly sliced
1   medium onion, sliced and separated into rings
2   cups thinly sliced carrots
½   cup sliced celery
1   cup vinegar

¼   cup vegetable oil
¼   cup sugar
1   teaspoon celery seed
1   teaspoon salt
¼   teaspoon pepper
    Leaf lettuce

Combine cucumbers, onion, carrots and celery in a large bowl. In a separate bowl, mix remaining ingredients except lettuce. Pour over vegetables and toss lightly. Cover and chill 8 to 10 hours. Drain and serve in a lettuce-lined bowl. Serves 6.

Salads

Sea Shell Party Salad

12	ounces shell macaroni, cooked and drained	1	teaspoon Worcestershire sauce
½	cup Italian salad dressing	¾	cup salad dressing or mayonnaise
2	green onions, thinly sliced		
½	cup chopped green pepper	2	teaspoons prepared mustard
2	cups chopped celery	1	teaspoon salt
2	cups cubed cooked ham	1	teaspoon Tabasco sauce (optional)
1	cup cubed Cheddar cheese		
1	cup chopped black olives		

Marinate cooked macaroni in Italian dressing at least 2 hours or overnight. Drain. Add onions, green pepper, celery, ham and cheese. In a separate bowl, combine remaining ingredients. Toss with macaroni mixture. Serve on lettuce or spinach with tomato wedges or use to stuff tomatoes. Serves 10 to 12.

Vidalia onion may be substituted for green onion.

Artichoke-Rice Salad

1	8-ounce package chicken-flavored rice	½	green pepper, chopped
2	6-ounce jars marinated artichoke hearts, liquid reserved	12	pimiento-stuffed olives, sliced
		⅓	cup mayonnaise
4	green onions, chopped	¾	teaspoon curry powder

Prepare rice according to package directions. Quarter artichoke hearts. Mix rice with artichoke hearts, onions, green pepper and olives. In a separate bowl, combine reserved artichoke liquid, mayonnaise and curry powder; pour over rice mixture. Mix well. Refrigerate overnight and serve chilled. Serves 8.

Salads

Curried Rice Salad

4	large mushrooms, thinly sliced	2	tablespoons finely chopped fresh parsley
1	tablespoon vegetable oil	1	tablespoon dry sherry
2	small zucchini, quartered lengthwise and cut into ½-inch pieces	3	tablespoons lemon juice
		1	teaspoon salt
1	small onion, finely chopped	1	teaspoon curry powder
1	cup long grain rice, cooked and cooled	⅛	teaspoon cayenne pepper
		⅓	cup vegetable oil
⅓	cup finely chopped green pepper		Lettuce

In a skillet, cook mushrooms in oil for 2 minutes. Add zucchini and onion and cook for 1 minute. In a large bowl, combine vegetable mixture with cooked rice, green pepper and parsley.

For the dressing, combine sherry, lemon juice, salt, curry powder and cayenne in a small bowl. Add oil in a stream, whisking continuously. Pour dressing over rice mixture and toss well. Place on lettuce. Serve at room temperature. Serves 4 to 6.

For a main dish, add chopped cooked chicken or turkey.

Rice Salad

3	cups cold cooked rice	½	cup sliced pitted black olives
2	cups broccoli florets, crisp-cooked	¼	cup chopped parsley
		¼	cup chopped pimiento
1	cup green beans, crisp-cooked		Prepared Italian dressing
			Salt and pepper to taste
½	cup chopped celery		Cherry tomatoes for garnish
½	cup finely chopped onion		

Gently toss rice and vegetables together. Add dressing and toss again. Salt and pepper to taste. Garnish with halved cherry tomatoes. Serves 6 to 8.

A combination of any or all of the vegetables may be used.

Salads

Sesame Chicken Salad

8   chicken breast halves, cooked, boned and chopped
1   pound snow peas, sliced
diagonally
1   8-ounce can sliced water
chestnuts, drained

8   green onions, tops included,
sliced
1   cup sesame seed, toasted
Salt and pepper to taste

Dressing:
4   tablespoons dry sherry
2   egg yolks
3   tablespoons lemon juice
2   tablespoons Dijon-style
mustard

2   tablespoons soy sauce
2   teaspoons sugar
½   teaspoon ground ginger
1   cup vegetable oil
Dash Tabasco sauce

Combine chicken, snow peas, water chestnuts, onions, sesame seed, salt and pepper. In separate bowl, combine sherry, egg yolks, lemon juice, mustard, soy sauce, sugar and ginger. Add oil gradually until well mixed. Add Tabasco. Pour over chicken and toss. Serve slightly chilled. Serves 8.

Grandma's Hot German Potato Salad

8-10 medium potatoes
1   pound bacon
½   cup flour
½   cup sugar
1   tablespoon salt

1   teaspoon pepper
½   cup vinegar
½   cup water
3   onions, finely chopped

Boil potatoes in enough water to cover until partially tender, about 10 minutes. Drain, cool, peel and slice. In a skillet, fry bacon until crisp. Remove from skillet and drain, reserving drippings. To prepare sauce, add flour, sugar, salt, pepper, vinegar and water to bacon drippings remaining in skillet. Cook until thick, about 5 minutes. In a large Dutch oven, layer ¼ of each: potatoes, onions, sauce and crumbled bacon. Repeat to make four layers. Bake at 275 degrees for 3½ hours. Serves 12 to 14.

Salads

Sour Cream Potato Salad

⅓   cup chopped fresh dill or 1
     tablespoon dried dill weed
1   teaspoon salt
¼   teaspoon pepper
1   tablespoon chopped onion
     or to taste
¼   cup vegetable oil
¼   cup cider vinegar

7   cups peeled, boiled, sliced
     potatoes
½   cup chopped celery
½   cup peeled, chopped
     cucumber
¾   cup sour cream
¾   cup mayonnaise

Combine dill, salt, pepper, onion, oil and vinegar, and gently add warm potatoes, tossing to coat. Chill. In another bowl, mix remaining ingredients. Chill. Before serving, gently combine potato and sour cream mixtures until well blended. Serves 10 to 12.

Tarragon Dill Slaw

1   medium head cabbage,
     shredded
2   carrots, shredded
¼   cup finely chopped onion
2   teaspoons dill weed

1   cup mayonnaise
2   tablespoons tarragon vinegar
½   teaspoon celery seed
     Salt and white pepper to
     taste

Combine shredded vegetables and onion and stir in dill weed thoroughly. Make a dressing of the remaining ingredients and toss with vegetables until well coated. Serves 8 to 10.

Salads

Chinese Slaw

¾ cup sugar
¾ cup vinegar
Dash Tabasco sauce
1 16-ounce can French-style green beans
1 16-ounce can Chinese vegetables
1 2-ounce jar chopped pimientos
1 16-ounce can small green peas
1 8-ounce can sliced water chestnuts
1 4-ounce can sliced mushrooms
½ cup chopped celery
1 large red onion, thinly sliced
Salt and pepper to taste

Heat sugar, vinegar and Tabasco sauce until sugar dissolves. Drain canned vegetables, combine with remaining ingredients and add warmed mixture, stirring to coat vegetables. Adjust seasonings. Chill 6 hours or longer, stirring several times. Serves 10.

This is an excellent make-ahead salad for a dinner party. It looks especially attractive in a glass salad bowl.

Two-Week Slaw

1 medium head cabbage, grated
2 onions, thinly sliced
1 cup sugar
1 cup vinegar
¾ cup vegetable oil
1 teaspoon dry mustard
1 tablespoon salt
1 teaspoon poppy seed

Alternate layers of cabbage and onions in a plastic container; top with sugar. In a saucepan, combine remaining ingredients, bring to a boil, and pour over cabbage. Cool; then cover and refrigerate for 3 days. This slaw will keep refrigerated for 2 weeks. Serves 8 to 10.

Salads

Summer Fruit Salad

2   large pink grapefruit
1   pint strawberries
1   tablespoon sugar
2   large avocados, peeled and chopped

1   Red Delicious apple, unpeeled, cored and chopped
Boston lettuce

The night before serving, peel and section grapefruit. Wash and halve strawberries and mix with 1 tablespoon sugar. Add to grapefruit mixture. Refrigerate. Shortly before serving add avocado and apple. Mound on lettuce. Serve with Poppy Seed Dressing. Serves 6.

Poppy Seed Dressing:
1½   cups sugar
2   teaspoons dry mustard
2   teaspoons salt
⅔   cup vinegar

3   tablespoons onion juice (optional)
2   cups vegetable oil
3   tablespoons poppy seed

Using food processor or electric mixer, combine sugar, mustard, salt, vinegar and onion juice. Gradually add oil, beating constantly until mixture is thick, about 5 minutes. Stir in poppy seed. Yields 3 cups.

Dressing may be prepared ahead and refrigerated. Bring to room temperature before serving.

Green Grape Salad

5   cups seedless green grapes
1½   cups cubed salad pickles
1   8-ounce package cream cheese, softened

2   cups chopped celery
1   teaspoon grated onion (optional)

Mix all ingredients. Chill in 9 x 13-inch pan. Do not freeze. Serve on lettuce. Serves 8 to 10.

Salads

Pickled Peach Halves

1	1-pound, 13-ounce can peach halves in heavy syrup, liquid reserved	½	cup sugar
		¼	teaspoon ground allspice
		½	teaspoon whole cloves
¼	cup cider vinegar	½	stick cinnamon

In a saucepan, combine reserved peach syrup, vinegar, sugar and spices. Boil 5 minutes. Add peaches and simmer 5 minutes. Chill peaches overnight in syrup. Serves 6 to 8.

Excellent with poultry or ham, it also makes a special garnish when each peach half is topped with a spoonful of prepared mincemeat for a holiday meal.

Avocado Bacon Boats

12	slices bacon, cooked and drained	¼	teaspoon salt
		1	tablespoon lemon juice
½	cup sour cream	3	avocados, halved
2	tomatoes, peeled and chopped		Lemon juice
			Paprika
2	tablespoons chopped green onion		

Crumble bacon and combine with sour cream, tomatoes, onion, salt and lemon juice. Scoop out unpeeled avocados, leaving a firm shell and brush lightly with lemon juice to prevent discoloration. Chop removed avocado and fold into bacon mixture. Spoon into shells, sprinkle with paprika and serve immediately. Serves 6.

Avocado with Caviar

3	ripe avocados	1	cup sour cream
	Lemon juice	1	2-ounce jar red caviar
1	10½-ounce can beef consommé, refrigerated overnight	6	lemon wedges

Cut avocados in half; remove seed and peel. Brush each half thoroughly with lemon juice and fill with consommé. Spoon on desired amount of sour cream and top with caviar. Serve on lettuce with a lemon wedge. Serves 6.

Salads

Molded Grapefruit Salad

2	envelopes unflavored gelatin	3	tablespoons lemon juice
1	cup cold water	¾	cup chopped celery
1	cup boiling water	½	cup slivered almonds
¾	cup sugar	1	avocado, peeled and thinly
3	large grapefruit, sectioned,		sliced
	juice reserved		Blue cheese dressing

Mix gelatin and cold water. Add boiling water and stir until dissolved. Add sugar, grapefruit juice and lemon juice. Chill until thickened and slightly set. Stir in celery and almonds. Pour mixture into oiled 6 to 8-cup salad mold. Press alternating grapefruit and avocado slices down into gelatin mixture. Chill until firm. Unmold and serve with blue cheese dressing. May be made in individual molds. Serves 10 to 12.

Cherry Sherry Salad

1	6-ounce package cherry	¼-½	cup dry sherry
	gelatin	1½	cup seedless grapes
1⅓	cups boiling water	1	cup chopped pecans
1	16½-ounce can pitted dark		
	cherries, juice reserved		

Dissolve gelatin in boiling water. Add cold water to reserved cherry juice to make 1¾ cups liquid and add to gelatin. Stir in sherry. Refrigerate until slightly thickened. Cut grapes and cherries in half. Place fruit and pecans in oiled 6-cup salad mold or individual molds. Add gelatin mixture and chill until firm. Unmold and serve with mayonnaise. Serves 8 to 10.

Canned pears may be substituted for grapes.

Salads

Cranberry Salad

2 cups fresh cranberries	1 cup boiling water
1 cup sugar	½ cup finely chopped apples
2 tablespoons lemon juice	½ cup finely chopped celery
½ cup orange juice	½ cup chopped pecans
2 envelopes unflavored gelatin	

In a saucepan, combine cranberries, sugar, lemon juice and orange juice and cook until cranberries are soft. Dissolve gelatin in boiling water. Add cranberry mixture, apples, celery and pecans. Pour into oiled 6-cup salad mold or 8 x 8-inch pan. Chill until firm. Unmold and serve on lettuce. Serves 6 to 8.

Niven's Congealed Vegetable Salad

2 3-ounce packages lemon gelatin	1 tablespoon finely chopped onion
2 cups boiling water	1 radish, thinly sliced
6 tablespoons vinegar	1 2-ounce jar chopped pimiento, drained
¼ teaspoon salt	½ cup finely chopped celery
1 15½-ounce can crushed pineapple, undrained	½ cup shredded carrots
1 cup shredded cabbage	

In a large bowl, dissolve gelatin in boiling water. Add other ingredients and mix well. Pour into oiled individual salad molds or 8 x 8-inch pan. Chill until firm. Cut in squares. Serves 6 to 8.

Cucumber Salad

1 3-ounce package lime gelatin	1 small onion, finely chopped
¾ cup boiling water	1 cup mayonnaise
1 cucumber	1 cup cottage cheese
	Dash salt

Dissolve gelatin in water and chill until slightly set. Without removing the skin, slice cucumber in very thin slices. Add cucumber and remaining ingredients to gelatin. Mix well and pour into 8 oiled individual molds. Chill until firm. Unmold and serve on lettuce. Serves 8.

Salads

Asparagus Salad

2   envelopes unflavored gelatin
1½ cups water, divided
¾   cup sugar
½   cup vinegar
1   tablespoon chopped onion
1   cup chopped celery
2   tablespoons lemon juice
1   teaspoon salt
2   4-ounce jars chopped pimiento, drained

1   10½-ounce can asparagus, drained and cut in 1-inch pieces
1   8-ounce can water chestnuts, drained and coarsely chopped
1   cup chopped pecans
   Mayonnaise

Sprinkle gelatin into ½ cup of cold water in mixing bowl. Set aside. In a saucepan, bring sugar, vinegar and 1 cup water to a boil. Combine with gelatin and stir to dissolve. Stir in onion, celery, lemon juice and salt. Chill about 25 minutes or until slightly set. Fold in pimiento, asparagus, water chestnuts and pecans, reserving 2 tablespoons of pecans for garnish. Pour into lightly oiled 6 to 8-cup mold. Chill until firm. Unmold and top with mayonnaise and pecans. Serves 8 to 10.

Jamye's Tomato Aspic

3   16-ounce cans stewed tomatoes
3   envelopes unflavored gelatin
1   8-ounce can water chestnuts, drained and chopped

1   3-ounce jar pimiento-stuffed olives, drained and chopped
1   14-ounce can artichoke hearts, drained and quartered
1   teaspoon onion salt

Purée tomatoes in blender or food processor. Dissolve gelatin in ¾ cup of tomato mixture. Heat remaining mixture until simmering. Remove from heat and add water chestnuts, olives, artichokes, onion salt and dissolved gelatin mixture. Chill in oiled individual molds until firm. Unmold, serve on lettuce and top with homemade mayonnaise. Serves 12.

Salads

Aunt Sue's Tomato Aspic with Homemade Mayonnaise

Tomato Aspic:

4   cups tomato juice
½   teaspoon celery salt
6-8 whole cloves
1   teaspoon Worcestershire
     sauce
2   tablespoons fresh basil or
     2 teaspoons dried basil
½   small onion, finely chopped

2   tablespoons fresh dill weed
     or 2 teaspoons dried dill
     weed
1-2 celery stalks, leaves included
2   3-ounce packages lemon
     gelatin
     Sliced pimiento-stuffed olives
½   cup sliced celery

In a saucepan, combine all ingredients except gelatin, olives and celery slices. Bring to a boil, reduce heat and simmer for 20 minutes. Strain to remove spices and vegetables. Add gelatin to liquid, mixing well, and chill until slightly congealed. Stir in olives and celery and pour into 9 x 13-inch casserole or oiled 6 to 8-cup salad mold. Chill until firm. Unmold and serve on a bed of lettuce, topping with Homemade Mayonnaise. Serves 6 to 8.

Homemade Mayonnaise:

2   eggs
1   tablespoon vinegar
1   tablespoon lemon juice
1   teaspoon dry mustard or
     Dijon-style mustard

½   teaspoon salt
     Dash pepper
2   cups peanut oil or 1 cup
     each peanut and olive oil

In a food processor, mix all ingredients except oil. With processor running, drip oil slowly into the mixture; blend thoroughly. Refrigerate until used. Serve on tomato aspic, fresh tomatoes or other congealed salads. Yields 3 cups.

Can be made ahead and will keep in refrigerator for 2 weeks.

Salads

Frozen Tomato Salad

1½	envelopes unflavored gelatin	1	tablespoon finely chopped
⅓	cup water		green onion
1	16-ounce can tomatoes, well	1	teaspoon Worcestershire
	drained		sauce
1⅓	cups mayonnaise	1	teaspoon salt
2	tablespoons lemon juice		Dash freshly ground pepper
2	drops Tabasco sauce		

Dissolve gelatin in water and pour into blender or food processor. Add remaining ingredients and process until well blended, pushing food down the sides of container as needed. Pour into paper-lined muffin tins and freeze. When well frozen, remove from muffin tins and return to freezer in air-tight container and use as needed. To serve, remove paper, place on lettuce and top with Horseradish Dressing. Serves 12.

Unusual and a very good aspic alternative.

Horseradish Dressing

1	cup mayonnaise	4	teaspoons prepared
½	cup sour cream		horseradish, undrained
¼	teaspoon dry mustard	2	teaspoons chopped chives
¼	teaspoon garlic powder		

Combine all ingredients except chives in blender or food processor, whipping until well blended. Add chives. Refrigerate. Yields 1½ cups.

This dressing is good with Frozen Tomato Salad and also with roast beef or fried shrimp.

Roquefort Dressing

3	ounces Roquefort cheese,	1	tablespoon lemon juice
	crumbled		Dash Worcestershire sauce
3	ounces blue cheese,	1	cup sour cream
	crumbled		
1	3-ounce package cream		
	cheese, softened		

Combine cheeses. Add lemon juice and Worcestershire. Mix in sour cream. Chill at least 2 hours. Serves 12.

Salads

White Wine Vinegar Dressing

¼	cup white wine vinegar	½	teaspoon pepper
¼	cup lemon juice	2	teaspoons sugar
1	cup salad oil	1	teaspoon dry mustard
2	teaspoons salt	2	cloves garlic

Mix all ingredients and refrigerate overnight. Remove garlic before serving. Yields 1½ cups.

Excellent dressing for spinach salad.

Celery Seed Dressing

⅓	cup sugar	1	small onion, chopped
1	teaspoon salt	1	cup vegetable oil
1	teaspoon dry mustard	1	tablespoon celery seed
⅓	cup vinegar		

Combine all ingredients, mixing well. Chill thoroughly. Yields 1½ cups.

This dressing is delicious served over a salad of lettuce, orange sections, chopped pecans and onion slices.

Touchdown Salad Dressing

1	cup olive oil	1¼	teaspoons poppy seed
¼	cup white vinegar	½	teaspoon salt
¼	cup lemon juice	½	teaspoon dry mustard
2	tablespoons powdered sugar		

Combine all ingredients in a jar, cover and shake vigorously. Chill. Shake before serving. Yields 1½ cups.

Delicious over melon balls.

Breads

Breads

*Other Bread recipes may be found in **Southern Classics.**

Glazed Lemon Bread

1½	cups flour	½	cup butter, melted
1	cup sugar	2	eggs, beaten
1	teaspoon baking powder	¼	teaspoon almond extract
1	teaspoon salt	1	teaspoon grated lemon rind
½	cup milk	½	cup chopped walnuts

Glaze:

2	tablespoons lemon juice	¼	cup sugar

In a large bowl, combine flour, sugar, baking powder and salt. In a small bowl, blend milk, butter, eggs and almond extract and add to dry ingredients. Stir just to mix. Fold in lemon rind and nuts. Pour into a greased 5 x 9-inch loaf pan and bake at 350 degrees for 50 minutes. Remove from oven and leave in pan. Mix lemon juice and sugar and immediately spoon over hot loaf. Cool in pan for 15 minutes. Remove and cool completely before slicing. Yields 1 loaf.

Banana Bread

⅔	cup vegetable shortening	1	teaspoon baking soda
1	cup sugar	1	teaspoon salt
4-5	large bananas, chopped	2	eggs
2	cups flour	1	cup chopped pecans

Cream shortening and sugar. Add bananas and beat well. Add dry ingredients and beat in eggs one at a time. Fold in pecans. Pour into greased and floured 5 x 9-inch loaf pan. Bake at 350 degrees for 50 to 60 minutes.

Zucchini Bread

3	eggs	½	teaspoon salt
¾	cup vegetable oil	¼	teaspoon baking powder
¾	cup sugar	2	teaspoons baking soda
¾	cup brown sugar	1	tablespoon ground cinnamon
2	cups chopped unpeeled zucchini	1	tablespoon vanilla
2	cups flour	1	cup chopped pecans

Combine all ingredients. Pour mixture into 2 greased 5 x 9-inch loaf pans and bake 1 hour at 325 degrees. Yields 2 loaves.

Breads

Apple Bread

4 eggs
⅔ cup water
1 cup vegetable oil
1 16-ounce can unsweetened applesauce
3 cups sugar
3½ cups flour

1 teaspoon ground nutmeg
1 teaspoon ground cinnamon
2 teaspoons baking soda
½ teaspoon salt
1½ cups chopped pecans (optional)

In a large bowl, combine eggs, water and oil. Add applesauce, then remaining ingredients, stirring well. Pour mixture into 3 well greased 5 x 9-inch loaf pans and bake at 350 degrees for 1 hour. Yields 3 medium loaves.

Pumpkin pie filling may be substituted for applesauce.

Old-Fashioned Orange Muffins

2½ cups flour
2 teaspoons baking powder
½ teaspoon salt
¾ cup butter, softened
1⅔ cups sugar
3 eggs, beaten

1 teaspoon vanilla
½ cup orange juice
Rind of 2 oranges, grated (8 teaspoons)
Powdered sugar (optional)

Sift together flour, baking powder and salt. Set aside. Cream butter and sugar. Add eggs, vanilla, orange juice and rind. Gently stir in dry ingredients until batter is moist but still lumpy. Grease miniature muffin tins with oil and dust with flour. Fill half full with batter. Bake 15 minutes at 350 degrees. Remove from oven and dust with powdered sugar if desired. Yields 3 dozen miniature muffins.

Breads

Blueberry Oatmeal Muffins

1	cup plus 2 tablespoons quick-cooking rolled oats	½	teaspoon freshly grated nutmeg
1	cup buttermilk	¼	cup butter, softened
1	tablespoon vanilla	¾	cup brown sugar
1	cup flour	1	egg
1	tablespoon baking powder	¼	cup finely chopped walnuts
½	teaspoon baking soda	1½	cups blueberries
1	teaspoon salt		

Mix oats, buttermilk and vanilla in small bowl; set aside. Sift together flour, baking powder, baking soda, salt and nutmeg in small bowl; set aside. In a large bowl, cream butter and sugar; add egg and mix. Stir in nuts. Fold in flour mixture, then oatmeal mixture. Fold in blueberries. Fill greased or paper-lined muffin tins ½ full. Bake 20 minutes or until lightly browned at 400 degrees. Yields 12 to 18 muffins.

Robin's Apple Muffins

3½	cups flour	1½	cups vegetable oil
2	cups sugar	1	teaspoon vanilla
1	teaspoon salt	3	cups peeled, finely chopped apples
1	teaspoon baking soda		
1	teaspoon ground cinnamon	½	cup chopped toasted pecans
2	eggs		

Sift together flour, sugar, salt, baking soda and cinnamon and set aside. Combine eggs, oil and vanilla and add to dry ingredients, stirring until moistened. Fold in apples and pecans. Fill greased and floured or paper-lined muffin tins ½ full. Bake 20 to 30 minutes at 350 degrees. Yields 24 muffins.

Breads

Bran Muffins

2	cups sugar	2	teaspoons baking soda
1	cup dark brown sugar	1	cup vegetable oil
3	cups flour	4	eggs
2	cups whole wheat flour	4	cups buttermilk
2	tablespoons ground cinnamon (optional)	1	15½-ounce box raisin bran cereal
2	teaspoons salt	½-1	cup raisins

In a large bowl, mix dry ingredients except cereal and raisins. In a separate bowl, combine all liquid ingredients and mix well. Add the liquid mixture to the dry ingredients, stirring only until moistened. Fold in cereal and raisins. Fill greased or paper-lined muffin tins ⅔ full and bake at 375 degrees for 15 to 18 minutes. Yields 48 muffins.

This batter will keep in the refrigerator for 6 weeks and may be used as needed or given as gifts.

Apricot Bran Muffins

1	cup finely chopped dried apricots	½	teaspoon salt
1	cup flour	1¼	cups 100% bran cereal
½	cup sugar	1	cup milk
2½	teaspoons baking powder	1	egg
½	teaspoon baking soda	¼	cup vegetable oil
		1	cup chopped pecans

Mix apricots with small amount of measured flour to keep pieces from sticking together. Combine remaining flour, sugar, baking powder, baking soda and salt; set aside. In a large bowl, mix bran with milk until moistened. Let stand 5 minutes. Mix in egg and oil. Add flour mixture, stirring until just combined. Gently stir apricots and nuts into mixture. Fill greased or paper-lined muffin tins about ¾ full. Bake 20 minutes at 375 degrees. Yields 12 large muffins.

Breads

Dede's Ginger Muffins

1	cup butter
1	cup molasses
2	eggs
1	cup sugar
2½	cups flour
1½	teaspoons baking soda
1½	teaspoons ground ginger

1½	teaspoons ground cinnamon
½	teaspoon ground nutmeg
½	teaspoon ground cloves
4	teaspoons grated orange rind
½	cup boiling water
4	tablespoons sour cream
	Dash of salt

In a small saucepan, melt butter with molasses. Cool. Beat eggs and sugar until fluffy. Sift together flour, baking soda, ginger, cinnamon, nutmeg and cloves. Alternately add egg mixture and dry ingredients to molasses and butter, stirring well after each addition. Add remaining ingredients. Blend well. Fill well greased miniature muffin tins ½ full. Bake at 350 degrees for 15 minutes or until puffed. Turn onto rack to cool. Yields 9 dozen miniature or 3 dozen large muffins.

Muffins may be frozen between layers of waxed paper in plastic container.

French Cinnamon Muffins

1½	cups flour
1½	teaspoons baking powder
½	teaspoon salt
¼	teaspoon ground mace

⅓	cup butter, softened
½	cup sugar
1	egg
½	cup milk

Glaze:

½	cup sugar
1	teaspoon ground cinnamon

½	cup butter, melted

Combine flour, baking powder, salt and mace and set aside. Cream butter and sugar. Add egg; then add dry ingredients and milk alternately. Pour into greased miniature muffin tins. Bake 15 minutes at 350 degrees.

After muffins have been baked, combine sugar and cinnamon. Dip hot muffins in melted butter and roll in sugar mixture. Serve warm. Yields 40 miniature muffins.

Wrap in foil and warm in oven to reheat. May be frozen unglazed; defrost before heating, dip in melted butter and roll in sugar mixture.

Breads

Dill Bread

1	package dry yeast	2	teaspoons dried dill weed
¼	cup warm water	1	teaspoon salt
1	cup cottage cheese	¼	teaspoon baking soda
2	tablespoons sugar	1	egg
1	tablespoon finely chopped onion	2½-3	cups flour
			Egg white (optional)
1	tablespoon butter, melted		Sesame seed (optional)

Dissolve yeast in warm water and set aside. In a saucepan, heat cottage cheese to lukewarm. Remove from heat. In a large mixing bowl, combine cottage cheese, sugar, onion, butter, dill, salt, soda and egg. Mix well. Stir in yeast. Add flour to make stiff dough and beat well. Cover; let rise in warm place until doubled in size, about 50 to 60 minutes. Stir down; turn into well-greased 9 to 10-inch quiche or pie pan or a 5 x 9-inch loaf pan. Let rise until doubled in size, 30 to 40 minutes. Brush with egg white and sprinkle with sesame seed, if desired. Bake at 350 degrees 30 to 40 minutes for round loaf or 40 to 50 minutes for loaf. Yields 1 loaf.

Freezes well. Delicious served warm.

English Muffin Bread

1	cup milk	1	package dry yeast
2	tablespoons sugar	1	cup warm water
1	teaspoon salt	5½	cups flour
3	tablespoons butter		Cornmeal

In a saucepan, scald milk; stir in sugar, salt and butter. Cool to lukewarm. In a large mixing bowl, dissolve yeast in water. Add milk mixture, then 3 cups flour. Beat until smooth. Add remaining flour to make a soft dough. On floured surface, knead about 2 minutes, until dough can form a sticky ball. Place in a greased bowl, cover and let rise until doubled, about 1 hour. Punch down and divide in half. Roll out each half into a 7 x 14-inch rectangle. Roll tightly from the 7-inch end, sealing ends and bottom. Roll each loaf in cornmeal. Place seam side down in 2 greased 5 x 9-inch loaf pans. Cover and let rise until doubled, about 1 hour. Bake 25 minutes at 400 degrees. Remove from pans to cool on wire racks. Yields 2 loaves.

Delicious toasted. Freezes well.

Breads

Pumpernickle Bread

1	tablespoon cornmeal	1	1-ounce square
1	tablespoon butter		unsweetened chocolate,
½	cup chopped onion		melted and cooled
2	packages dry yeast	1	cup 100% bran cereal
2¼	cups lukewarm water	3	cups rye flour
⅓	cup dark molasses	2	tablespoons caraway seed
1	tablespoon salt	3½-4 cups unbleached flour	
2	tablespoons vegetable oil		

Grease large baking sheet and sprinkle with cornmeal; set aside. Melt butter in small saucepan. Add onions and sauté about 5 minutes; set aside. Combine yeast and warm water in large mixing bowl. Add molasses, salt, oil, chocolate and cereal. Beat at low speed until mixed. Add rye flour, caraway seed and sautéed onions. Beat at medium speed for 2 minutes. With wooden spoon, stir in 2½ to 3 cups unbleached flour. Turn out on lightly floured surface and knead until smooth and elastic, about 10 minutes. Add more flour as needed. (Dough will be sticky.)

Place in large greased bowl. Cover and let rise in a warm place about 1 hour, until doubled in size. Punch down and divide in half. Shape each half into an oval, turning edges under to make a smooth top. Place on baking sheet, cover and let rise 45 minutes. Bake at 350 degrees 35 to 45 minutes, or until loaves sound hollow when tapped. Yields 2 oval loaves.

Breads

Herbed Cheese Bread

1	cup buttermilk	5	cups sifted flour, divided
2	tablespoons sugar	1½	cups grated Cheddar cheese
2½	teaspoons salt	1	egg
1	tablespoon vegetable	½	cup chopped parsley
	shortening	1	tablespoon Italian seasoning
1	package dry yeast	½	teaspoon onion salt
1	cup very warm water		Melted butter
½	teaspoon baking soda		

Scald buttermilk with sugar, salt and shortening. Cool to lukewarm. Dissolve yeast in warm water and add to buttermilk mixture. Stir in soda and 2 cups flour. Beat in cheese and gradually add remaining flour. Turn out on floured board and knead until smooth. Place in a large greased bowl, turn to coat, cover and let rise until doubled, about 1 hour.

In a small bowl, mix egg with parsley, Italian seasoning and onion salt. Punch down dough, divide in half and roll into two 6 x 18-inch rectangles. Spread with egg mixture, roll up and place each loaf seam side down in greased 5 x 9-inch loaf pan. Cover, let rise until double and bake at 350 degrees for 45 minutes. Remove from pans, brush with melted butter and cool on racks. Yields 2 loaves.

Best when hot from the oven.

 When baking bread, all ingredients and utensils should be at room temperature.

After first rising, bread can be punched down and refrigerated, covered, before second rising.

To ensure even baking, oven should be preheated to correct temperature.

Breads

Austin's Whole Wheat Buttermilk Bread

4½-5	cups flour, divided	2	tablespoons wheat germ
1	cup whole wheat flour	1	package dry yeast
3	tablespoons sugar	1	cup water
2½	teaspoons salt	⅓	cup vegetable oil
¼	teaspoon baking soda	1	cup buttermilk

In a large mixing bowl, stir together 1½ cups flour, whole wheat flour, sugar, salt, baking soda, wheat germ and dry yeast. Combine water, oil and buttermilk in a saucepan and heat until warm. Add liquid gradually to dry ingredients with electric mixer and blend for 2 minutes at medium speed. Add 1 cup flour and beat at high speed 2 minutes. With wooden spoon, add enough of remaining flour to make a dough that is soft but not sticky. Turn out onto floured board and knead about 8 minutes until smooth and elastic, adding flour as necessary.

Place in greased bowl, cover and let rise until doubled in bulk. After dough has risen, punch down and divide in half. Shape into 2 loaves, place in 2 greased 5 x 9-inch loaf pans and cover with greased waxed paper. Let rise about ½ inch above pan rim; remove paper. Bake at 375 degrees for 40 minutes. Turn pans around once halfway through baking period for even browning. Remove and immediately turn out on wire racks. Yields 2 loaves.

 Bake bread in center rack of oven for more even browning.

Yeast breads are done when they are golden brown and make a hollow sound when lightly tapped.

For evenly sliced bread, cool and slice with an electric knife; wrap in foil to reheat if desired.

Breads

Panache's Whole Wheat Bread

3	packages dry yeast	3	tablespoons butter
1	cup lukewarm water	1	tablespoon salt
3	cups rolled oats	2	cups whole wheat flour
3	cups hot water	10-12	cups all-purpose or bread
1	cup molasses		flour
1	cup bran flakes		

Combine yeast and lukewarm water in small bowl and set aside. In a very large mixing bowl, combine oats, hot water, molasses, bran flakes, butter and salt. Cool to lukewarm and add yeast mixture. Stir in whole wheat flour and 8 cups white flour. Add enough additional flour to make a stiff dough. Cover with greased plastic wrap and let rise until doubled. Punch down, turn onto floured surface and knead about 10 minutes, adding more flour as necessary. Divide into thirds, shape into loaves and put in greased 5 x 9-inch loaf pans. Cover with greased plastic wrap and a clean dish towel; let rise until doubled. Bake 30 to 40 minutes or until brown at 350 degrees. Remove from pans and cool on wire rack. Yields 3 loaves.

Dough may be refrigerated for up to 24 hours after it is punched down following first rising. Then proceed as usual. The second rising will take longer if dough has been refrigerated.

Recipe may be halved for a more manageable amount of dough and baked in two smaller loaf pans.

Breads

Very Light Dinner Rolls

1	cup milk	2	packages dry yeast
¼	cup sugar	½	cup warm water
6	tablespoons butter, divided	2	eggs, beaten
1	teaspoon salt	4-5	cups bread flour

Glaze:

1	egg, beaten with 1 tablespoon water	Poppy seed or sesame seed

In a saucepan, heat milk, sugar, 4 tablespoons butter and salt until sugar dissolves. Set aside to cool. In a large bowl, dissolve yeast in warm water. Add cooled milk mixture, eggs and 2 cups flour, beating until well mixed. Add enough remaining flour to form a dough and knead until smooth, about 10 minutes. Place dough in a greased bowl, cover and let rise in a warm place until double in size, about 1 hour. Melt remaining 2 tablespoons butter. Punch down dough and divide into 3 pieces. Roll each piece into a 12-inch circle and brush with melted butter. Cut each circle into 12 wedges. Starting at wide end, roll each wedge to form crescents. Cover and let rise 1 hour. Brush with glaze and sprinkle with poppy or sesame seed. Bake 10 minutes at 400 degrees. Yields 36 rolls.

Potato Rolls

2	packages dry yeast	½	cup butter, softened
½	cup sugar	½	cup unseasoned mashed potatoes
1	tablespoon salt		
1½	cups warm water	6½	cups flour
2	eggs		Melted butter

Dissolve yeast, sugar and salt in warm water; let stand until bubbles form. Add eggs, butter, mashed potatoes and 3 cups flour. With electric mixer at high speed, beat until smooth. Using wooden spoon, gradually stir in remaining flour. Use hands to work in flour until dough is stiff and leaves the sides of bowl. Turn out on floured board, cover and let rest 15 minutes. Shape into rolls. Let rolls rise on greased baking sheet, covered, until double in bulk, about 1 hour. Brush with melted butter and bake at 400 degrees for 12 minutes or until golden. Yields 36 rolls.

Unbaked rolls may be frozen up to 6 months; rolls may be removed and baked as needed.

Breads

Popovers

3	eggs, well beaten	1	cup milk
½	teaspoon salt	2	teaspoons vegetable oil
1	cup flour	1	teaspoon sugar

Generously grease muffin tins. Preheat oven to 500 degrees. Combine all ingredients until well blended. Fill muffin tins ½ full. Place immediately in oven. Bake 10 minutes at 500 degrees; reduce heat to 250 degrees and bake for 10 more minutes. Popovers are done when the sides are firm. Yields 12 popovers.

Ice Box Rolls

2	cups milk	1	teaspoon sugar
½	cup sugar	¼	cup lukewarm water
2	teaspoons salt	2	eggs, beaten
3	tablespoons butter	6½	cups flour
2	packages dry yeast		

Scald milk and combine with ½ cup sugar, salt and butter. Cool to 85 degrees (lukewarm). Dissolve yeast and 1 teaspoon sugar in water. Let proof; then stir into cooled milk mixture. Add eggs plus 4 cups flour. Mix well. Add remaining flour or as much as needed to make ball of dough. Place dough in oiled bowl, turn to coat dough evenly, cover and place in refrigerator overnight. Remove from refrigerator and shape like Parker House rolls. Place on greased baking sheet and let rise 2 hours. Bake at 400 degrees for 12 minutes or until brown. Yields 4 dozen.

To make Parker House rolls, form dough into small balls and flatten with rolling pin. With pencil or handle of wooden spoon press a line into center of each round. Brush with melted butter and fold over.

Breads

Family Biscuits

⅔   cup vegetable shortening   ⅔   cup milk
2   cups self-rising flour

Mix together shortening and flour with fork or pastry cutter. Stir in milk as needed to make a dough. On a floured surface, press out to ¼-inch thickness and cut with floured biscuit cutter or other round object of desired size. Bake on an ungreased baking sheet at 425 degrees for 10 minutes or until brown. Yields 10 to 12 biscuits.

For drop biscuits, increase milk slightly and drop by spoonfuls on ungreased baking sheet.

Cream Cheese Biscuits

½   cup butter, softened   ⅛   teaspoon salt
2   3-ounce packages cream   1   cup flour
     cheese, softened

Cream butter and cheese with electric mixer; add salt and flour. When dough forms, remove and scrape blades. Knead for a few minutes with floured hands. Cover and refrigerate one hour or place in freezer 10 minutes. Roll out on floured surface to ¼-inch thickness. Cut with small floured biscuit cutter. Place on lightly greased baking sheet. Bake 15 minutes or until brown at 400 degrees. Yields 24 small biscuits.

Breads

Broccoli Cornbread

1   10-ounce package frozen
    chopped broccoli
1   large onion, chopped
½   cup butter
4   eggs, beaten

1   cup cottage cheese
1   teaspoon salt
1   8½-ounce package
    cornbread mix

Cook and drain broccoli. Sauté onion in butter until transparent. Combine broccoli, onion, eggs, cottage cheese, salt and cornbread mix. Pour into lightly greased 9 x 13-inch pan. Bake at 375 degrees for 50 minutes or until golden. Cut into squares. Serves 12.

Versatile Sweet Dough

2   packages dry yeast
½   cup warm water
1   cup milk, scalded
⅓   cup butter, melted

1   teaspoon salt
½   cup sugar
2   eggs, beaten
4-5 cups flour

Sprinkle yeast over warm water (105 to 115 degrees). Set aside. Combine milk, butter, salt, sugar and eggs. Stir in 1 cup flour. Add yeast and remaining flour, 1 cup at a time to make a soft dough. Knead on well floured surface until smooth and elastic, about 5 minutes. Place dough in warm buttered bowl, turning to coat. Cover and let rise until doubled, about 1½ hours. Punch down and let rest 10 minutes. Use to make Caramel Pecan Rolls or Apple Coffee Cake.

Breads

Caramel Pecan Rolls

1	recipe Versatile Sweet Dough	1	cup sugar
4	tablespoons butter, softened	3	teaspoons ground cinnamon

Topping:

½	cup butter, softened	2	tablespoons water
1	cup dark brown sugar	4-5	dozen pecan halves
2	tablespoons corn syrup		

Roll sweet dough into two 15 x 20-inch rectangles. Spread each with half the butter, sugar and cinnamon. Roll up jelly roll fashion, beginning at long edge. Cut each into 9 slices. Combine topping ingredients and divide mixture among 18 well greased muffin tins. Place a dough slice on top of mixture and let rise 1 hour. Bake at 350 degrees for 20 minutes. Turn bottom side up to cool. Freeze if not used immediately. Yields 18 rolls.

Apple Cinnamon Coffee Cake

1	recipe Versatile Sweet Dough	4	tablespoons butter
4-5	cups peeled, thinly sliced tart apples	¼	cup sugar
		½-1	teaspoon cinnamon

Divide dough into three balls. Pat each into well greased 9-inch deep-dish pie pans or cake pans. Let rise 1 hour. Place prepared apples on dough, dot with butter and sprinkle with mixture of cinnamon and sugar. Bake at 350 degrees for 25 to 30 minutes. Yields 3 coffee cakes.

Freezes beautifully.

Breads

Sour Cream Breakfast Cake

Dough:

1	cup sour cream	2	packages dry yeast
½	cup sugar	½	cup warm water
1	teaspoon salt	2	eggs, beaten
½	cup butter, melted	4	cups flour

In a small saucepan, warm sour cream. Stir in sugar, salt and butter. Let mixture cool. Sprinkle yeast over warm water in large mixing bowl and let dissolve. Add to dissolved yeast the sour cream mixture, then eggs, mixing well. Add flour ½ cup at a time, mixing after each addition. Cover dough tightly and refrigerate overnight, no more than 24 hours.

Cream Cheese Filling:

2	8-ounce packages cream cheese, softened	⅛	teaspoon salt
¾	cup sugar	2	teaspoons vanilla or
1	egg, beaten		1 teaspoon vanilla and
			1 teaspoon almond extract

Cream the cheese and sugar; add remaining ingredients and mix well. Set aside.

Divide dough into 4 equal parts. Roll each into a 12 x 18-inch rectangle. Spread each with ¼ of filling, leaving 1-inch margin around edges. Roll up lengthwise (jelly roll fashion), seal seam and tuck ends under. Place seam side down on greased baking sheet. Make several slits across top to reveal filling. Cover with towel and let rise about 1 hour. Bake at 375 degrees for 12 to 15 minutes.

Glaze:

1	cup powdered sugar	1	teaspoon vanilla
2	tablespoons milk		Dash salt

Mix together glaze ingredients and spread over warm coffee cakes. Cool completely on rack.

When completely cool, wrap in foil for later reheating. Breakfast cakes also freeze well. Yields 4 breakfast cakes.

Breads

Poppy Seed Coffee Cake

2-3	tablespoons poppy seed		4	eggs
1	cup buttermilk		2	cups flour
1	cup butter		1	teaspoon baking soda
1½	cups sugar		1	teaspoon vanilla

In a small bowl, soak poppy seed in buttermilk. Set aside. In a large bowl, cream butter and sugar. Add eggs, one at a time, beating well after each addition. Mix together flour and soda and add alternately with buttermilk-poppy seed mixture. Add vanilla and mix well. Pour into greased bundt pan or 10-inch tube pan. Bake at 350 degrees for 55 to 60 minutes. Cool thoroughly in pan before removing to slice. May be frozen.

Variation: Use ½ to ¾ teaspoon almond extract instead of vanilla.

Golden Cake Bread

1	package dry yeast		2	eggs, beaten
¼	cup warm water		2	teaspoons vanilla
1	cup milk		1	teaspoon salt
½	cup butter		4-4½	cups flour
½	cup sugar			

In a large mixing bowl, dissolve yeast in water. Scald milk in small saucepan, remove from heat and stir in butter and sugar. Cool to lukewarm and add to yeast. Stir in eggs, vanilla and salt. Add 1 cup flour; beat well. Add remaining flour ½ cup at a time, beating well after each addition. Cover and let rise for 1 hour. Punch down, cover and let rise 45 minutes. Generously flour hands. Remove dough and divide evenly between two greased 5 x 7-inch loaf pans. Let rise 45 minutes. Bake 25 to 30 minutes at 350 degrees. Remove from pans immediately after baking. Cool on racks. Yields 2 loaves.

Breads

Blueberry Cake

1	cup butter, softened	½	cup milk
2	cups sugar	½	teaspoon vanilla
3	eggs	2	cups blueberries
3	cups flour	2	teaspoons sugar
1½	teaspoons baking powder	2	teaspoons flour
⅛	teaspoon salt		Powdered sugar
¼	teaspoon ground mace		

In a large bowl, cream butter and sugar. Add eggs and mix well. Combine flour, baking powder, salt and mace; add to creamed mixture alternately with milk, blending well after each addition. Stir in vanilla. Coat blueberries with sugar and flour and fold into batter. Pour into greased and floured 10-inch bundt pan. Bake at 350 degrees for 60 minutes or until golden brown. Cool slightly and serve sprinkled with powdered sugar.

Breakfast Squares

2	8-ounce cans refrigerated crescent rolls	1	teaspoon vanilla or almond extract
2	8-ounce packages cream cheese, softened	1	tablespoon lemon juice
¾	cup sugar	1	egg white, beaten
		¼	cup chopped pecans or almonds

Press one package of rolls in the bottom of a greased 9 x 13-inch pan. Mix together cream cheese, sugar, vanilla and lemon juice. Spread on dough. Top with remaining package of rolls. Brush with egg white and sprinkle with nuts. Bake at 350 degrees for 30 to 35 minutes. Serve warm. Yields 24 squares.

Breads

Fluffy Buttermilk Pancakes

1½	cups flour	3	eggs, separated
1	tablespoon sugar	1⅔	cups buttermilk or sour milk
1	teaspoon baking powder	3	tablespoons butter, melted
¾	teaspoon salt		and cooled
1	teaspoon baking soda		

Sift dry ingredients together. In a small bowl, beat egg whites until stiff. Set aside. Beat yolks in large bowl until lemon colored. Stir in buttermilk, then sifted ingredients until just blended. Blend in butter. Fold in beaten egg whites. Cook on greased, preheated griddle turning once. Yields 15 medium pancakes.

Overnight French Toast

8	slices French bread, ¾-inch thick	2	tablespoons orange juice
4	eggs	½	teaspoon vanilla
1	cup milk	¼	cup butter, divided
1	tablespoon sugar		Fresh fruit
⅛	teaspoon salt		Powdered sugar

Place bread in a 9 x 13-inch baking dish. Combine eggs, milk, sugar, salt, orange juice and vanilla, beating well. Pour mixture over bread slices. Turn slices to coat evenly. Cover and refrigerate overnight. To cook, melt 2 tablespoons butter in a large skillet. Sauté 4 slices of the French bread in butter for 4 minutes on each side or until lightly browned. Repeat procedure with remaining butter and bread slices. Top each slice of toast with fresh fruit (peaches, strawberries, blueberries) and sprinkle with powdered sugar. Serve immediately. Serves 4.

Breads

Strawberry Butter

½   pint strawberries, hulled   3   tablespoons powdered sugar
1   cup butter, softened

Mash strawberries and combine with butter and sugar until smooth. Yields 1½ cups.

Especially delicious on toast, muffins and pound cake.

Cranberry Butter

⅓   pound raw cranberries   1   tablespoon lemon juice
½   cup butter, softened   1½   cups powdered sugar

Blend cranberries in blender or food processor for 1 minute or until well chopped. Add all other ingredients and blend for 3 minutes. Yields 1 cup.

Delicious on toast or bran muffins.

Vegetables
& Side
Dishes

Vegetables & Side Dishes

*Other Vegetable and Side Dish recipes may be found in **Southern Classics.***

Vegetables and Side Dishes

Artichokes in Sauce

3	14-ounce cans artichoke hearts, drained	3	tablespoons butter, melted
¾	cup mayonnaise	1	tablespoon lemon juice
½	cup sour cream or plain yogurt	1	tablespoon capers
½	cup grated Parmesan cheese	1	teaspoon salt
			Dash garlic salt
			Dash pepper

Place artichokes in a buttered shallow 1½-quart baking dish. Combine remaining ingredients and pour over artichokes. Bake 20 minutes at 350 degrees. Serves 4 to 6.

Baked Artichokes and Mushrooms

½	pound fresh mushrooms	16	slices bacon, cooked and crumbled
2	8-ounce cans tomato sauce	2	teaspoons parsley
2	tablespoons white wine	2	tablespoons grated Parmesan cheese
1	14-ounce can artichoke hearts, drained and quartered		

Remove stems from mushrooms, keeping caps whole. Slice stems and add to tomato sauce and set aside. Sprinkle a buttered 7 x 11-inch baking dish with wine. Arrange mushroom caps and artichoke hearts in alternating rows. Sprinkle bacon on top. Pour tomato sauce mixture over vegetables. Top with parsley and cheese. Bake 30 minutes at 350 degrees. Serves 4.

Green Beans with Dill

1	teaspoon dried dill weed	½	teaspoon sugar
¾	pound fresh green beans, washed and ends trimmed	½	teaspoon salt
		1	tablespoon butter

Fill a large pot half full with water. Bring to a rapid boil. Crumble dill weed into water and add green beans. Boil 8 to 10 minutes or until tender. Drain beans well. Return beans to pot. Add sugar, salt and butter. Toss over heat for about 1 minute. Serve hot. Serves 4.

Vegetables and Side Dishes

String Bean Special

2   10-ounce packages frozen
     French-style green beans
2   tablespoons butter
½   cup finely chopped onion
3   2-ounce packages slivered
     almonds
2   tablespoons flour
1   teaspoon salt
½   teaspoon pepper

½   teaspoon dry mustard
1   teaspoon Worcestershire
     sauce
     Dash garlic powder (optional)
1   cup milk
1   cup sour cream
1   cup grated sharp Cheddar
     cheese

Cook green beans until tender. Drain and set aside. Melt butter in a saucepan. Add onion and almonds. Cook over medium heat until onion is transparent, stirring occasionally. Remove from heat and blend in flour, salt, pepper, mustard, Worcestershire and garlic powder. Heat until mixture bubbles. Remove from heat and gradually add milk and sour cream. Cook over low heat 2 or 3 minutes, stirring constantly. Add drained green beans to sauce. Toss gently until well coated. Turn into an ungreased 2-quart baking dish. Sprinkle cheese on top. Bake uncovered 10 to 15 minutes at 350 degrees. Serves 6 to 8.

Penny's Green Beans

2   medium onions, chopped
1   green pepper, chopped
4-5 slices bacon, coarsely
     chopped
2   10-ounce packages frozen
     French-style green beans,
     thawed and drained

1   28-ounce can stewed
     tomatoes, partially drained
1   4-ounce can button
     mushrooms, drained
     Salt and pepper to taste
2   cups grated Cheddar cheese

Sauté onion and green pepper with bacon in skillet until bacon is crisp. Drain and place in an ungreased 3-quart casserole. Stir in beans, tomatoes, mushrooms, salt and pepper. Top with cheese. Bake covered at 300 degrees for 30 to 35 minutes. Serves 8 to 10.

Vegetables and Side Dishes

Super Bean Trio

3	medium onions, chopped	1	8-ounce can midget butter
1	clove garlic, finely chopped		beans, drained
4	tablespoons bacon drippings	½	cup brown sugar
1	16-ounce can pork and	¼	cup ketchup
	beans	1	teaspoon dry mustard
1	15-ounce can red kidney	1	teaspoon salt
	beans	½	teaspoon black pepper

Sauté onions and garlic in bacon drippings. Combine remaining ingredients. Add onions and garlic. Pour into a greased 2-quart casserole. Bake uncovered 45 minutes at 350 degrees. Serves 10 to 12.

Broccoli Delicious

1	14-ounce can artichoke hearts, drained and quartered	¼	teaspoon Worcestershire sauce
½	cup butter, softened	2	10-ounce packages frozen chopped broccoli, cooked and drained
1	8-ounce package cream cheese, softened		Cooked crumbled bacon
1½	teaspoons lemon juice		

Grease a 1½-quart baking dish. Place artichokes on bottom. Cream butter, cheese, lemon juice and Worcestershire. Add broccoli and mix well. Pour mixture over artichokes. Sprinkle bacon on top. Bake 25 minutes at 350 degrees. Serves 6 to 8.

Spinach may be substituted for broccoli.

Broccoli Puff

1	pound fresh broccoli, cut in spears, cooked and drained	⅔	cup sour cream
		⅔	cup cottage cheese
	Salt and pepper to taste	⅓	cup grated Parmesan cheese

Place broccoli in a lightly buttered 8 x 11½-inch baking dish. Season with salt and pepper. Combine remaining ingredients and spread on top of broccoli. Broil 10 to 12 minutes or until browned and bubbly. Serves 4 to 6.

Asparagus may be substituted for broccoli.

Vegetables and Side Dishes

Never-Fail Hollandaise

2	egg yolks	½	cup butter
2	tablespoons lemon juice		Salt and pepper to taste

Beat egg yolks and lemon juice in a small bowl until well blended. Place in a saucepan over low heat. Add butter cut into pieces. Stir until butter melts and mixture thickens. Add salt and pepper. Serve at room temperature. Serves 4 to 6.

Do not refrigerate or reheat.

Carrots Consommé

½	pound carrots, peeled and sliced	2	tablespoons brown sugar
2	tablespoons finely chopped onion	2	tablespoons butter
		1	10½-ounce can beef consommé

Combine all ingredients in a saucepan. Cover and simmer until carrots are tender. Serves 6.

Crusty-Topped Cauliflower

1	large head cauliflower	½	cup mayonnaise
2	teaspoons Dijon-style mustard	½-¾	cup grated Cheddar cheese

Cook cauliflower whole in a covered pan with a small amount of boiling, salted water for 20 minutes or until tender. Drain. Combine mustard and mayonnaise and spread over cauliflower in a baking dish. Sprinkle with cheese and bake at 350 degrees for 10 minutes or until cheese melts. Serves 6.

Vegetables and Side Dishes

Celery Almondine

1	chicken bouillon cube, crushed	⅛	teaspoon garlic powder
1	teaspoon MSG	⅛	teaspoon ground ginger
1	tablespoon minced dried onion	½	cup slivered almonds
½	teaspoon sugar	2	tablespoons butter, melted
		4	cups diagonally cut celery

Combine bouillon, MSG, onion, sugar, garlic powder and ginger. Set aside. Sauté almonds in butter. Add celery. Sprinkle in spice mixture and stir. Cook covered 20 to 25 minutes over medium to low heat, stirring occasionally. Serves 4 to 6.

Corn Pie

2	tablespoons butter	1	cup milk
2	cups fresh corn, cut from cob	2	eggs, beaten
2	tablespoons flour	1	cup grated Cheddar cheese
1	teaspoon salt	2-3	tablespoons butter
1	tablespoon sugar	10	round buttery crackers, crumbled

Melt butter in a small skillet and sauté corn until tender. In a mixing bowl, combine flour, salt and sugar. Add corn, milk, eggs and cheese. Place mixture in a lightly buttered 8-inch square casserole and dot with butter. Sprinkle with cracker crumbs. Bake uncovered at 350 degrees for 30 minutes or until center is set. Serves 6.

 Freeze an onion 20 minutes before chopping for fewer tears.

To absorb odors when cooking cauliflower or strong greens, place the end crusts of bread on top of lid.

To retain color in cauliflower, add a little milk to cooking water.

Vegetables and Side Dishes

Eggplant Croquettes

2	ripe plump eggplants			Dash ground allspice
1	cup chopped fresh parsley	2	eggs, well beaten
3	cloves garlic, finely chopped	½	cup grated Gruyère or Swiss cheese
2	tablespoons finely chopped green onion	2	cups breadcrumbs
	Salt and cayenne pepper to taste	½-1	cup vegetable oil, as needed

Peel eggplants and cut in half lengthwise. Place in cold, salted water. Bring to boil, reduce heat, cover and cook for 5 to 7 minutes. Drain eggplants and squeeze out water. Purée in a vegetable mill or blender. Combine purée with parsley, garlic, onion, salt, cayenne pepper and allspice. Mix well. Add eggs, cheese and breadcrumbs. Drop mixture by the teaspoon into hot oil; fry on both sides until well browned. Serves 6 to 8.

Excellent side dish for pork roast.

Greenwood Sherried Fruit

1	15½-ounce can pineapple slices, cut in halves	1	15-ounce jar spiced apple rings
1	29-ounce can pear halves	½	cup butter
1	29-ounce can cling peach halves	2	tablespoons flour
1	17-ounce can apricot halves	½	cup sugar
		1	cup sherry

Drain fruit and layer in a deep 3-quart casserole, placing apple rings on top. In a double boiler, melt butter and blend in flour, sugar and sherry. Cook mixture until thick as cream. Pour over fruit and refrigerate overnight. Before serving, bake uncovered 30 minutes at 350 degrees. Serves 12.

This is a nice side dish with ham, fowl, crab or shrimp.

Vegetables and Side Dishes

Summer Curried Peaches

8	fresh peaches, unpeeled and halved or quartered	2	teaspoons curry powder
¾	cup brown sugar	1	16-ounce can crushed pineapple, undrained
6	tablespoons butter, melted		

Layer half of peaches in an 8-inch square baking dish. Mix sugar, butter and curry powder. Pour half over the peaches. Layer remaining peaches. Pour pineapple over peaches. Top with rest of sugar mixture. Bake until bubbly at 325 degrees. Do not overcook. Serves 8.

Baked Pineapple

2	eggs	5	slices white bread, cubed
¼	cup sugar	½	cup butter, melted
1	20-ounce can crushed pineapple in own juice, undrained		

In a small bowl, beat eggs and sugar. Add pineapple and mix well. In a large bowl, toss bread cubes with melted butter. Stir in pineapple mixture; pour into a greased 8-inch square baking dish. Bake 30 minutes at 350 degrees. Serves 6 to 8.

May be served as a side dish with ham or roast pork. May also be used as a dessert topped with sweetened whipped cream or vanilla ice cream.

Cranberry Relish

1½	cups fresh cranberries	¾	cup sugar
½	cup orange juice		Dash salt
1	orange, unpeeled, cut in pieces and seeded	½	cup pecans

Put all ingredients except pecans in blender. Cover and blend 20 seconds or until finely chopped. Add pecans; turn blender on and off several times to chop pecans. Chill before serving. Store in refrigerator up to 1 week. Yields about 1 pint.

Traditionally served with turkey or pork.

Vegetables and Side Dishes

Duxelles

4	tablespoons butter	½	teaspoon salt
3	tablespoons finely chopped shallots	⅛	teaspoon cayenne pepper
½	pound fresh mushrooms, chopped	1	tablespoon finely chopped fresh parsley
2	tablespoons flour	1½	tablespoons finely chopped fresh chives
1	cup whipping cream	½	tablespoon lemon juice

In heavy frying pan, melt butter. Add shallots and mushrooms. Cook, stirring, for about 4 minutes but do not brown. Cook slowly over low heat for 20 minutes. Stir in remaining ingredients and continue cooking until almost all of liquid has evaporated. Refrigerate until chilled. Serves 8 to 10.

This freezes well. Duxelles may be served over Beef Wellington, as stuffing for blanched zucchini boats or as filling for crêpes or omelets.

Mushroom Casserole

1½	pounds mushrooms, sliced		Salt and pepper to taste
1	onion, chopped	2	tablespoons chopped parsley
½	cup butter		
2	tablespoons flour	¼	cup bread crumbs
1	cup sour cream	¼	cup butter

In a skillet, sauté mushrooms and onion in butter until onion is transparent. Stir in flour and cook 5 to 10 minutes over low heat. Blend in sour cream, salt and pepper. Stir in chopped parsley. Place in a shallow 1½-quart buttered casserole. Sprinkle with bread crumbs and dot with butter. Bake uncovered at 350 degrees for 25 minutes. Serves 6 to 8.

Vegetables and Side Dishes

Baked Mushrooms

1	pound mushrooms	¼	cup grated Parmesan cheese
3	tablespoons butter	2	teaspoons chopped fresh dill
2	tablespoons finely chopped onion	1	cup whipping cream or half and half
¼	teaspoon salt	2	egg yolks, slightly beaten
⅛	teaspoon white pepper	3	tablespoons soft bread crumbs
1	tablespoon flour		

Rinse mushrooms; pat dry and slice. In large skillet, melt butter. Add mushrooms, onion, salt and white pepper. Cover and simmer 8 minutes. Stir in flour and cheese; cook 3 minutes. Place in buttered 8-inch square baking dish or individual ramekins. Sprinkle with dill. Mix cream with egg yolks. Pour over mushrooms and sprinkle with bread crumbs. Bake uncovered at 425 degrees for 12 to 15 minutes or until brown. Serves 6.

May be served as an appetizer on toast rounds.

Mushroom Quiche

1	10-inch pie shell, unbaked	1	teaspoon salt, divided
4	tablespoons butter, divided	4	eggs
2	tablespoons finely chopped onion	1	cup whipping cream
		⅛	teaspoon pepper
1	pound mushrooms, thinly sliced	⅛	teaspoon ground nutmeg
1	teaspoon lemon juice	½-1	cup grated Gruyère or Swiss cheese

Preheat oven to 450 degrees. Bake pie shell 10 minutes or until lightly browned; cool. Reduce oven temperature to 350 degrees. Melt 3 tablespoons butter in skillet. Add onion and sauté for 1 minute. Stir in mushrooms, lemon juice and ½ teaspoon salt. Cover pan and simmer 10 minutes. Uncover pan, increase heat and boil 5 to 10 minutes until liquid evaporates, stirring occasionally. Beat eggs and cream together. Add remaining salt, pepper and nutmeg. Stir in mushroom mixture. Pour into pie shell. Sprinkle with cheese and dot with remaining tablespoon butter. Bake at 350 degrees 35 minutes or until knife inserted in center comes out clean. Serves 6.

Vegetables and Side Dishes

Stuffed Onions

6	medium onions	¼	cup sliced mushrooms
2	tablespoons vegetable oil	2	tablespoons chopped pecans
	Paprika	¼	teaspoon salt
¼	cup butter	¼	cup herb seasoned stuffing
¼	cup half and half	1	tablespoon butter, melted
¼	cup chopped black olives		Grated Parmesan cheese

Peel onions. Cut a thick slice from the top and scoop out centers of each onion. Set aside tops and centers. Cook shells in boiling salted water for 25 minutes or until tender. Drain well. Brush each shell with oil and sprinkle with paprika. Coarsely chop reserved tops and centers of onions. In a saucepan, melt butter and sauté chopped onions until tender. Stir in half and half, olives, mushrooms, pecans and salt. Spoon into cooked onion shells and top with a mixture of stuffing and 1 tablespoon melted butter. Sprinkle with paprika and Parmesan cheese. Bake in greased shallow pan for 15 minutes at 350 degrees. Serves 6.

Shrimp-Stuffed Potatoes

6	medium baking potatoes	1	4¼-ounce can shrimp, drained, or ½ pound raw shrimp, cooked and cleaned
½	cup butter, softened		
½	cup half and half		
4	teaspoons onion juice		
1	cup grated Cheddar cheese		Paprika, cooked crumbled bacon and parsley for garnish
1	teaspoon salt		
½	teaspoon paprika		

Scrub potatoes and bake at 425 degrees for 40 to 60 minutes or until done. When cool to touch, but still warm, cut potatoes in half lengthwise. Carefully scoop out pulp leaving a firm ¼-inch shell. Mash potato pulp in a large bowl. Blend in butter, half and half, onion juice, cheese, salt and paprika. Stir in shrimp and mix well. Stuff potato shells with mixture. Sprinkle with paprika and bacon. Bake for 15 minutes at 425 degrees. Before serving, garnish with parsley. Serves 12.

Vegetables and Side Dishes

Sweet Potato Casserole

Syrup:

¼ cup brown sugar
2 tablespoons orange juice

2 tablespoons butter

Heat all ingredients until melted. Set aside.

Casserole:

2 cups cooked or canned
       sweet potatoes
2 eggs, beaten
¼ cup brown sugar
¼ cup orange juice

6 tablespoons butter, melted
1 teaspoon salt
1 teaspoon ground cinnamon
¼ teaspoon ground cloves
⅔ cup pecan halves

In a large mixing bowl, mash sweet potatoes. Stir in eggs. Add remaining ingredients, except pecans, and mix well. Place mixture in a greased 2-quart baking dish. Arrange pecans on top and pour syrup over contents. Bake uncovered 40 minutes at 375 degrees. Serves 6.

Wild Rice with Pecans

1 cup wild rice
2-3 14½-ounce cans chicken
        broth
½ cup butter, melted

½ cup sliced green onions,
        tops included
½-1 cup unsalted pecans, toasted

Cook rice according to directions, substituting chicken broth for water. When rice is done, blend in butter, onions and pecans. Serve hot. Serves 6 to 8.

For variety, add 1 pound cooked drained sausage, sautéed mushrooms or grated cheese.

Vegetables and Side Dishes

Garlic Rice

½   cup butter
½   cup vermicelli, broken into
     1-inch pieces
1   cup uncooked rice
½   pound mushrooms, sliced
     (optional)

1   teaspoon salt
1   teaspoon garlic powder
2⅔   cups chicken broth

Melt butter in a large covered skillet. Add vermicelli and brown until golden. Add rice, mushrooms, salt, garlic powder and chicken broth. Bring to a boil, cover and simmer for 20 minutes, or until liquid is absorbed. Serves 8.

If a more colorful dish is desired, chopped green pepper and chopped parsley may be added with mushrooms. Seafood lovers may add sautéed shrimp before serving.

Spanish Rice

3   cups cooked rice
¼   cup butter, melted
4   eggs, beaten
2   cups grated sharp Cheddar
     cheese
1   10-ounce package frozen
     chopped spinach, cooked
     and drained
1   3-ounce can sliced
     mushrooms, drained

1   cup milk
1   tablespoon finely chopped
     onion
1   tablespoon Worcestershire
     sauce
1½   teaspoons salt
½   teaspoon dried marjoram
½   teaspoon dried thyme
½   teaspoon dried rosemary

Mix all ingredients together. Pour into lightly buttered 2-quart baking dish. Place casserole in a shallow pan filled with water. Bake uncovered at 350 degrees for 30 to 45 minutes or until heated. Serves 6 to 8.

Vegetables and Side Dishes

Robin's Confetti Rice

¼	cup butter	¾	cup sliced celery
1½	cups uncooked rice	¾	cup slivered almonds, toasted
3	cups hot chicken broth	½	cup chopped fresh parsley
¾	cup grated carrots		(optional)

In a skillet, melt butter. Add rice and coat well with butter. Heat together for 5 minutes. In a 3-quart casserole, combine rice and chicken broth. Cover and bake 45 minutes at 350 degrees. Stir in carrots, celery and almonds. Cover and bake an additional 10 minutes. Garnish with parsley before serving. Serves 6.

Baked Red Rice

6	slices bacon, cooked and crumbled, drippings reserved	2	medium onions, finely chopped
¾	cup uncooked rice	1	tablespoon dried basil
2	16-ounce cans tomatoes, undrained and chopped		Tabasco sauce to taste
2	green peppers, finely chopped		Worcestershire sauce to taste
			Salt and pepper to taste

Rub bottom and sides of a 2-quart baking dish with 1 to 2 tablespoons bacon drippings. Combine rice, tomatoes, green peppers, onions, bacon and seasonings. Stir gently with fork. Cover and bake 1 hour and 15 minutes at 350 degrees, stirring occasionally. Serves 6 to 8.

Fried Rice

1	cup cooked rice, cooled	¼	cup water
1	large onion, chopped	¼	teaspoon salt
3	large lettuce leaves, cut in 1-inch squares	⅛	teaspoon pepper
2	tablespoons soy sauce	4	slices bacon, chopped
1	teaspoon sherry	1	large tomato, chopped

Mix rice, onion and lettuce and add soy sauce, sherry, water, salt and pepper. In a skillet, fry bacon for 3 minutes. Add rice mixture and cook 3 minutes. Remove from heat and add tomato. Serves 4.

A great way to use leftover rice.

Vegetables and Side Dishes

Oriental Rice

½ cup finely chopped dried
   apricots
¾ cup uncooked rice
2 tablespoons olive oil
2 tablespoons vegetable oil
2 teaspoons salt
⅛ teaspoon cayenne pepper
1 teaspoon curry powder
1½ cups water

4-5 tablespoons mayonnaise
¼ cup seedless raisins
1½ tablespoons finely chopped
   onion
½ cup finely chopped green
   pepper
¼ cup slivered almonds,
   chopped
¼ cup chopped cashews

Cover apricots with water to soak. In a large saucepan, combine rice, oils, salt, cayenne, curry and water. Bring to a boil and remove from heat. Transfer to an ungreased 2-quart casserole dish and bake covered for 30 minutes at 350 degrees. Remove from oven and fluff with fork. Add drained apricots and remaining ingredients and refrigerate. Serve cold. Serves 6.

Great as a cold salad for a picnic or informal entertaining.

Lentil and Brown Rice Pilaf

4 tablespoons butter
1 medium onion, chopped
1 clove garlic, finely chopped
½ cup chopped green pepper
1 14½-ounce can chicken broth
1 cup water

¼ cup sherry
½ cup dried lentils, washed
   and drained
½ cup uncooked brown rice
Salt and pepper to taste
Chopped parsley

In a medium-size skillet, melt butter and sauté onion, garlic and green pepper. Add chicken broth, water and sherry. Bring to a boil. Add lentils and rice. Return to a boil. Cover and simmer 50 to 55 minutes or until lentils are tender. Add salt and pepper. Sprinkle with chopped parsley. Serves 6.

Good instead of rice as an accompaniment for spicy meat dishes.

Vegetables and Side Dishes

Hot Spinach Molds on Tomato Rings

2	10-ounce packages frozen chopped spinach	¼	teaspoon pepper
3	tablespoons butter, melted	1	tablespoon white vinegar
6	eggs, slightly beaten	¼	teaspoon dried savory
1⅓	cups milk	8-9	tomato slices, ¼-inch thick
2	medium onions, grated		Salt and pepper to taste
1¼	teaspoons salt		Sour cream with horseradish for topping

Cook spinach and drain well. In a bowl, combine spinach, butter, eggs, milk, onion, salt, pepper, vinegar and savory. Preheat oven to 350 degrees. Pour mixture into 8 or 9 well buttered custard cups. Place cups in a shallow roasting pan in 1 inch of hot water. Bake 35 to 40 minutes or until set. Remove pan, cover entire pan with foil and let stand. Salt and pepper tomato slices. Uncover pan, loosen edges of each cup. Lay tomato slice, seasoned side down, on top of each cup. Invert cup, unmolding spinach onto tomato. Top with mixture of sour cream and horseradish to taste. Serves 8 to 9.

Sally's Spinach Pie

1	10-inch pie shell, unbaked		Dash black pepper
2	10-ounce packages frozen chopped spinach	1	16-ounce carton ricotta cheese
1	small onion, finely chopped	½	cup half and half
3	tablespoons butter	½	cup grated Parmesan cheese
½	teaspoon salt	3	eggs, beaten
½	teaspoon ground nutmeg		

Bake pie shell at 400 degrees for 5 minutes and remove from oven. Cook and drain spinach. In a large skillet, sauté onion in butter until transparent. Add salt, nutmeg, pepper and spinach. In a separate bowl, combine ricotta, half and half, Parmesan and eggs. Stir in spinach mixture. Pour into pie shell. Bake 50 minutes at 350 degrees or until inserted knife comes out clean.

May be made the day before and refrigerated before baking.

Vegetables and Side Dishes

Italian Spinach Casserole

2   10-ounce packages frozen chopped spinach
¼   cup butter
½   cup onion, chopped
1   8-ounce package cream cheese
1   egg, slightly beaten
2   tablespoons Italian bread crumbs

2   tablespoons Parmesan cheese, grated
1   cube chicken bouillon
Additional bread crumbs and Parmesan cheese for topping
3-4   tablespoons butter

Cook and drain spinach. In a skillet, melt butter and sauté onion. Add spinach. Cube cream cheese and add to spinach, stirring until cheese melts. Add egg, bread crumbs, Parmesan cheese and bouillon. Mix well. Pour into a greased 9-inch square baking dish. Sprinkle with additional Parmesan cheese and crumbs if desired and dot with butter. Bake uncovered 20 to 25 minutes at 350 degrees. Serves 6 to 8.

Garden Stuffed Yellow Squash Boats

8-10   medium yellow squash
½   cup chopped green pepper
1   medium tomato, chopped
1   medium onion, chopped
2   slices bacon, cooked and crumbled

½   cup grated sharp Cheddar cheese
½   teaspoon salt
Dash pepper
Butter

Cook whole squash in salted water about 10 minutes, or until tender. Drain and cool. Cut in half or cut a thin slice from top of each squash forming boats; remove seeds. Combine remaining ingredients, except butter, and mix well. Spoon into lightly salted shells. Dot with butter. Place in a buttered 9 x 13-inch baking pan and bake uncovered for 20 minutes at 400 degrees. Serves 8 to 10.

Any combination of finely chopped vegetables may be used in stuffing.

Vegetables and Side Dishes

Nanny's Guinea Squash Pie

2	large eggplants	3-4	slices bread, cut into small
	Salt and pepper		crumbs
1	small onion, chopped	1½	cups grated sharp Cheddar
2	eggs, well beaten		cheese

Peel, slice and cook eggplant in salted water until tender. Drain well and mash. Salt and pepper to taste. Add onion, eggs, crumbs and cheese, reserving enough crumbs and cheese for topping. Mix well. Place in buttered 1½-quart casserole. Top with reserved crumbs and cheese. Bake uncovered at 350 degrees for 45 minutes. Serves 4 to 6.

Squash may be substituted for eggplant.

Zucchini, Eggplant and Tomato Casserole

1	medium eggplant	2	teaspoons dried basil
	Salt	1	teaspoon dried oregano
⅓	cup olive oil	1	tablespoon brown sugar
1	clove garlic, finely chopped		Salt and freshly ground
2	large onions, sliced		pepper to taste
3	zucchini, sliced	¼	cup grated Parmesan cheese
6	large ripe tomatoes, skinned		
	and chopped		

Peel and slice eggplant ½-inch thick. Salt slices and let stand for 15 minutes or longer. Heat oil in a heavy skillet and sauté garlic and onion until transparent. Rinse eggplant, pat dry, cube and add to onion. Cook, stirring, until eggplant is lightly browned. Add zucchini, tomatoes, basil, oregano, brown sugar, salt and pepper. Pour into a 3 to 4-quart casserole; sprinkle with cheese. Bake covered for 20 minutes at 350 degrees. Uncover and bake 10 minutes longer or until vegetables are tender. Serves 6 to 8.

Excellent with chicken or veal.

Vegetables and Side Dishes

Company Squash

8	medium yellow squash	1	tomato, sliced (optional)
½	cup chopped onion	1	cup bread crumbs
1	cup sour cream	1	cup grated Cheddar cheese
½-¾	teaspoon salt	½	cup butter, melted
¼	teaspoon pepper	4	slices bacon, cooked and
¼	teaspoon dried basil		crumbled

Wash squash, trim ends and slice. Cook squash and onion in small amount of salted water. Drain well and mash. Mix sour cream, salt, pepper and basil with squash. Pour into 2-quart or 7 x 11-inch buttered casserole dish. Layer tomato slices on top. Combine bread crumbs, cheese and butter; sprinkle over squash. Top with bacon and bake uncovered at 300 degrees for 30 minutes. Serves 6 to 8.

Zucchini "Pizza"

3	cups grated zucchini	1-2	jalapeño peppers, finely
3	eggs, well beaten		chopped (optional)
⅓	cup flour	1	tablespoon fresh oregano or
	Salt to taste		1 teaspoon dried oregano
2½	cups grated mozzarella	1½	teaspoons fresh basil or
	cheese		½ teaspoon dried basil
½	cup chopped black olives	3	tomatoes, thinly sliced
⅔	cup finely chopped green		Salt and pepper to taste
	onions		
½	cup finely chopped Italian		
	pickled peppers		

Preheat oven to 450 degrees. Generously butter a 9 x 13-inch baking pan. Press excess liquid from zucchini. Add eggs, flour and salt. Mix well and spread in pan. Bake uncovered for 8 minutes. Remove and reduce temperature to 350 degrees. Cover with cheese. Combine olives, onion, peppers and jalapeños. Spread over cheese. Top with herbs. Arrange tomatoes on top. Sprinkle with salt and pepper. Bake uncovered for 25 minutes. Serves 4 to 6.

Good as a main course for lunch or supper.

Vegetables and Side Dishes

Zucchini Pie with Basil

1	9-inch pie shell, unbaked	¼	teaspoon white pepper
2	zucchini, cut into ¼-inch slices	½	cup slivered almonds, toasted
3	tablespoons butter	2	eggs, slightly beaten
1	tablespoon dried basil, crushed		Dash Worcestershire sauce
¾-1	tablespoon coarse salt	½-¾	cup grated Gruyère or Swiss cheese
			Freshly grated nutmeg

Preheat oven to 375 degrees. Bake pie shell for 10 minutes. Remove and cool on rack. In a skillet, sauté zucchini in butter for 1 minute, stirring constantly. Add basil, salt and white pepper and cook over medium heat until zucchini is tender. Layer almonds in bottom of pie shell. Spread zucchini mixture over almonds. Mix eggs and Worcestershire and pour over zucchini. Top with cheese and sprinkle nutmeg in center of pie. Bake in middle of oven for 25 to 30 minutes. Serves 6.

For an appetizer, this may be baked in miniature pie shells. It may also be made without a pie shell.

Scalloped Tomatoes and Artichoke Hearts

½	cup chopped onion	1	14-ounce can artichoke hearts, drained and quartered
3	tablespoons chopped shallots		
½	cup butter, melted	½	teaspoon dried basil
1	2-pound 3-ounce can whole tomatoes, drained	2	tablespoons sugar
			Salt and pepper to taste

Sauté onions and shallots in butter. Add tomatoes, artichokes and basil. Heat for 2 minutes, stirring gently. Season with sugar, salt and pepper. Pour into a 1-quart casserole. Bake uncovered 20 minutes at 325 degrees. Serves 4 to 6.

Vegetables and Side Dishes

Broccoli-Stuffed Tomatoes

6	whole tomatoes	6	teaspoons chopped onion
2	cups broccoli flowerets		Salt and pepper to taste
6	slices bacon, cooked and crumbled		Hollandaise sauce (See index)

Scoop out tomato pulp leaving ¼-inch shell. Invert shells and drain on paper towels. Blanch flowerets; drain and chop coarsely. Add bacon and onion. Salt and pepper tomato shells; fill with broccoli mixtue. Place in a shallow baking dish and bake 15 minutes at 400 degrees. Pour Hollandaise over each tomato. Serves 6.

Vera Cruz Tomatoes and Spinach

3	strips bacon	½	cup sour cream
¼	cup chopped onion		Dash Tabasco sauce
10	ounces fresh spinach, snipped, or 1 10-ounce package frozen chopped spinach, thawed and drained	4	medium tomatoes
			Salt to taste
		½	cup grated mozzarella cheese

Cook bacon. Remove bacon, drain and crumble. Sauté onion in bacon drippings until tender. Stir in spinach and cook 3 to 5 minutes. Remove from heat and stir in sour cream, Tabasco and crumbled bacon. Cut centers out of the tomatoes. Drain and sprinkle with salt. Fill with spinach mixture. Bake 20 to 25 minutes at 375 degrees. Top with cheese and bake 2 to 3 more minutes until cheese melts. Serves 4.

Tomato Pie

1	9-inch deep-dish pie shell, unbaked	½	teaspoon pepper
5	large tomatoes, peeled and thickly sliced	3	teaspoons dried basil
			Garlic powder to taste
½	teaspoon salt	¾	cup mayonnaise
		1¼	cups grated Cheddar cheese

Bake pie shell 10 minutes at 375 degrees. Remove from oven. Layer tomatoes in shell sprinkling each layer with salt, pepper, basil and garlic powder. Combine mayonnaise and cheese. Spread over tomatoes. Bake at 350 degrees for 35 minutes or until browned and bubbly. Let stand 5 minutes before serving. Serves 6 to 8.

Southern Classics

Southern Classics

Southern Classics

Southern Iced Tea

3　quarts water, divided
3　tablespoons loose tea
3　lemons, halved and juiced

1½　cups sugar
　　Fresh mint leaves

Boil 1 quart of water. To this add 3 heaping tablespoons of loose tea and all of lemon rinds, juice and pulp. Let steep for 10 minutes. In another container, mix 2 quarts of water and sugar. Stir until dissolved. Strain the tea mixture into the sugared water and stir. Serve over ice. Garnish with mint. Yields 3 quarts.

Cheese Straws

1　cup butter
1　pound sharp Cheddar
　　cheese, grated
2½　cups flour

½　teaspoon cayenne pepper
1　teaspoon salt
1　teaspoon baking powder

Allow butter and cheese to reach room temperature; cream together. Add flour, cayenne, salt and baking powder. Blend thoroughly. Press through a cookie press onto an ungreased baking sheet. Bake at 350 degrees for 10 to 15 minutes. Watch carefully to prevent overbaking. Store in an airtight container. Yields 14 to 16 dozen.

Buttermilk Biscuits

2　cups flour
1　teaspoon baking powder
½　teaspoon baking soda

½　teaspoon salt
½　cup vegetable shortening
⅔　cup buttermilk

Sift together flour, baking powder, baking soda and salt. Using a pastry cutter, cut in shortening until consistency of coarse corn meal. Add buttermilk and toss gently with a fork until moist. Form dough into a ball. Place on waxed paper and roll dough to thickness of ½ inch. Cut with a 2-inch round cookie cutter dipped in flour. Place on greased baking sheet and bake 10 minutes at 450 degrees. Yields 15 to 18 2-inch biscuits.

Southern Classics

Hot 'Uns

2	cups self-rising flour, unsifted	⅓	cup vegetable oil
		⅔	cup milk

Put flour in a bowl and make a well in the center. Combine liquids and stir into flour. If mixture is too sticky, add a little flour; if too dry, add milk by the teaspoon. Turn onto lightly floured surface; knead gently a few times. Roll to ½-inch thickness. Cut with floured biscuit cutter or juice glass. For soft, high biscuits, place close together on an ungreased baking sheet. For crusty biscuits, place on baking sheet 1-inch apart. Bake in preheated oven at 425 degrees for 10 to 12 minutes. Yields 10 to 12 biscuits.

Sweet Potato Biscuits

3	cups flour	2	cups mashed cooked sweet potatoes
2	heaping tablespoons baking powder		
1	teaspoon salt	½	cup sugar
1	cup vegetable shortening	¼	cup milk

Sift together flour, baking powder and salt. Cut in shortening with fork or pastry cutter. Combine warm sweet potatoes and sugar, mixing well. Add milk. Combine sweet potato and flour mixtures. Blend well. Place on floured surface and roll to desired thickness or about ½ inch. Cut with biscuit cutter. Bake on lightly greased baking sheet at 400 degrees for 10 minutes. Yields 2 to 3 dozen.

Great with pork, country ham or smoked turkey.

Southern Classics

Grandmother's Spoon Bread

2	cups water	2	eggs, beaten
1	cup white corn meal	1	cup milk
1	teaspoon salt	1	teaspoon vegetable oil

In a saucepan, combine water, corn meal and salt. Cook over medium heat until thick, stirring occasionally. Add eggs and milk. Stir well. Spread oil in the bottom of an 8 x 8-inch metal pan. Place pan in a heated oven until oil is very hot. Pour batter into hot pan. Bake at 475 to 500 degrees for 20 minutes or until golden brown. Serve with butter. Serves 4 to 6.

Spoon bread may not be made ahead because it will fall; prepare for immediate serving.

Corn Dodgers

2	cups fine corn meal	3	eggs
1	cup self-rising flour		Chopped onion, if desired
1	tablespoon baking powder	1¼-1½	cups milk, as needed
2	tablespoons sugar		Vegetable oil
1	tablespoon salt		

Mix all dry ingredients together. Add eggs and onion. Mix with enough milk to make batter that will drop from spoon without running. Batter will drop better if made 2 or 3 hours ahead. Drop by tablespoonful into hot oil and deep fry until golden brown.

These Corn Dodgers (Hush Puppies) are served at Lee's Inlet Kitchen, Murrells Inlet, South Carolina.

Kitty's Skillet Corn Bread

1	tablespoon bacon drippings	1	teaspoon salt
1	egg	1	teaspoon baking powder
½	teaspoon baking soda	1	cup corn meal
1	cup buttermilk		

Melt bacon drippings in 8-inch iron skillet in 450 degree oven. Beat egg add baking soda to buttermilk and add to egg. Combine salt, baking powder and corn meal. Add to buttermilk mixture. Pour in hot bacon drippings and return mixture to skillet. Bake 30 minutes in 450 degree oven. Serves 4.

Southern Classics

Blueberry Muffins

½ cup butter, softened	½ teaspoon salt
1 cup sugar	1 teaspoon ground cinnamon
2 eggs, beaten	¼ teaspoon ground nutmeg
½ cup milk	2 cups fresh or frozen
2 cups flour	blueberries
2 teaspoons baking powder	2 tablespoons sugar for topping

Cream together butter and sugar. Add eggs and mix well. Stir in milk. Combine all dry ingredients and mix with liquid mixture, using a wooden spoon. Fold in blueberries. Grease muffin tins and fill each ⅔ full. Sprinkle tops lightly with sugar. Bake 20 minutes or until brown at 375 degrees. Yields 12 to 18 muffins.

Melon Ball and Shrimp Salad

2 pounds shrimp, cooked, cleaned and chilled	1½ tablespoons curry powder
2 tablespoons lemon juice	⅓ cup sour cream
2 teaspoons grated onion	1 large honeydew melon
1 cup chopped celery	1 large canteloupe
1½ teaspoons salt	Bibb lettuce
1 cup mayonnaise	Fresh mint or parsley for garnish

Combine shrimp, lemon juice, onion, celery, salt and mayonnaise. In a separate bowl, blend curry powder into sour cream. Combine the two mixtures. Mix well and chill. Halve melons, remove seeds and form fruit into small balls using a melon scoop. Before serving, combine melon balls and shrimp. Serve on Bibb lettuce and garnish with mint or parsley. Serves 6 to 8.

Wonderful as first course for a formal dinner.

Southern Classics

She-Crab Soup

3	tablespoons butter	½	teaspoon salt
3	tablespoons flour		Pepper to taste
4	cups half and half	1	pound crabmeat
2	tablespoons grated onion	6	tablespoons dry sherry
1	teaspoon Worcestershire sauce		Crumbled cooked egg yolk (optional)
	Dash ground nutmeg		

In top of double boiler, melt butter and stir in flour. Add half and half gradually, stirring until sauce thickens. Add onion, Worcestershire, nutmeg, salt, pepper and crabmeat. Cook over low heat for 20 minutes and adjust seasonings. To serve, put a tablespoon of sherry in each bowl and fill with soup. Top with crumbled egg yolk, if desired. Serves 6.

Inlet-Style Clam Chowder

½	pound fat back, sliced	2½	quarts tomato juice
8	large potatoes, chopped	1	6-ounce can tomato paste
2	large onions, chopped		Salt and pepper to taste
¼	cup chopped celery	1	quart clams, chopped
1	quart clam juice		

In a large skillet, fry fat back. Remove. Sauté potatoes, onion and celery in drippings. Transfer sautéed vegetables to a large pot and add remaining ingredients, except clams. Chop fat back and add to mixture. Simmer until potatoes are done, stirring occasionally. Add clams and heat thoroughly. Yields 1 gallon.

This chowder is a favorite from Lee's Inlet Kitchen, Murrells Inlet, South Carolina.

Southern Classics

Grits

1 cup uncooked grits	½ cup milk
1 teaspoon salt	Butter, as desired
2 cups cold water	

In top of double boiler, combine grits, salt and water. Cook 1 hour, uncovered, stirring occasionally. Add more water if necessary during cooking to keep moist. Add milk and continue cooking, stirring well until mixture thickens. Just before serving, add butter and beat. Beating makes the grits smooth. Serves 4.

To be creative with leftover grits, refrigerate grits in a jelly jar or cylinder-shaped container. Next morning remove from container and slice into patties. Dip sliced grits in beaten egg and a mixture of cornmeal and flour. Fry in vegetable oil or bacon drippings until lightly browned.

Southern Baked Grits

1 cup uncooked grits	¼ teaspoon freshly grated nutmeg
2½ cups grated extra sharp Cheddar cheese	¼ teaspoon Tabasco sauce
8 tablespoons butter	¼ cup milk
3 eggs, well beaten	

Cook grits according to package directions. Stir in cheese, butter, eggs, seasonings and milk. Pour into buttered 2-quart casserole. Bake uncovered at 350 degrees for 40 minutes. Serves 8.

Sausage and Grits Casserole

1 pound hot sausage, browned and drained	3 eggs, beaten
3 cups cooked grits, slightly cooled	3 tablespoons butter, melted
1½ cups milk	10 ounces Cheddar cheese, grated
	Salt and pepper to taste

Mix all ingredients. Place in greased 2-quart casserole and bake uncovered at 350 degrees for 1 hour. Serves 6 to 8.

This casserole may be assembled the night before, refrigerated overnight and baked in the morning. It is also good for a family supper dish served with a salad. Reheats well in microwave.

Southern Classics

Southern Green Beans

2	pounds fresh green beans	½	teaspoon salt
3-4	thin slices salt pork	2	cups water

With small knife or potato peeler, remove strings from side of beans, remove and discard ends. Wash thoroughly. Place all ingredients in large saucepan. Bring to a boil, cover and simmer for at least 2 hours. Serves 8 to 10.

Fried Green Tomatoes

½	cup butter, bacon drippings or vegetable oil		Salt and pepper to taste
2-3	firm green tomatoes	½	cup flour

In a large heavy skillet over medium heat, melt about 4 tablespoons of butter until it begins to brown. Slice tomatoes ¼ to ½ inch thick. Salt and pepper tomato slices, and dredge both sides in flour until well covered. Cook in melted butter. Turn slices only once after first side has thoroughly browned and cook on other side. Add additional butter as needed to keep tomatoes from sticking to the pan. Serve hot. Serves 3 to 4.

Excellent with eggs and grits.

Fried Okra

1	pound fresh okra	Bacon drippings, margarine
	Salt and pepper to taste	or butter
	Yellow corn meal	

Slice okra into ⅓-inch pieces, discarding ends. Sprinkle with salt and pepper and roll in corn meal. Heat bacon drippings in a skillet and fry okra until lightly browned. Drain and serve hot. Serves 4.

Southern Classics

Carolina Vegetable Gumbo

½   cup chopped onion
¼   cup chopped green pepper
2   tablespoons butter
1   tablespoon sugar
1   tablespoon flour
¾   teaspoon salt
¼   teaspoon pepper
6   tomatoes, coarsely chopped,
    or 1 16-ounce can
    tomatoes, undrained

1½ cups fresh orka, sliced in ½-
    inch pieces, or 1 10-ounce
    package frozen cut okra,
    cooked
Water or tomato juice
    (optional)

In a large skillet, sauté onion and green pepper in butter until tender. Stir in sugar, flour, salt and pepper, blending well. Add tomatoes and okra and simmer for 45 minutes to 1 hour, adding water or tomato juice if needed. Serves 4.

May be served over rice.

Hoppin' John

1   cup dried black-eyed peas
4   cups water
2   teaspoons salt
4   slices bacon
1   medium onion, chopped

2   stalks celery, chopped
    (optional)
1   cup uncooked rice
1   teaspoon salt
¼   teaspoon pepper

Boil peas in water with salt until tender; reserve liquid. Fry bacon, remove from pan and crumble. Sauté onions and celery in bacon drippings until onions are clear. In rice steamer or double boiler, combine peas with 1 cup of reserved liquid. Add rice, bacon, onion, celery, salt and pepper. Cover and cook for 1 hour or until rice is done. Stir frequently with a fork. Serves 8.

A South Carolina tradition on New Year's Day, eating Hoppin' John brings good luck.

Southern Classics

Aunt Theo's Rice and Tomato Croquettes

2 tablespoons chopped onion
2 tablespoons butter
1 tablespoon chopped sweet red or green pepper
½ tablespoon chopped fresh parsley
4 whole cloves
1½ cups fresh tomatoes, boiled, drained and mashed or 1½ cups canned tomatoes, drained and mashed

1 cup water
½ cup uncooked rice
Salt and pepper to taste
Paprika to taste
2 egg yolks, slightly beaten
⅓ cup grated Cheddar cheese
3 cups bread crumbs
2 eggs, beaten
Vegetable oil

In a skillet, sauté onion in butter until tender. Add red pepper, parsley, cloves and tomatoes and cook 5 minutes. Pour into top of double boiler. Add water and rice; cover and cook until rice is tender, about 1 hour. Remove cloves; add salt, pepper, paprika, egg yolks and cheese. Chill thoroughly. Shape into croquettes, roll in crumbs, egg and again in crumbs. Fry in hot oil until lightly browned. Serves 6.

Corn Oysters

2 cups fresh white corn, uncooked, or 1 10-ounce package frozen white corn
2 egg yolks, beaten
¼ cup flour

Salt and pepper to taste
2 teaspoons sugar
2 egg whites, stiffly beaten
¼ cup vegetable shortening

In a bowl, combine corn, egg yolks, flour, salt, pepper and sugar. Mix well. Fold in egg whites. In a heavy skillet, heat shortening on medium-high heat. Drop batter from tablespoon into skillet. Brown corn oysters quickly on both sides. Drain on paper towels and serve very hot. Serves 4.

Southern Classics

Beaufort Stew

6	bay leaves	1	pound onion sausage or
	Salt as desired		other link sausage
	Pepper as desired	12	ears fresh corn, shucked
1½	pounds smoked link sausage	3½	pounds unpeeled raw shrimp

Fill large kettle with enough water to cover all ingredients. Add bay leaves, salt and pepper. Boil 15 to 20 minutes. Cut sausage into 2-inch lengths; add to water. Boil for 30 minutes. Break corn ears in half; add to mixture and boil 10 minutes. Add shrimp; boil 5 minutes. Drain water and serve immediately with seafood sauce and melted butter. Serves 12 to 15.

A 3-ounce package Crab Boil may be substituted for seasonings.

Dingle Shrimp Sauté

3	tablespoons butter	1	teaspoon Worcestershire
¼	lemon, rind included, finely		sauce
	chopped	1	pound raw shrimp, cooked
2-3	drops Tabasco sauce		and cleaned

Melt butter in a skillet. Sauté lemon and add sauces. Toss in shrimp. Serve hot. Serves 4.

Great for supper with grits, biscuits and fruit salad.

Southern Classics

Shrimp Pie

2 eggs, beaten
1 cup milk
2 teaspoons Worcestershire
   sauce
Salt and pepper to taste

1½ pounds medium raw shrimp,
    cooked and cleaned
8 saltine crackers, crumbled
4 tablespoons butter

Mix together eggs, milk, Worcestershire, salt and pepper. Add shrimp. Turn into a greased 1-quart casserole. Top with cracker crumbs and dot with butter. Bake uncovered 30 minutes at 350 degrees. If large shrimp are used, place casserole in pan of water while baking to prevent shrimp from becoming tough. Serves 4.

Stewed Shrimp for Breakfast

4 slices bacon
1 small onion, finely chopped
1½ cups small raw shrimp,
    cleaned
1 cup water
1½ tablespoons flour

2 teaspoons water
Salt and pepper to taste
1 teaspoon Worcestershire
  sauce
1 tablespoon ketchup
Cooked grits

Fry bacon until crisp; remove from pan and crumble. Sauté onion in bacon drippings; add shrimp and toss with onion several times. Add 1 cup water and simmer several minutes. Make a paste with flour and 2 teaspoons water and stir into shrimp mixture. Add salt, pepper, Worcestershire and ketchup. Simmer slowly until sauce thickens, about 15 minutes. Serve over hot grits and top with crumbled bacon. Serves 4 to 6.

Southern Classics

Crab Balls

¼	cup finely chopped onion	2	cups half and half
¼	cup finely chopped mushrooms	1	teaspoon salt
		1	teaspoon MSG (optional)
¼	cup finely chopped green pepper	1	teaspoon Worcestershire sauce
2	tablespoons chopped pimiento	½	teaspoon dry mustard
			Pepper to taste
1	tablespoon chopped green onion	2½	cups or 1 pound crabmeat
		1½–2	cups dry bread crumbs, divided
¼	cup butter		
2	tablespoons flour	1	cup Hollandaise Sauce

Sauté all vegetables in butter. Add flour, half and half and seasonings. Blend in crabmeat and 1 cup bread crumbs. Form into 8 balls about 2½ inches in diameter and roll in remaining bread crumbs. Place in lightly buttered individual ramekins. Bake at 350 degrees for 15 to 20 minutes. Remove from oven. Place 1 to 2 tablespoons Hollandaise Sauce on each crab ball and return to broiler for a few minutes. Serves 8.

Crab Cakes

1	pound crabmeat	1	tablespoon prepared mustard
1	egg, beaten		
2	tablespoons finely chopped onion	1	teaspoon salt
		½	teaspoon freshly ground pepper
2	tablespoons mayonnaise		
1	tablespoon Worcestershire sauce	1–1½	cups saltine cracker crumbs, divided
¾–1½	teaspoon Tabasco sauce		Vegetable oil

Mix first 9 ingredients plus ¾ cup cracker crumbs in a bowl. Form 6 patties and roll in remaining crumbs. Heat oil to 375 degrees. Fry patties until golden brown on each side. Drain on paper towel. Serves 6.

Delicious with Southern Baked Grits and broiled tomatoes.

Southern Classics

Seafood Gumbo

4	pounds okra, sliced	3	bay leaves
1¼	cups shortening, divided	½	teaspoon thyme
¾	cup flour	¼	cup Worcestershire sauce
4	onions, chopped		Tabasco sauce to taste
16-20	green onions, chopped		Salt and pepper to taste
4	cups chopped celery	8	quarts water
3	green peppers, chopped	8	pounds raw shrimp,
2	16-ounce cans stewed		cleaned
	tomatoes	2	pounds crabmeat
1	8-ounce can tomato sauce	3-3½	cups long grain rice,
2	tablespoons chopped fresh		cooked
	parsley		

Fry okra in ½ cup shortening for about 30 minutes, or until it is no longer stringy. Make a roux with ¾ cup shortening and the flour and cook until brown. Add onions, celery and green pepper; cook until tender. Stir in tomatoes, tomato sauce, parsley, bay leaves, thyme and okra. Add Worcestershire, Tabasco, salt and pepper. Pour in water and cook uncovered over low heat for at least 2 hours. Add shrimp and cook 30 minutes. Prepare rice. Stir crabmeat into gumbo mixture. Serve gumbo over rice in individual bowls. Serves 25.

Best prepared a day in advance.

Southern Classics

George's Catfish Stew

Salt and pepper
3 pounds catfish filets
4 stalks celery, chopped
1 green pepper, chopped
1 onion, chopped
1 pound bacon, cooked and chopped, drippings reserved
2 quarts ketchup
2 quarts tomatoes, crushed

Salt and pepper to taste
Crushed red pepper to taste
Ground red pepper to taste
Tabasco sauce to taste
Worcestershire sauce to taste
¼-½ cup brown sugar
1 pound potatoes, cooked, peeled and cubed, liquid reserved
Cooked rice

Salt and pepper fish filets. Bake for 20 minutes at 350 degrees in foil-lined baking pan. Reserve juices. Sauté celery, green pepper and onion in bacon drippings in large pot. Add bacon, ketchup and tomatoes to vegetable mixture. Simmer 20 minutes, stirring often. Add seasonings and brown sugar. Cut fish into bite-size pieces and add to mixture along with potatoes and fish stock. Simmer 1 hour. Add potato water if stew is too thick. Serve over rice. Yields 2 gallons.

Best made a day ahead.

Shad Roe with Sherry Lemon Butter

2 pairs shad roe
Flour seasoned with salt and pepper
6 tablespoons butter

1 cup dry sherry
⅓ cup lemon juice
Parsley for garnish

Dredge roe in seasoned flour. Heat butter in heavy skillet until butter begins to brown. Sauté roe for 4 to 5 minutes on each side or until lightly browned. Lower heat and transfer roe to heated serving dish. Add sherry and lemon juice to pan drippings. Reduce liquid to ¾ cup over medium heat, stirring constantly. Pour liquid over roe, garnish with parsley and serve immediately. Serves 2 to 4.

Southern Classics

Buttermilk Froglegs

8	small pairs froglegs or 4 large pairs froglegs	1	teaspoon salt
1-2	cups buttermilk	¼	teaspoon pepper
1	cup flour		Lemon pepper to taste
		6	tablespoons vegetable oil

Place cleaned and skinned froglegs in a dish and cover with buttermilk. Let stand at room temperature for 2 hours. Mix flour, salt, pepper and lemon pepper in a paper or plastic bag. Remove froglegs from buttermilk and shake individually in bag of flour mixture. Heat vegetable oil in skillet. Add coated froglegs to hot oil and fry until done. Serves 4.

Serve as breakfast meat with scrambled eggs and grits or as dinner main course with asparagus and Hollandaise Sauce. If froglegs are large and tend to be tough, brown in butter after coating and cook in small amount of water in a covered skillet until tender, about 10 minutes.

Fried Chicken

2	pounds chicken pieces	1	teaspoon salt
	Salt and pepper	¼	teaspoon pepper
1	cup flour		Vegetable oil

Season chicken pieces with salt and pepper. Combine flour, salt and pepper in a plastic or paper bag. Shake each piece individually in bag to coat well. Allow to stand at least 20 minutes before frying. Heat 2 inches of oil in a heavy skillet; add chicken, cover and fry over medium heat 10 minutes. Uncover and continue frying, turning chicken when underside is golden brown. Cover again and fry 10 minutes. Uncover and fry over medium-high heat until brown. The secret of good Southern fried chicken is to turn chicken only once. Serves 4 to 6.

Southern Classics

Cream Gravy

2   tablespoons pan drippings
2   tablespoons flour

1   cup milk
Salt and pepper to taste

Blend drippings and flour in skillet. Cook and stir until brown. Add milk and cook until thick. Season with salt and pepper. Serve over rice or hot biscuits. Yields 1 cup.

If there are no pan drippings, as with chicken that has been deep-fat fried, fry wing tips and necks in oil in a skillet to obtain drippings necessary to flavor the gravy. This gravy is light in color and thick.

Chicken Bog

2   2½-3-pound whole chickens
2   onions, chopped
    Water to cover
1½-2 cups uncooked rice
4-5 hard-cooked eggs, chopped

1   10¾-ounce can cream of
    mushroom soup (optional)
    Salt and pepper to taste
    Soy sauce

Remove livers, hearts and gizzards from chickens and reserve for other use. Cover chickens and onions with water in large pot. Simmer 1½ to 2 hours. Reserve stock. Remove meat from chicken; discard bones. Cook rice according to package directions, using chicken stock for liquid. In large bowl, combine rice, eggs, chicken, soup if desired, salt and pepper. Add additional chicken stock as needed for moistness. Put mixture in rice steamer and cook 1 hour. Serve with soy sauce. Serves 8.

Barbeque Sauce I

½   cup butter
½   teaspoon cayenne pepper
1   tablespoon pepper
¾   tablespoon dry mustard
1½ cups vinegar
1   tablespoon brown sugar
1   teaspoon salt

1   6-ounce can tomato paste
3   tablespoons Worcestershire
    sauce
5   tablespoons prepared
    mustard
5   tablespoons lemon juice

Melt butter in a medium-size saucepan. Add remaining ingredients and bring to a boil. Cool. Store in refrigerator for use on poultry, meats or shrimp. Yields 3 cups.

144

Southern Classics

Baked Country Ham

1	country ham	Glaze
	Whole cloves	

Cover and soak country ham for 24 hours in cold water. Scrub off all mold with stiff brush, using mild soap if needed. Rinse thoroughly. Simmer ham in enough water to cover in a covered pot for 20 minutes per pound. Pour off water, remove skin and trim off most of the fat. Score fat, stud with cloves and/or cover with favorite glaze. Bake at 425 degrees until fat is glazed. Slice very thin when serving.

Choice of glaze may include brown sugar combined with prepared mustard, orange juice or pineapple juice.

Tip-Top Pecan Pie

4	tablespoons butter, softened	¼	teaspoon salt
1	cup brown sugar	1	teaspoon vanilla
1	cup light corn syrup	1	cup chopped pecans
3	eggs	1	9-inch pie shell, unbaked

Cream butter and sugar. Gradually add syrup, beating constantly. In a small bowl, beat eggs and salt until light and fluffy. Add to creamed mixture. Stir in vanilla and pecans. Pour into pie shell. Bake at 325 degrees for 45 to 60 minutes or until knife inserted in center comes out clean. Serve warm, a must for all Southern pies. Serves 8.

This is a favorite from the Tip-Top Inn, Pawleys Island, South Carolina.

Southern Classics

Mrs. Strom Thurmond's Watermelon Pie

4	cups chopped watermelon rind	½	teaspoon ground nutmeg
	Water	½	teaspoon ground cinnamon
2	oranges, peeled and finely chopped	¼	teaspoon curry powder
			Dash cayenne pepper
2	tablespoons lemon juice	1	9-inch pie shell, baked
1	teaspoon grated lemon rind	1	cup crumbled gingersnaps
2	cups brown sugar	9	egg whites, beaten

Place watermelon rind in a large saucepan and barely cover with water. Bring to a boil and add oranges, lemon juice and lemon rind. Cook until watermelon is transparent. Stir in brown sugar and spices. Allow mixture to cool. Pour into pie shell and sprinkle with gingersnap crumbs. Spread beaten egg whites over top. Bake for 20 minutes at 325 degrees. Serves 8.

Senator Strom Thurmond was elected United States Senator from South Carolina in 1954.

Rum Cream Pie

4	egg yolks	1	cup whipping cream, whipped
1	cup sugar		
1	envelope unflavored gelatin	1	9-inch graham cracker pie shell, baked
½	cup water		
¼	cup rum		Chocolate curls for garnish

Beat egg yolks until lemon colored. Add sugar gradually and continue beating until well mixed. In top of a double boiler, soften gelatin in ½ cup water and heat to dissolve.

Gradually pour gelatin into egg mixture, beating constantly. Add rum to whipped cream and fold into egg mixture. Pour into pie shell and refrigerate overnight. Garnish with chocolate curls before serving. Serves 8.

Southern Classics

Swamp Fox Peach Pie

Crust:

1½	cups flour
¼	teaspoon salt
¼	teaspoon sugar
6	tablespoons butter, chilled
2	tablespoons vegetable shortening
4-5	tablespoons ice water

Filling:

5	cups peaches, peeled and sliced
1	teaspoon almond extract
1	cup sugar
¾	cup dark brown sugar
¼	cup flour
¼	teaspoon salt
2	tablespoons lemon juice
3	tablespoons butter
1	teaspoon ground cinnamon
1	teaspoon ground nutmeg
1	tablespoon grated orange rind

Topping:

¼	cup dark brown sugar
2	tablespoons flour
2	tablespoons butter
½	teaspoon ground cinnamon

Cream:

1	cup whipping cream
1	tablespoon orange liqueur
1	teaspoon grated orange rind

For crust, mix flour, salt and sugar. Cut in butter and shortening. Gradually add ice water until moist. Knead 1 minute. Divide into 2 balls and refrigerate 1 hour. Roll out 1 ball for 9-inch pie pan. Prebake bottom crust for 10 minutes at 350 degrees.

Combine peaches, almond extract, sugars, flour, salt and lemon juice. Let stand 5 minutes. Drain and reserve liquid. Turn into pie shell and sprinkle with butter, cinnamon, nutmeg and orange rind. Add enough reserved liquid to cover fruit. Top with lattice crust formed from second ball of pastry.

For topping, mix brown sugar, flour, butter and cinnamon until crumbly. Spoon lightly into lattice holes. Bake at 400 degrees for 40 minutes on baking sheet. Baste with juices that run over and any remaining reserved liquid until crust is glazed. Just before serving, beat cream, orange liqueur and orange rind until stiff. Serve over pie. Serves 8.

Southern Classics

Sweet Potato Pie

1½	cups sweet potatoes, cooked and mashed	1	cup milk
⅔	cup brown sugar	1	9-inch deep-dish pastry shell, unbaked
½	teaspoon salt		Pecan halves (optional)
¼	teaspoon ground cinnamon		Sweetened whipped cream
2	eggs, beaten		for garnish
1	tablespoon lemon juice		

Combine sweet potatoes, brown sugar, salt, cinnamon, eggs, lemon juice and milk. Beat until smooth. Pour into pastry shell; add pecans if desired. Bake at 450 degrees for 15 minutes. Reduce to 325 degrees for 30 minutes or until set. Garnish with whipped cream.

Plum Pudding

1	pound raisins	1	cup chopped suet
¼	pound figs, chopped	1	cup chopped pecans
1	cup chopped candied fruit	1½	cups soft bread crumbs
¼	cup orange juice	3	eggs
¼	cup red wine	½	cup sugar
1½	cups flour	1	cup molasses
1	teaspoon baking powder	1	cup strawberry jam
1	teaspoon salt	½	cup water
¼	teaspoon ground cloves	1	cup light corn syrup
½	teaspoon ground cinnamon	12	candied cherries
½	teaspoon ground nutmeg		Brandy

Cover raisins, figs and candied fruit with orange juice and wine and let stand overnight. Sift flour with baking powder, salt, cloves, cinnamon and nutmeg. Add suet, pecans and bread crumbs. In a separate bowl, beat eggs with sugar, molasses and strawberry jam. Stir into flour mixture. Add fruit. Add additional orange juice or wine if batter is too stiff. Spoon mixture into greased individual molds, filling ⅔ full.

Place molds in large shallow pan and pour boiling water around them until pan is ½ full. Cover entire pan with aluminum foil and bake at 300 degrees for 1 hour. Cool; brush pudding with mixture of water and corn syrup. Decorate with candied cherries. Wrap each pudding in aluminum foil.

Make several months ahead. Store in cool place and baste every 3 to 4 weeks with brandy. To serve, steam molds until heated. Serves 12 to 14.

Southern Classics

Walnut-Raisin Spice Cake

Cake:

1½	cups finely chopped seedless raisins
1½	cups chopped walnuts, divided
1½	teaspoons baking soda
1½	cups boiling water
2¼	cups sifted flour
1½	teaspoons ground cinnamon

¼	teaspoon salt
¾	cup butter, softened
1½	cups sugar
2	eggs
2	egg yolks
1½	teaspoons lemon juice
1½	teaspoons vanilla

Frosting:

1	8-ounce package cream cheese, softened
⅔	cup butter, softened

3	teaspoons vanilla
1½	pounds powdered sugar

Grease and lightly flour 3 8-inch cake pans. Place raisins and 1 cup walnuts in medium mixing bowl. Add baking soda and stir in boiling water. Let mixture cool ½ hour. Sift flour with cinnamon and salt; set aside. In large bowl, beat butter until creamy. Add sugar a small amount at a time, beating until light and fluffy. Add eggs and egg yolks, one at a time, beating well after each addition. Add lemon juice and vanilla. With a wooden spoon, beat in flour mixture alternately with nut mixture, beginning and ending with flour mixture. Pour batter into prepared pans. Bake at 350 degrees for 25 to 30 minutes, or until top springs back when lightly pressed with finger and cake pulls away from edge. Cool on wire rack 5 minutes. Remove from pans and cool completely, right side up, on wire rack.

For frosting, in a large bowl, beat cream cheese, butter and vanilla until creamy. Add sugar and beat until light and fluffy. Put layers together using 1½ cups frosting. Use remaining frosting to cover top and sides of cake. With frosting spreader, make decorative swirls. Sprinkle remaining walnuts on top. Refrigerate until served. Serves 16.

Southern Classics

Blackberry Jam Cake

1	cup vegetable shortening	1	teaspoon ground cloves
1½	cups brown sugar	1	teaspoon ground nutmeg
3	cups flour	1	teaspoon baking soda
1	teaspoon cocoa	1	cup buttermilk
1	teaspoon ground cinnamon	3	eggs, beaten
1	teaspoon ground allspice	1	cup blackberry jam

Cream shortening and brown sugar. Sift together flour, cocoa, cinnamon, allspice, cloves and nutmeg. Dissolve baking soda in buttermilk. Add buttermilk and flour mixture alternately to creamed shortening. Add eggs and jam, mixing thoroughly. Pour batter into 2 9-inch round greased and floured cake pans. Bake at 350 degrees for 30 to 40 minutes or until done. Frost with chocolate icing. Yields 1 9-inch cake.

Bourbon Balls

1	12-ounce package vanilla wafers, crushed	3	tablespoons light corn syrup or honey
2	tablespoons cocoa	¼	cup bourbon, brandy or rum
1	cup sifted powdered sugar		Powdered sugar
1	cup chopped walnuts		

Mix crushed vanilla wafers, cocoa, powdered sugar and nuts. Add corn syrup and liquor, mixing thoroughly. Shape into 1-inch balls. Roll each in powdered sugar. Store in covered tin. Yields 3 dozen.

Best made 24 hours before serving.

Southern Classics

Frances Arthur's Artichoke Pickle

1	peck Jerusalem artichokes			Salt water
1	large cabbage		½	cup flour
1	dozen onions		1	tablespoon dry mustard
1	large cauliflower		1	tablespoon ground turmeric
4	green peppers		2	cups sugar
4	sweet red peppers		1	quart white vinegar

Chop vegetables coarsely and cover with salt water (1 cup salt per gallon of water). Soak overnight. Drain well. Mix flour, mustard and turmeric in a small bowl. Set aside. Bring sugar and vinegar to a boil. Add enough hot vinegar mixture to the flour mixture to make a smooth paste. Slowly add the paste to rest of hot vinegar, stirring constantly. When the sauce is smooth and boiling, add drained vegetables. Continue stirring mixture over heat until vegetables are heated through. Place in sterile pint jars and seal. Be sure that hot vinegar mixture covers vegetables. Extra vinegar may be added to stretch sauce before putting vegetables into jars. Process 10 minutes in a boiling water bath. Yields about 12 pints.

Excellent accompaniment for any green vegetable.

Bread and Butter Pickles

4	quarts (½ peck) cucumbers	2	tablespoons mustard seed
8	onions	1	teaspoon ground turmeric
½	cup salt	1	teaspoon celery seed
8	cups crushed ice	5	cups sugar
4	cups white vinegar		

Slice cucumbers and onions into thin rounds. Mix with salt and ice and place in crock. Weight down to keep submerged and leave for 3 to 4 hours. Drain. In a large saucepan, add the remaining ingredients and heat almost to a boil, stirring carefully. Pack cucumbers and onions into sterilized jars and cover with vinegar mixture. Seal jars, process in a boiling water bath for 10 minutes and store. Yields 6 to 8 quarts.

Do not use cider or homemade vinegar.

Southern Classics

Kosher-Style Dill Pickles

3	cups white vinegar	2	cloves garlic, sliced
3	cups water	3	teaspoons mustard seed
6	tablespoons salt	30-36	small cucumbers, washed
2	teaspoons dried dill weed		

In a 2-quart pot, combine vinegar, water and salt. Bring to a boil. In 2 1-quart jars, layer ¼ of dill, ½ of garlic and ½ of mustard seed in bottom of each jar. Pack one layer of cucumbers into jars. Sprinkle remaining dill on top. Pack another layer of cucumbers. Fill to within ½ inch of top with boiling brine. Seal and process in boiling water bath for 15 minutes. Yields 2 quarts.

Annie Sue's Refrigerator Pickles

7-8	cucumbers, thinly sliced	1	tablespoon salt
1	cup sliced onion		Pepper to taste
1	cup sliced green pepper	½	cup sugar
1	tablespoon celery seed	1	cup vinegar

Put vegetables and seasonings in tightly sealed container. Add vinegar and shake or stir well. Chill. Flavor improves with time. Keeps in refrigerator about 1 week. Yields 2 quarts.

Delicious served with crackers as an appetizer.

Southern Classics

Betty Herbert's Recycled Sweet Pickles

1	quart kosher dill pickles	2	cups sugar
1	cup vinegar	2	tablespoons pickling spice

Pour off pickle juice. Wash pickles and slice. Place in medium-size bowl. Mix vinegar, sugar and spice and pour over pickles. Let stand in refrigerator overnight. Return to quart jar and refrigerate. Yields 1 quart.

Amaretto Peach Preserves

9	pounds peaches, peeled and thickly sliced	3	lemons, thinly sliced
5	pounds sugar		Amaretto to taste

In a large pot, layer peaches and sugar. Place lemons on top. Bring rapidly to transparent stage over medium-high heat, stirring constantly. Lower heat and cook until syrup thickens. Skim foam and add Amaretto to taste. Pour into hot sterilized jars and seal immediately. Yields 20 to 25 half-pints.

 For pickles, select young, tender, unwaxed cucumbers that show no signs of bruising.

Use fresh whole spices for best flavor in pickles. Tie loosely in cheesecloth and add to brine when heated. Pickles should be stored in cool, dark, dry place to retain crispness.

Southern Classics

Spiced Blueberry-Peach Jam

4	cups peeled, chopped peaches (4 pounds)	5½	cups sugar
4	cups blueberries	½	teaspoon salt
2	tablespoons lemon juice	1	stick cinnamon
½	cup water	½	teaspoon whole cloves
		¼	teaspoon whole allspice

Place fruit in Dutch oven; add lemon juice and water. Cover, bring to a boil and simmer 10 minutes, stirring occasionally. Add sugar and salt. Tie spices in cheesecloth and add to fruit. Boil rapidly, stirring constantly, until mixture thickens. Remove from heat, remove spices and skim foam. Pour into 6 or 7 half-pint jars. Seal jars and process 10 minutes in boiling water bath. Yields 6 or 7 half-pints.

Cranberries in Wine

1½	cups sugar	¼	cup orange juice
¼	cup claret or Burgundy wine	4	cups raw cranberries
4	tablespoons grated orange rind	1	tablespoon currant jelly

In a saucepan, combine sugar, wine, orange rind and juice. Bring to a boil. Add cranberries. Simmer over medium heat, shaking pan often, until all cranberries break open. Stir in currant jelly and simmer 1 minute. Chill thoroughly. Serve as condiment for poultry or game. Yields 1 quart.

This will keep in the refrigerator up to 2 weeks.

Southern Classics

Pear Chutney

3½	pounds pears, peeled and chopped	1	pound raisins
3	cups sugar	1	teaspoon ground cloves
1	cup cider vinegar	1	teaspoon ground cinnamon
2	whole oranges, finely chopped	1	teaspoon ground allspice
		1	teaspoon ground ginger
		1	cup chopped pecans

Combine all ingredients except pecans. Simmer for 2 hours or until thick. Add pecans and cook 2 minutes. Pour immediately into hot sterilized jars and seal. Yields 7 half-pints.

Hot Pepper Jelly

6	green peppers	2½	6-ounce bottles liquid pectin or 5 individual packages
20	hot peppers		
5	pounds sugar	10	drops green or 30 drops red food coloring
3	cups white vinegar		

Remove seeds from green peppers; trim stems from hot peppers. Place peppers in blender and process until smooth. Combine sugar and vinegar in a large pot, stirring to mix well. Add peppers; boil 8 to 10 minutes, stirring as needed. Remove from heat; strain into another large pot. Discard pepper residue. Put large pot of strained pepper liquid over heat and add liquid pectin and food coloring; stir to mix and bring to a boil. Ladle into half-pint jars and seal. Yields 12 to 14 half pints.

Wear gloves when handling hot peppers.

Southern Classics

Boiled Peanuts

4	pounds green peanuts, in shell	6	quarts water
		6-10	tablespoons salt

Select and wash green peanuts (available June through August). Place in a large kettle with water and salt. Cover, bring to a boil and boil slowly for 1½ to 2 hours. Water should be briny. More water and salt may be added during cooking if necessary. Test for doneness. Peanuts should be soft inside, but not mushy. Allow to soak for 30 minutes. Drain. Serves 6.

Peanuts may be frozen in plastic bags after cooling. To reheat, place in salted water, bring to a boil, drain and enjoy!

Spicy Sugared Pecans

1	cup sugar	¼	cup hot water
1	teaspoon ground cinnamon	1½	cups pecans
⅛	teaspoon cream of tartar	½	teaspoon vanilla

Bring sugar, cinnamon, cream of tartar and water to a boil. When mixture reaches 234 degrees (soft ball) on candy thermometer, stir in nuts and vanilla, continuing to stir until mixture sugars. Pour on platter and separate nuts. Store in airtight container. Yields ¾ pound.

Wonderful as a holiday gift.

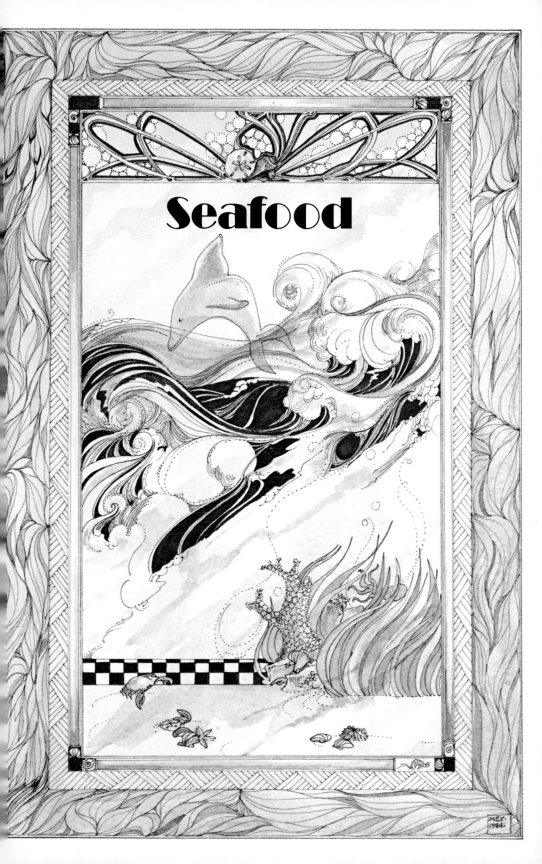

Seafood

Seafood

*Other Seafood recipes may be found in **Southern Classics.**

Seafood

Shrimp Pastry Log

3	tablespoons butter	1	10 x 15-inch sheet puff pastry
4	canned artichoke hearts,	10	ounces sliced Swiss cheese
	drained and halved	12	jumbo shrimp, cooked and
½	pound fresh mushrooms,		cleaned
	halved	1	egg, beaten
1	tablespoon dried parsley	½	teaspoon chopped fresh
1	tablespoon garlic salt		parsley

Melt butter in a large skillet over medium-high heat. Add artichoke hearts, mushrooms, parsley and garlic salt. Sauté for about 2 minutes until mushrooms are tender. Let mixture cool. Drain well.

Grease large, rimmed baking sheet. Place puff pastry on baking sheet. Overlap cheese slices lengthwise along right half of dough, leaving a 1-inch border at long (15-inch) edge and ½-inch border at each end. Arrange artichoke hearts on cheese, spacing evenly. Spoon mushrooms over artichoke hearts. Arrange row of shrimp over mushrooms. Brush border with some of beaten egg. Fold left half of dough over filling, pressing edges firmly with fork to seal. (Log may be prepared to this point up to 8 hours ahead, covered with foil or plastic wrap and refrigerated.)

Preheat oven to 475 degrees. Brush pastry with beaten egg and sprinkle with fresh parsley. Bake 15 minutes. Reduce oven temperature to 375 degrees and continue baking until golden, about 15 to 20 minutes. Slice. Serves 4.

Shrimp Casserole

½	pound mushrooms, sliced	1	tablespoon Worcestershire
1	medium onion, finely		sauce
	chopped		Salt and pepper to taste
2	tablespoons butter	¼	teaspoon paprika
2	tomatoes, chopped	3	pounds raw shrimp, cooked
2	tablespoons flour		and cleaned
½	cup whipping cream		Bread crumbs
¼	cup sherry		Grated sharp Cheddar cheese

In a large skillet, sauté mushrooms and onion in butter. Add tomatoes and simmer for 10 minutes. Blend flour with cream and add to skillet along with sherry, Worcestershire, salt, pepper and paprika. Add shrimp, mix and place in a 2-quart buttered casserole dish. Top with bread crumbs and cheese. Bake uncovered 20 minutes at 350 degrees. May be served over rice. Serves 8.

Seafood

Easy Shrimp Casserole

2 cups cleaned raw shrimp	Salt and pepper
2 cups cooked rice	Buttered bread crumbs or
1 cup mayonnaise	cracker crumbs
1 cup tomato-vegetable juice	

Mix all ingredients except crumbs in a greased 2-quart casserole. Sprinkle bread or cracker crumbs on top and bake uncovered at 350 degrees for 30 minutes. Serves 4 to 6.

Crabmeat may be substituted for shrimp or a combination may be used. Casserole may be topped with slivered almonds.

Shrimp Rice

1 pound cleaned raw shrimp	1 tablespoon lemon juice
4 tablespoons butter	2 tablespoons chopped fresh
1½ cups cooked rice	parsley
4 tablespoons chopped fresh	1½ teaspoons dry vermouth
chives	Salt and pepper to taste

Sauté shrimp in butter over low heat until shrimp begin to turn pink. Add remaining ingredients, stirring to heat thoroughly. Serve immediately. Serves 4 to 6.

This recipe requires very fresh shrimp.

 Slice large shrimp length-wise to give the appearance of having used more shrimp in a casserole.

Seafood

Curried Rice and Shrimp

1	cup butter	4	cups cooked rice
1	teaspoon curry powder	2	tablespoons lemon juice
½	teaspoon celery seed	½	cup chopped salted peanuts
1	medium onion, chopped	6	slices bacon, cooked and
1	small green pepper, chopped		crumbled
1	pound raw shrimp, cooked		
	and cleaned		

In a skillet, melt butter and add curry powder and celery seed. Add onion and green pepper and sauté until soft. Stir in shrimp and toss until well coated. Combine mixture with rice, lemon juice, peanuts and bacon. Place in a greased 3-quart casserole and bake uncovered at 325 degrees for 20 minutes. Serves 8 to 10.

May be served as a main dish or as an accompaniment for game.

Far Eastern Shrimp

1-1½	pounds raw shrimp, cleaned	½	tablespoon grated fresh
5	tablespoons oil		ginger
1	large potato, peeled and	1½	teaspoons ground cumin
	chopped	¼	teaspoon chili powder
2	medium tomatoes, chopped	1	teaspoon salt
1	medium onion, grated	¼	cup water
½	teaspoon ground turmeric		Condiments

In a skillet, sauté shrimp in oil for 3 to 4 minutes and remove. In same oil, sauté potatoes, tomatoes and onions. Add turmeric, ginger, cumin, chili powder and salt. Cook for 5 minutes over medium heat. Add water and shrimp. Bring to a boil, lower heat and simmer, covered, for 15 minutes. Serve over rice with some or all of the following condiments: chopped hard-cooked egg, chopped peanuts, raisins, chutney, chopped cooked bacon or orange slices. Serves 4.

Lamb or chicken may be substituted for shrimp.

Seafood

Creole Shrimp Bake

½   cup chopped celery
½   cup chopped green pepper
1   large onion, chopped
1   tablespoon butter
½   pound grated sharp
      Cheddar cheese
3   pounds raw shrimp, cooked
      and cleaned

1   6-ounce can sliced
      mushrooms, undrained
1   tablespoon Worcestershire
      sauce
1   10¾-ounce can tomato soup
3   cups cooked rice
      Salt and pepper

In a large saucepan, sauté celery, green pepper and onion in butter until transparent. Combine with half of grated cheese and remaining ingredients. Season with salt and pepper. Place in a 3-quart casserole and sprinkle with remaining cheese. Bake uncovered at 350 degrees for 45 minutes. Serves 8.

Shrimp Creole

6   slices bacon
½   cup chopped green pepper
½   cup chopped celery
½   cup chopped onion
2   16-ounce cans tomatoes,
      drained
½   cup chili sauce
4-5   dashes Tabasco sauce

1   teaspoon Worcestershire
      sauce
¼   teaspoon black pepper
1   teaspoon salt
1   pound raw shrimp, cooked
      and cleaned
      Cooked rice

In a skillet, fry bacon. Remove from skillet and set aside. Sauté green pepper, celery and onion in bacon drippings. Add remaining ingredients except shrimp and rice. Cook slowly until thick, stirring occasionally. Before serving, add shrimp, stirring until shrimp are heated through. Serve over rice and sprinkle with crumbled bacon. Serves 4 to 6.

Seafood

Shrimp Hollandaise

Hollandaise Sauce:

3	egg yolks	⅛	teaspoon pepper
2	tablespoons lemon juice	½	cup butter, heated until
¼	teaspoon salt		foaming

Shrimp:

1	pound raw shrimp, cleaned	½	teaspoon salt
1	tablespoon lemon juice	⅛	teaspoon cayenne pepper
2	tablespoons olive oil	1	cup Hollandaise Sauce

To prepare Hollandaise, blend yolks and lemon juice in blender at top speed for 2 minutes. Add salt and pepper. Continue blending, pouring in hot butter by drops until sauce thickens. Yields 1 cup.

Arrange shrimp in a 1½-quart baking dish. Sprinkle with lemon juice, olive oil, salt and cayenne pepper. Broil 2 to 3 minutes; turn and broil again 2 to 3 minutes. Spoon Hollandaise over shrimp and broil until lightly browned. Serves 3 to 4.

Sauce may be made ahead and refrigerated. Reheat over warm water in a double boiler.

Open-Face Shrimp Sandwich

2	cups mayonnaise	3	green onions, finely chopped
½	cup ketchup	2½	pounds raw shrimp
4	tablespoons Worcestershire	8	slices whole wheat bread
	sauce		Butter
6	drops Tabasco sauce	¼	cup white wine
2	cloves garlic, grated	8	slices Swiss cheese
2	tablespoons lemon juice		

Several hours before serving, mix mayonnaise, ketchup, Worcestershire, Tabasco, garlic, lemon juice and onions to make sauce; refrigerate.

Boil, drain and peel shrimp. Toast whole wheat bread; butter both sides. Mound shrimp on toast. Add wine to sauce and pour over shrimp. Top with cheese. Place under broiler until cheese melts. Serve immediately. Serves 8.

Seafood

Boiled Shrimp

2 quarts water
2 teaspoons whole allspice
4 peppercorns
1 slice lemon, with rind
8 tablespoons salt
1 bay leaf

2 small stalks celery, leaves included
1 pound raw shrimp
Melted butter and dry vermouth

In a large pot, bring water to a boil with allspice, peppercorns, lemon, salt, bay leaf and celery. Add shrimp. When water returns to a boil, remove from heat. Leave shrimp in pot: small shrimp for 1 minute, medium shrimp for 2 to 3 minutes, large shrimp for 4 minutes, jumbo shrimp for 6 to 8 minutes. When shrimp are done, pour through colander to drain. Serve hot with a mixture of butter melted with dry vermouth or with favorite seafood sauce. Serves 2.

Jane's Baked Shrimp

2 pounds large or jumbo raw shrimp, unpeeled
2 cups salad oil
2 cups lemon juice
4 teaspoons Italian salad dressing mix
4 teaspoons seasoned salt

2 teaspoons seasoned pepper
2 teaspoons Worcestershire sauce
8 tablespoons brown sugar
4 tablespoons soy sauce
1 cup chopped green onion

Wash shrimp and drain. Mix remaining ingredients and stir well. Place shrimp in half of the mixture in a 2-quart baking dish. Reserve remaining marinade for sauce. Cover baking dish with foil. Bake at 350 degrees for 30 minutes, or until shrimp are pink. Remove shrimp with slotted spoon to serve.

Warm remaining marinade on stove. Pour in individual bowls to use for dipping shrimp. Serves 6 to 8.

French bread may be served as a side dish to dip into heated sauce.

Seafood

Barbequed Shrimp

2	cups butter	3	cloves garlic, finely chopped
2	cups olive oil	1	teaspoon paprika
¾	cup Worcestershire sauce	4	teaspoons salt
6	tablespoons pepper	8	pounds medium or jumbo
4	lemons, sliced		raw shrimp, unpeeled
1½	teaspoons Tabasco sauce		French bread

Heat butter and olive oil in a saucepan. Add Worcestershire, pepper, lemons, Tabasco, garlic, paprika and salt. Mix thoroughly and simmer 5 to 7 minutes. Divide shrimp between 2 Dutch ovens and pour heated sauce over each batch. Cook over medium heat for about 3 to 4 minutes, or until shrimp begin to turn pink. (Shrimp may be prepared up to this point and refrigerated overnight.) Bake uncovered at 450 degrees for 10 minutes, turning shrimp once. Serve in a soup bowl with French bread on the side for dipping in the sauce. Serves 8.

Beer Batter Shrimp

½	cup flour		Dash paprika
½	cup beer	1-2	teaspoons lemon juice
¼	teaspoon salt	1-2	pounds raw shrimp, cleaned
¼	teaspoon pepper		Vegetable oil for frying

Mix flour, beer, salt, pepper, paprika and lemon juice. Pat shrimp dry and dip in batter. Deep fry 3 to 4 minutes or until golden. Serves 4.

Also good for frying fish filets.

Seafood

Cold Crabmeat Omelets

Tomato Mayonnaise and Filling:

1   egg
1   teaspoon Dijon-style mustard
½   teaspoon Worcestershire sauce
      Salt and pepper to taste
1   cup vegetable oil
2   tablespoons bottled chili sauce

2   tablespoons finely chopped parsley
2   tablespoons finely chopped green onions
1   teaspoon cognac
1   tablespoon lemon juice
1   pound crabmeat

Omelets:

8   large eggs
2   tablespoons finely chopped parsley
1   teaspoon dried tarragon
¼   cup whipping cream

      Salt and pepper to taste
2-4   teaspoons butter
¾   cup peeled, cubed tomato
      Parsley for garnish

To make tomato mayonnaise, whisk together egg, mustard, Worcestershire, salt and pepper. Gradually add oil, beating constantly. Add chili sauce, parsley, onions and cognac. Blend well. In a mixing bowl, sprinkle lemon juice over crabmeat and toss lightly. For filling, add ½ tomato mayonnaise to crab mixture, reserving remaining mayonnaise to serve over omelet.

To prepare omelets, beat together eggs, parsley, tarragon, cream, salt and pepper. In a small omelet pan, heat ½ teaspoon butter. Add ¼ of egg mixture. Sprinkle ¼ of tomato cubes on top. Cook until firm. When set, turn quickly, add another ¼ teaspoon butter and cook until done. Turn flat omelet out onto waxed paper. Repeat, making 3 more omelets. To assemble omelets, place ¼ crab filling in center of each omelet and fold over. Garnish with parsley and serve with reserved tomato mayonnaise. Serves 4.

Seafood

Carolina Creamed Crab in Pastry Shells

Pastry:

2 cups flour	⅓ cup unsalted butter
1 teaspoon salt	5-7 tablespoons ice water
½ cup shortening	Melted butter

Sift together flour and salt. Blend together shortening and butter. Gradually add flour mixture. Add ice water, 1 tablespoon at a time, until dough begins to stick together. Form dough into ball and chill 15 minutes. Roll dough ⅛-inch thick and cut with cookie cutter or drinking glass. Line greased muffin tins with dough. Cover and freeze unbaked dough in muffin tins at least 1 day. When ready to bake, remove from freezer and brush each shell with melted butter. Bake at 350 degrees for 30 minutes or until golden brown. Yields 12 to 16 pastry shells.

Store in airtight container; do not freeze shells after baking.

Crab Filling:

3 tablespoons butter, melted	2 cups crabmeat
3 tablespoons flour	½ cup thinly sliced or chopped fresh mushrooms
½ cup condensed chicken broth	2 tablespoons sherry
1 cup half and half	Salt to taste
2 egg yolks, slightly beaten	

In a saucepan, whisk together butter and flour. When mixture begins to bubble, add broth and half and half; stir until blended. Beat egg yolks in a small bowl and add some of the hot sauce. Gradually add rest of sauce to eggs, stirring well. Return to saucepan and add crabmeat, mushrooms, sherry and salt. Heat thoroughly and serve in pastry shells. Yields 4½ to 5 cups filling. Serves 6 to 8.

May be prepared in miniature muffin tins and served as an appetizer.

Seafood

Crab and Artichoke Casserole

4 cups whipping cream
½ cup butter
3 tablespoons finely chopped onion
½ cup flour
½ cup Madeira wine
2 tablespoons lemon juice
4 cups crabmeat, cleaned and drained

3 14-ounce cans artichoke hearts, drained and quartered
2¼ cups shell macaroni, cooked and drained
2 cups grated Gruyère cheese

In saucepan, bring cream to a boil. While cream is heating, melt butter in large heavy skillet. Stir in onion and flour and cook over low heat until flour is pale yellow. Remove from heat and add cream. Return to heat and stir until sauce comes to a boil. Reduce heat and add wine. Sprinkle lemon juice over crab. In a 6-quart buttered casserole, combine crab, artichokes, macaroni and sauce. Top with cheese. Bake uncovered 25 to 30 minutes at 350 degrees. Serves 10 to 12.

Crab Bake

1 pound crabmeat
3 tablespoons lemon juice
3 hard-cooked eggs, chopped
Salt and pepper to taste
½ teaspoon prepared horseradish

1 teaspoon Tabasco sauce
3 tablespoons mayonnaise
⅔ cup grated sharp Cheddar cheese
Buttered bread crumbs

Rinse and clean crabmeat; drain well. Mix all ingredients except bread crumbs. Place in individual buttered shells or buttered 1½-quart casserole. Top with bread crumbs. Bake uncovered 30 minutes at 350 degrees. Serves 6.

May be prepared a day ahead.

Seafood

Deviled Crab

2	pounds crabmeat	1	teaspoon dry mustard
6	hard-cooked eggs	½	teaspoon Tabasco sauce
½	cup butter, melted	¼	teaspoon pepper
1	teaspoon salt	2	tablespoons lemon juice
2	tablespoons Worcestershire sauce		Buttered bread crumbs

Rinse and clean crabmeat. Set aside to drain. Halve hard-cooked eggs and put yolks in a bowl. Add melted butter, salt, Worcestershire, mustard, Tabasco, pepper and lemon juice. Add crabmeat and toss gently. Mash egg whites with a fork and stir into mixture. Place in individual crab shells or ramekins and top with buttered bread crumbs. Bake uncovered at 350 degrees 10 to 15 minutes until hot but not dry. Serves 12.

May be made a day ahead or frozen.

Edisto Beach Crab Casserole

20	crabs, cooked and cleaned or 2 6½-ounce cans crabmeat, drained	½-1	cup chopped onion
		2	hard-cooked eggs, chopped
2	cups mayonnaise	1	teaspoon prepared mustard
½	cup milk		Salt and pepper to taste
1	cup chopped celery	1	stack round buttery crackers

Combine crabmeat, mayonnaise, milk, celery, onion, eggs, mustard, salt and pepper. Crush 10 crackers and stir into mixture. Pour into lightly buttered 8-inch square casserole dish. Top with remaining crackers, crushed. Bake uncovered 30 minutes or until lightly browned at 350 degrees. If additional crabmeat is used, increase amount of mayonnaise to keep casserole moist. Serves 4 to 6.

This recipe was handed down from a long-time Edisto Island cook.

Seafood

Waccamaw Crab Quiche

1	9-inch pie shell	8	ounces crabmeat, well drained
3	green onions, finely chopped	2	tablespoons dry vermouth
3	tablespoons butter, melted	3	eggs
¼	teaspoon salt	1	cup half and half
¼	teaspoon pepper	1	tablespoon tomato paste
		½	cup grated Swiss cheese

Bake pie shell for 8 minutes at 400 degrees. Sauté onions in butter until tender. Add salt, pepper, crab and vermouth. Bring to a boil. Remove from heat. Beat together eggs, half and half and tomato paste. Stir in crab mixture. Pour into pie shell and top with cheese. Bake 25 to 30 minutes at 375 degrees. Quiche is done when knife inserted comes out clean. Serves 4 to 6.

May be frozen, unbaked, for later use.

Crabmeat Quiche

6	eggs, beaten	1	pound crabmeat, well drained
1½	cups plain yogurt		
½	cup dry white wine	2-3	cups grated Monterey Jack cheese
	Dash Worcestershire sauce		
	Dash white pepper	2	9-inch deep-dish pie shells, unbaked
½	teaspoon salt		
¼	teaspoon dried dill weed		

Combine eggs, yogurt, wine, Worcestershire, white pepper and salt. Add dill weed, crushing it between fingers. Place crab and cheese in unbaked pie shells. Pour mixture over all. Bake at 350 degrees for 40 to 50 minutes. Quiche is done when golden brown and knife inserted comes out clean. Serves 8 to 10.

Seafood

Seafood Trio

½	cup butter	1	teaspoon dry mustard
¾	cup chopped onion	½	teaspoon Worcestershire
¾	cup chopped green pepper		sauce
1	6-ounce can sliced mushrooms, drained	1	12-ounce package frozen cooked lobster meat
⅔	cup flour	2	6½-ounce cans crabmeat
2	teaspoons salt	1	12-ounce package frozen
¼	teaspoon pepper		cooked shrimp
4	cups milk	12	ounces shell macaroni,
1½	cups grated Cheddar cheese		cooked and drained
1	tablespoon lemon juice	1	tablespoon chopped parsley

Melt butter in large saucepan. Stir in onion, green pepper and mushrooms and cook until onion is soft, about 5 minutes. Remove from heat. Blend in flour, salt and pepper. Stir in milk gradually. Return to heat and continue cooking until thickened, stirring constantly. Stir in cheese, lemon juice, mustard and Worcestershire; cook until cheese melts. Break lobster into large pieces. Add seafood to sauce, reserving a few lobster claws and shrimp for garnish. Heat mixture to boiling. Place most of macaroni in bottom of a buttered 3-quart casserole and cover with seafood and sauce. Border with remaining macaroni and garnish with parsley and reserved lobster and shrimp. Warm thoroughly in oven at 350 degrees before serving. Serves 8 to 10.

Seafood au Gratin with Artichoke Hearts

4	tablespoons butter	2	teaspoons Dijon-style mustard
4	tablespoons flour	1	cup white wine
1	cup milk	1	14-ounce can artichoke
2	8-ounce packages cream cheese		hearts, drained and chopped
1	pound raw shrimp, cleaned and coarsely chopped	½	pound Swiss cheese, grated
1	pound crabmeat		White pepper to taste

In a large saucepan, melt butter and add flour. Stir constantly for 1 minute over low heat. Add milk gradually and stir until mixture thickens. Add cream cheese, a little at a time, stirring with a whisk. Add remaining ingredients. Cook no more than 10 minutes over low heat, stirring constantly. Serve over rice or toast points. Serves 6 to 8.

Seafood

Ten-Boy Seafood Curry

8	tablespoons butter, divided	1	pound mushrooms, thinly sliced
6	tablespoons flour		
3	cups half and half, divided	3	teaspoons curry powder
2	tomatoes, chopped	2	pounds raw shrimp, cooked and cleaned
1	green pepper, finely chopped		
2	stalks celery, finely chopped	½	pound crabmeat
2	tart apples, peeled, cored and finely chopped	½	pound lobster, cooked
		¼	cup dry sherry

In a saucepan, melt 6 tablespoons butter and stir in flour. Gradually add 2 cups half and half. Continue cooking, stirring until sauce thickens. Set aside. In a large pan, sauté until tender tomatoes, green pepper, celery, apples and mushrooms in remaining butter. Add curry and sauté 1 minute longer. Stir in sauce and simmer for 15 minutes.

Ten minutes before serving, add 1 cup half and half, shrimp, crabmeat, lobster and sherry. Heat until warmed through. Serve in electric frying pan or chafing dish. "Ten-boy" refers to the 10 small bowls of condiments served with seafood. Suggested condiments are: chopped salted peanuts, chopped pimiento, shredded coconut, bacon bits, plain yogurt, raisins, chopped cucumber, sliced black olives, mango chutney and green onion tops. Serves 8 to 10.

Peg's Crab and Shrimp Salad

½	pound crabmeat, cleaned and drained	½	teaspoon salt
		⅛	teaspoon pepper
1	pound raw shrimp, cooked, cleaned and chopped	1	tablespoon Worcestershire sauce
1	medium green pepper, chopped	1	cup mayonnaise
		1	cup herb seasoned stuffing
1	medium onion, chopped		Butter
1	cup chopped celery		

Mix together crab, shrimp, green pepper, onion, celery, salt, pepper, Worcestershire and mayonnaise. Spread in a buttered 2-quart casserole dish and top with stuffing and butter. Bake for 30 minutes at 350 degrees. Serve hot. Serves 6 to 8.

Serve in ramekins or use as filling for tiny cream puffs (omitting stuffing and butter).

Seafood

Hot Seafood Salad

½   pound fresh scallops,
      coarsely chopped
½   pound small raw shrimp,
      cleaned
1   cup dry white wine
1   tablespoon butter
2   cups sliced mushrooms
1   cup sour cream
1   cup chopped celery
¼   cup slivered almonds, toasted

¼   cup crumbled blue cheese
¼   cup chopped green pepper
2   tablespoons finely chopped
      onion
1-2   tablespoons lemon juice
      Salt to taste
½   cup seasoned dry bread
      crumbs
      Lemon wedges

In a medium-size saucepan, combine scallops, shrimp and wine. Simmer over low heat 3 minutes. Drain off liquid. In a skillet, melt butter and sauté mushrooms until tender; reserve butter. In a mixing bowl, combine scallops, shrimp, mushrooms, sour cream, celery, almonds, cheese, green pepper, onion, lemon juice and salt. Stir well. Spoon mixture into 4 individual serving dishes or 2-quart casserole. Combine bread crumbs and reserved butter, stirring well. Sprinkle bread crumbs over seafood mixture. Bake 10 to 15 minutes at 300 degrees. Before serving, garnish with lemon wedges. Serves 4.

Seafood Spinach Fettuccine

1   8-ounce package spinach
      fettuccine noodles
2   10-ounce packages frozen
      chopped spinach
1   cup grated Monterey Jack
      cheese

1   cup half and half
1   pound fresh scallops
1   pound raw shrimp, cleaned
2   cups sliced fresh mushrooms
4   tablespoons butter
      Salt and pepper to taste

Cook noodles as directed on package. Set aside. Cook spinach as directed. In a large serving bowl, combine noodles, spinach, cheese and half and half. Sauté scallops, shrimp and mushrooms in butter until cooked. Add salt and pepper. Spoon seafood over spinach fettuccine mixture and serve. Serves 6 to 8.

Seafood

Crawfish Cardinale

3	green onions, finely chopped	½	teaspoon Tabasco sauce
6	tablespoons butter, divided	2	teaspoons lemon juice
2	tablespoons flour	2	tablespoons brandy
1	cup half and half	1	pound crawfish tails, boiled
¼	cup ketchup		and peeled
¾	teaspoon salt	8	thin lemon slices for garnish
¼	teaspoon white pepper		Paprika for garnish

In a skillet, sauté onions in 4 tablespoons butter for 5 minutes. Set aside. In separate saucepan, melt remaining butter. Blend in flour; add half and half and ketchup, stirring until sauce thickens. Add salt, pepper, Tabasco and lemon juice. Flame brandy and add to sauce. Add reserved onions and crawfish tails. Divide mixture into 8 greased ramekins or a 9 x 13-inch casserole and bake 12 to 15 minutes at 350 degrees. Garnish with lemon slices and paprika. Serve over rice. Serves 8.

Cooked, peeled shrimp may be substituted for crawfish.

Carolyn's Company Scallops

1	pound fresh scallops	1	10¾-ounce can Cheddar
2	tablespoons butter		cheese soup
1	4-ounce can sliced		Dash pepper
	mushrooms, drained		Dash dried thyme
2	tablespoons finely chopped		Dash ground marjoram
	onion	2	tablespoons bread crumbs
2	teaspoons lemon juice		Paprika

In a saucepan, cook scallops in water over low heat for 10 minutes. Drain well. Divide among four individual baking dishes or place in a 1-quart casserole dish. In a medium-size saucepan, melt butter. Add mushrooms and onions, cooking until tender. Add lemon juice, soup, pepper, thyme and marjoram. Pour over scallops. Top with bread crumbs. Sprinkle with paprika. Bake uncovered at 350 degrees for 15 minutes or until hot. Serve over rice, if desired. Serves 4.

Shrimp may be used instead of scallops.

Seafood

Coquille Saint-Jacques

½ pound fresh mushrooms, sliced
1 medium onion, sliced
4 tablespoons butter, divided
1 pound fresh scallops
¼ cup dry sherry

¼ cup flour
1 cup half and half
½ teaspoon salt
⅛ teaspoon white pepper
1 teaspoon lemon juice
4 frozen patty shells, baked

In a saucepan, sauté mushrooms and onion in 1 tablespoon of butter. Add scallops and sherry and bring to a boil. Reduce heat and simmer, uncovered for 8 minutes, stirring occasionally. In a medium saucepan, melt remaining butter over low heat. Blend in flour and whisk until smooth. Cook 1 minute, stirring constantly. Blend in half and half while cooking over medium heat, stirring constantly. When mixture is thick and bubbly, stir in salt, white pepper and lemon juice. Add sauce to scallops, stirring gently, and cook uncovered until heated. Spoon into patty shells. Serves 4.

Serve with salad and steamed vegetables.

Coquillage Alexander

½ large onion, finely chopped
½ cup butter
½ pound fresh mushrooms, sliced
1 pound bay scallops
1 cup dry white wine
3-4 tablespoons flour

1½ cups whipping cream
1 14-ounce can artichoke hearts, drained and coarsely chopped
¼ teaspoon dried tarragon
4 tablespoons dry sherry

In a skillet, sauté onion in butter 5 minutes. Add mushrooms, cook another 5 minutes. In a small saucepan, poach scallops in wine 10 minutes. Reserve ¼ cup liquid and drain remainder. Sprinkle flour over onion and mushrooms, add cream and reserved liquid and cook over medium heat until sauce thickens. Add scallops, artichoke hearts, tarragon and sherry. Serve immediately. If refrigerated, bake uncovered at 350 degrees for 30 minutes or until bubbly. Serve in ring of piped mashed potatoes or over rice. Serves 4 to 6.

Seafood

Fairey Oyster Pie

½	pound saltine crackers, crumbled	1	cup butter, divided
48	ounces select oysters, drained	1¼	cups milk
1	teaspoon salt, divided	1	teaspoon Worcestershire sauce
	Freshly ground black pepper to taste	2-3	dashes Tabasco

Layer a third of cracker crumbs in a greased 3-quart casserole. Layer half of oysters. Sprinkle with ½ teaspoon salt and ground pepper. Place half of butter in slices on top of oysters. Layer half of remaining crumbs and all of remaining oysters. Top with ½ teaspoon salt, pepper, and remaining butter in slices. Put remaining crumbs on top. Combine milk, Worcestershire and Tabasco and pour over casserole. Preheat oven to 400 degrees and bake 15 to 20 minutes or until thoroughly hot. Do not overcook. Oven may be set on broil for last few minutes to complete browning, if needed. Serves 10 to 12.

Excellent as a side dish with holiday ham or turkey.

Mrs. Richard Riley's Oyster and Ham Pie

1	pint oysters	½	cup white wine
1	medium onion, chopped	½	cup milk
½	cup plus 2 teaspoons butter, divided	1½	cups chopped cooked ham
½	cup flour	2	cups green peas, cooked and drained

Drain oysters and reserve liquid. Sauté onion in 2 teaspoons butter until transparent. Set aside. Melt remaining butter; add flour, stirring until smooth. Add oyster liquid, wine and milk. Cook until thick, stirring often. Remove from heat and add oysters, onion, ham and peas. Pour into a buttered 2-quart casserole. Bake uncovered 15 minutes at 400 degrees. Serves 4.

Richard Riley became Governor of South Carolina on January 11, 1979.

Seafood

Seafood Stuffed Flounder

½ pound crabmeat, cleaned and drained
1 pound raw shrimp, cleaned
½ pound fresh scallops, chopped
4 tablespoons butter
Garlic salt to taste
Salt and pepper to taste

2 slices processed cheese or ½ cup grated Cheddar cheese
1 cup whipping cream
8 medium flounder filets
Salt and lemon pepper
Lemon slices and parsley for garnish

Sauté crabmeat, shrimp and scallops in butter; add garlic salt, salt, pepper and cheese, stirring until cheese melts. Lower heat, add cream and continue stirring until sauce is smooth. Place about ¼ cup of sauce on each filet, roll up filet and secure with toothpick. (Retain some sauce.) Place rolled filets in foil-lined broiler pan. Sprinkle lightly with salt and lemon pepper. Bake 20 minutes covered, and 5 minutes uncovered at 400 degrees. Thin leftover sauce with milk or water. To serve, top filet with sauce; garnish with lemon slice and parsley. Serves 8.

Flounder Parmesan

1 pound flounder filets
3 tablespoons grated Parmesan cheese

½ cup mayonnaise
1 teaspoon grated onion
¼ teaspoon Tabasco sauce

Place filets in an oven-proof casserole and broil for 4 minutes. Mix together remaining ingredients. Spread sauce over filets. Broil an additional 3 minutes or until sauce is golden. Serves 4.

 Thaw frozen fish filets in milk for fresher flavor.

Seafood

Almond Butter Sauce

2	tablespoons slivered almonds	2	teaspoons finely chopped fresh parsley
½	cup butter, divided		
2	tablespoons chopped pimiento (optional)	2	teaspoons lemon juice
		1	teaspoon salt

Sauté almonds in 2 tablespoons of butter until golden. Cool. Cream remaining butter and add almonds, pimiento and seasonings. May be stored for two weeks in refrigerator. Yields ¾ cup.

Wonderful with fried or broiled seafoods.

Buerre Blanc

¼	cup dry white wine	1	cup butter, softened
¼	cup white wine vinegar	¼	teaspoon kosher salt
1½	tablespoons chopped shallots	¼	teaspoon white pepper

In a saucepan, combine wine, vinegar and shallots and reduce to 2 tablespoons over high heat. Cool slightly, then gradually add butter, whisking until well blended. Add salt and pepper. Serve warm with any type of fish. Serves 6.

Also good over asparagus.

Meats

Meats

*Other Meat recipes may be found in **Southern Classics.***

Meats

Company Tenderloin and Spicy Beef Spread

1	whole beef tenderloin	½	cup butter, softened
	Kosher salt	¼	cup mayonnaise
1	8-ounce package cream	¼	cup prepared horseradish,
	cheese, softened		drained

Rub tenderloin with salt until well coated. Cook for 15 minutes at 500 degrees. Reduce to 350 degrees and cook 45 minutes. Use meat thermometer to assure desired degree of doneness.

Meanwhile, blend cream cheese and butter until fluffy. Stir in mayonnaise and horseradish. Mix well. Slice tenderloin; serve spread in separate bowl. Allow ½ pound tenderloin per person. Spread serves 6 to 8.

This may be served as an appetizer with party round bread.

Marinated Tenderloin

1	whole beef tenderloin	1	teaspoon garlic powder
1	cup soy sauce	1	teaspoon grated ginger
¾	cup vegetable oil	1	green onion, top included,
3	tablespoons honey		chopped
2	tablespoons vinegar		Parsley

Trim tenderloin to remove fat. Combine remaining ingredients and pour over tenderloin. Marinate overnight. Preheat oven to 400 degrees. Place tenderloin in 9 x 13-inch pan lined with foil and pour marinade over. Bake for 30 to 40 minutes or until meat reaches desired stage of doneness. Remove from oven, slice and garnish with parsley. Serves 8 to 10, or about 2 to 3 servings per pound.

Meats

Steak au Poivre

¼ cup fresh whole peppercorns
4 individual tenderloin or rib eye steaks, completely trimmed
2-3 tablespoons vegetable oil

3 tablespoons butter
¼ cup plus 1 teaspoon cognac, divided
½ cup whipping cream
Salt

Crush peppercorns and use to coat both sides of steaks. Heat oil (enough to coat bottom) in a large skillet. Sauté steaks over medium-high heat until lightly browned. Remove steaks from pan and discard oil. Add butter and return steaks to pan. Add ¼ cup cognac and ignite; allow to cook over heat until flames die out. Remove steaks to serving platter and keep warm. Add cream to pan and stir with wooden spoon over medium-high heat until cream boils and thickens. Add 1 teaspoon cognac and salt to taste. Spoon sauce over steaks and serve immediately. Serves 4.

Carrie's London Broil with Mushroom Sauce

1 2-pound flank steak
2 tablespoons peanut oil

Coarse salt
Freshly ground black pepper

Rub both sides of flank steak with oil, a small amount coarse salt and a generous amount of pepper. Broil 4 to 5 minutes on each side, depending on desired degree of doneness. Set aside for 5 minutes before slicing thinly on the diagonal. Serves 6.

Mushroom Sauce:
1 tablespoon butter
1½-2 cups sliced fresh mushrooms
Freshly ground pepper to taste
½ cup dry white wine
½ cup canned beef broth

¼ teaspoon dried tarragon, crushed
1½ teaspoons cornstarch dissolved in 3 teaspoons water

In a skillet, melt butter. Add mushrooms and sprinkle with pepper. Sauté 3 to 4 minutes. Add wine and cook briefly over high heat. Add beef broth and tarragon. Reduce heat and simmer 10 minutes. Add dissolved cornstarch. Cook 2 to 3 minutes and serve with meat. Serves 6.

If cooking the meat on a grill, do not rub with oil. Allow 10 minutes for rare beef.

Meats

Grilled Chuck Roast

1	4-5 pound chuck roast, 2 inches thick	1	tablespoon lemon juice
	Unseasoned meat tenderizer	¼	cup bourbon
1	5-ounce bottle soy sauce	1	teaspoon Worcestershire sauce
¼	cup brown sugar	1½	cups water

Sprinkle all sides of roast with tenderizer and pierce with fork. Let stand for approximately 1 hour. Combine soy sauce, brown sugar, lemon juice, bourbon, Worcestershire and water. Marinate roast in refrigerator for 24 hours in sauce. Grill roast over hot coals, basting frequently with sauce, for 30 to 45 minutes for medium-rare beef. Slice very thin. Serves 8 to 10.

Marinated Shish Kabob

Marinade:

1	cup vegetable oil	2	teaspoons salt
½	cup soy sauce	1	teaspoon pepper
¼	cup Worcestershire sauce	¼	cup lemon juice
2	tablespoons dry mustard		Garlic salt to taste

Shish Kabob:

1-2	pounds sirloin or tenderloin, cubed	Cherry tomatoes
	Small onions	Pineapple chunks
	Green pepper, cut in pieces	Fresh mushrooms

Mix marinade ingredients and pour over beef cubes. Refrigerate 24 hours, turning occasionally.

Before assembling, cook onions and green pepper in boiling water until softened. Place meat on skewers, alternating with vegetables and fruit. Grill over hot coals until done. Serves 4 to 6.

Meats

David's Deviled Swiss Steak

1	large onion, sliced	¼	teaspoon pepper
1	clove garlic, finely chopped	1½	pounds cubed steak
4	tablespoons vegetable oil	1	16-ounce can tomatoes,
¼	cup flour		undrained
1	teaspoon dry mustard	½-1	teaspoon dried basil,
1½	teaspoons salt		crushed

In a Dutch oven, sauté onion and garlic in oil. Remove, drain and reserve oil. Mix flour, mustard, salt and pepper and coat meat well with mixture. Brown meat on each side in oil, adding more oil if needed. Add onions, garlic, tomatoes and basil. Cover tightly. Bake at 325 degrees for 25 minutes or until tender. Serves 6.

Moussaka

1	pound ground beef	2½	pounds eggplant
1	cup chopped onions	2	cups cottage cheese
3	8-ounce cans tomato sauce	2	eggs
¼	cup water	8	tablespoons grated
1	teaspoon dried oregano		Parmesan cheese, divided
1¼	teaspoons salt, divided	¼	teaspoon dried rosemary
¼	teaspoon pepper	¼	teaspoon ground mace

Brown beef and drain. Add onion and stir over high heat for 5 minutes. Stir in tomato sauce, water, oregano, 1 teaspoon salt and pepper. Cover and simmer for 30 minutes, stirring occasionally. Peel and slice eggplant into ½-inch slices. Boil in salted water until tender. Drain well. In a bowl, blend together cottage cheese, eggs, 2 teaspoons Parmesan, ¼ teaspoon salt, rosemary and mace.

In an ungreased 9 x 13-inch baking dish, spread half of meat mixture. Sprinkle 2 tablespoons Parmesan on top. Add half of eggplant slices. Spread cottage cheese mixture on top. Sprinkle with 2 tablespoons Parmesan. Top with remaining eggplant and sprinkle with 2 tablespoons Parmesan. Add remaining meat mixture and rest of Parmesan. Bake at 375 degrees for 30 minutes or until bubbly. Let stand 5 minutes before slicing. Serves 6 to 8.

Greek Styfado

½	cup butter	1	small cinnamon stick
3	pounds lean beef, cubed	½	teaspoon whole cloves
	Salt and pepper to taste	2	tablespoons currants, raisins
2	6-ounce cans tomato paste		or currant jelly
⅔	cup red table wine	¼	teaspoon ground cumin
4	tablespoons red wine vinegar		(optional)
2	tablespoons brown sugar	2½	pounds small white onions,
1	clove garlic		peeled
1	bay leaf		Rice or cooked noodles

Melt butter in a Dutch oven. Brown meat and season with salt and pepper. In a large bowl, mix together remaining ingredients except onion and rice or noodles. Pour mixture over browned beef in butter. Do not stir. Cover meat and sauce with whole raw onions. Cover onions with an inverted ovenproof plate. (A covering of aluminum foil works well if it is placed directly on the onions and extends to the sides of the Dutch oven.) Place lid on Dutch oven and bake at least 3 hours at 325 degrees. Serve over rice or cooked noodles. Serves 6.

Meats

Mexican Casserole

4	pounds ground chuck	1	cup sliced black olives
1	medium onion, chopped	24	corn tortillas
3	cloves garlic, finely chopped		Vegetable oil
¼	cup chili powder	4	cups cottage cheese
6	cups tomato sauce	2	eggs
1	teaspoon sugar	1	pound Monterey Jack
1½	tablespoons salt		cheese, sliced
2	4-ounce cans chopped green chilies, drained	2	cups grated Cheddar cheese

Suggested Toppings:

1	cup chopped green onions	1	cup sliced black olives
1	cup sour cream		

Brown meat in a Dutch oven. Add onions and garlic and sauté . Sprinkle with chili powder. Add tomato sauce, sugar, salt, chilies and 1 cup olives. Simmer 15 minutes. Fry tortillas in vegetable oil until soft but not brown. Drain and slice into quarters. Beat together cottage cheese and eggs and set aside. Spread ⅓ of meat sauce in a 6-quart casserole dish. Cover with ½ each: Monterey Jack slices, cottage cheese mixture and tortillas. Repeat layers and top with remaining meat sauce. Top with grated Cheddar cheese. Bake uncovered 30 minutes at 350 degrees. Serve with green onions, sour cream and black olives. Serves 12.

Delightful with guacamole salad and frozen margaritas.

Meats

Cannelloni

1	8-ounce box manicotti shells	2	chicken livers, cooked and chopped
2	tablespoons butter		
2	tablespoons olive oil	5	tablespoons grated Parmesan cheese
3	cloves garlic, finely chopped		
1	medium onion, finely chopped	½	teaspoon dried oregano
			Salt and pepper to taste
1	pound ground round steak	2	eggs, beaten
1	10-ounce package frozen chopped spinach, thawed	2	tablespoons whipping cream

Cook manicotti and drain well. Set aside. In a skillet, heat butter and oil. Add garlic and onion; cook for 5 minutes. Add beef, brown well and drain if needed. Add spinach. Cook until almost all moisture has evaporated from mixture. Add chicken livers, cheese, oregano, salt and pepper. Beat eggs with cream and add to mixture. Mix well. Stuff manicotti tubes with this mixture and set aside.

Cream Sauce:

2	tablespoons butter	½	cup whipping cream
2	tablespoons flour	½	teaspoon salt
½	cup milk		White pepper to taste

In a saucepan, melt butter. Gradually add flour, cooking for 2 minutes without browning. Add milk and cream, stirring constantly until thick. Blend in seasonings, mixing well. Set aside.

Tomato Sauce:

1	tablespoon olive oil	½	teaspoon sugar
½	small onion, finely chopped	¼	teaspoon salt
1	16-ounce can tomatoes, undrained		Pepper to taste
1½	tablespoons tomato paste	3	tablespoons grated Parmesan cheese
½	teaspoon dried basil	3	tablespoons butter

In a skillet, heat olive oil. Add onion, stirring until transparent. Blend in tomatoes, tomato paste and remaining seasonings. Simmer partially covered for 30 minutes.

To assemble, coat the bottom of a 9 x 13-inch glass dish with the tomato sauce. Make a single layer of stuffed manicotti; then cover with cream sauce. Cover cream sauce with tomato sauce and sprinkle with Parmesan cheese. Dot with butter. Bake at 350 degrees until bubbly. Brown top under broiler. Serves 6 to 8.

Meats

Lasagna

1	pound ground beef	3	eggs
¾	teaspoon salt	1	pound cream-style cottage cheese
⅛	teaspoon pepper		
½	teaspoon dried oregano	1	tablespoon dried parsley
1	small onion, sliced	¼	cup grated Parmesan cheese
2	tablespoons vegetable oil	4	slices processed mozzarella cheese
1	15-ounce can tomato sauce		
½	cup water		
1	8-ounce package lasagne noodles		

Sprinkle beef with salt, pepper and oregano. Toss with a fork to distribute seasonings. Brown beef and onion in oil heated in a skillet, stirring to crumble meat; drain. Add tomato sauce and water. Bring to a boil, reduce heat and simmer 20 minutes. Cook lasagna noodles according to package directions. Beat eggs; add cottage cheese and parsley. In a 9 x 13-inch baking dish, alternate layers of noodles, beef mixture, Parmesan cheese and cottage cheese mixture, ending with beef. Bake at 375 degrees for 20 minutes. Put mozzarella cheese on top for the last 5 minutes of baking. Serves 8.

Meats

Mock Ravioli

8	ounces sea shell or bow knot macaroni	¼	teaspoon dried basil
1	medium onion, chopped	¼	teaspoon dried rosemary
2	cloves garlic, divided		Salt and pepper to taste
½-1	pound ground beef	½	cup bread crumbs
1	10-ounce package frozen chopped spinach, cooked and well drained, liquid reserved	1	cup grated Cheddar cheese
		¼	cup vegetable oil
		2	eggs, well beaten
			Salt and pepper to taste
			Grated Parmesan cheese
1	6-ounce can tomato paste	1	8-ounce can mushroom sauce or mushroom sauce from Chicken Loaf (see index)
1	8-ounce can tomato sauce		
½	teaspoon dried oregano		

Cook macaroni until tender; drain. Sauté onion and 1 clove garlic with ground beef until meat browns; drain. Add ¾ cup reserved spinach liquid, tomato paste, tomato sauce and seasonings. Simmer 15 to 20 minutes. Finely chop or put through meat grinder the spinach, bread crumbs, remaining clove of garlic and cheese. To this mixture add oil, eggs, salt and pepper; mix well. In a buttered 9 x 13-inch baking dish, alternate layers of pasta, spinach mixture and meat sauce. Top with Parmesan cheese, cover and refrigerate several hours or overnight. Before baking, top with mushroom sauce. Bake uncovered at 350 degrees for 30 minutes or until bubbly. Serves 6.

Spaghetti

3	pounds ground beef or 2 pounds ground beef and 1 pound hot bulk sausage	1	cup water
		2	6-ounce cans tomato paste
			Salt and pepper to taste
3	medium onions, chopped	2	3-ounce cans mushroom stems and pieces, undrained
1	green pepper, chopped		
3	cloves garlic, finely chopped	2	16-ounce packages spaghetti pasta
2	teaspoons dried basil		
2	teaspoons dried oregano		Grated Parmesan cheese for garnish
4	8-ounce cans tomato sauce		

In a Dutch oven, cook beef and sausage with onion and green pepper; drain. Add remaining ingredients except pasta and cheese. Simmer uncovered for several hours or at least 45 minutes. Stir frequently. Cook pasta according to package directions and serve topped with sauce and Parmesan cheese. Serves 12 to 16.

Sauce may be thinned with tomato juice or water while cooking.

Meats

Spaghetti Pie

8	ounces linguini	1	8-ounce can tomatoes,
2	tablespoons butter		undrained and chopped
½	cup grated Parmesan cheese	1	teaspoon dried oregano,
2	eggs, well beaten		crushed
1	pound ground beef	½	teaspoon garlic salt
½	cup chopped onion	1	cup cottage cheese
¼	cup chopped green pepper	⅔	cup grated mozzarella cheese
1	6-ounce can tomato paste		

Cook linguini, drain and stir in butter, Parmesan and eggs. Place mixture in a greased 10-inch pie plate and shape into a crust. In a skillet, sauté beef, onions and green pepper until beef is brown and vegetables are tender; drain. Stir in tomato paste, tomatoes and seasonings. Simmer 30 to 45 minutes. Spread cottage cheese over noodle crust. Add tomato-meat mixture and bake 30 minutes at 350 degrees. Top with mozzarella and bake until cheese melts, about 5 minutes. Serves 6.

Italian Eggplant Casserole

1	large eggplant	1	green pepper, chopped
½	cup milk		Salt and pepper to taste
1	egg, beaten	2	15-ounce cans tomato sauce
½	cup flour	1	8-ounce package sliced
	Vegetable oil		mozzarella cheese
1	pound ground beef	½	cup grated Cheddar cheese
1	onion, chopped		Dried oregano to taste

Peel and slice eggplant. Dip slices in milk, then egg. Dredge in flour. In a large skillet, heat oil and cook eggplant until brown. Remove from skillet and drain. In the same skillet sauté beef, onion and green pepper until vegetables are tender; drain. Add salt, pepper and tomato sauce. In a greased 8 x 11½-inch casserole, place alternate layers of eggplant, cheese slices and beef mixture. Top with grated cheese and oregano. Bake uncovered at 350 degrees until bubbly. Serves 6.

Meats

Curry Hot Pot

1½	pounds stew beef	1	10½-ounce can beef bouillon
2	tablespoons vegetable oil		
2	onions, peeled and sliced	2	teaspoons salt
1	apple, cored and cubed	¼	teaspoon pepper
1	tablespoon curry powder	1	tablespoon brown sugar
2	tomatoes, chopped	2	hard-cooked eggs, sliced, for garnish
¼	cup golden seedless raisins		
1	tablespoon flour		Chopped fresh parsley

Cut beef into small chunks. Heat oil in large saucepan and brown meat. Add onions, apple and curry powder and sauté until onion is tender. Stir in remaining ingredients except garnish; cover and simmer 1 to 2 hours, or until meat is tender. Serve over rice and garnish with eggs and parsley. Serves 6.

For a homemade version of curry powder, use the following spices, varying the amounts according to individual tastes:

1	*teaspoon ground cardamom*	*1*	*teaspoon ground fenugreek (available at specialty and health food stores)*
1	*teaspoon ground cinnamon*		
1	*teaspoon ground coriander*		
1	*teaspoon ground cumin*	*1*	*teaspoon ground cayenne pepper (or less if desired)*
2	*teaspoons ground tumeric*		

Yields 8 teaspoons.

Mrs. Richard Riley's Beef Casserole

1	pound lean ground beef	1	8-ounce package cream cheese, softened
1	teaspoon salt		
1	teaspoon sugar	1	cup sour cream
	Dash garlic salt	1	onion, chopped
1	16-ounce can tomato sauce	¼	cup grated green pepper
1	8-ounce package narrow noodles	1	cup grated Cheddar cheese

Brown beef and add salt, sugar and garlic salt. Drain well. Add tomato sauce and remove from heat. Cook noodles according to directions; drain. Mix cream cheese, sour cream, onion and green pepper. In a buttered 2-quart casserole dish, layer half of noodles, half of cream cheese mixture and half of meat. Repeat layers, ending with meat and top with Cheddar cheese. Bake at 350 degrees for 20 to 25 minutes. Serves 6.

Richard Riley became Governor of South Carolina on January 11, 1979.

Meats

Chipped Beef and Artichoke Sauce

1	14-ounce can artichoke hearts, drained	¼	teaspoon salt
3	tablespoons butter	1	cup sour cream
3	tablespoons flour	¼	cup dry white wine
¾	cup milk	1	cup shredded chipped beef
		¾	cup chopped black olives

Cut artichoke hearts in bite-size pieces. Melt butter in large saucepan. Stir in flour until blended. In a separate pan, heat milk to boiling and add all at once to butter and flour mixture. Stir vigorously until smooth and thick. Add remaining ingredients, heating until warm. Serves 6 to 8.

Excellent served over scrambled eggs, grits, toast points or English muffins. May be reheated in a double boiler.

Chili

1	pound ground beef	1	bay leaf
¼-½	cup chopped green pepper	1	tablespoon chili powder or to taste
½	cup chopped onion		
2	cups canned tomatoes	1	clove garlic, finely chopped
1	10¾-ounce can tomato soup	1	16-ounce can red kidney beans, undrained
½	teaspoon paprika		
⅛	teaspoon cayenne pepper		Salt to taste

Brown beef, adding green pepper and onion as meat cooks. Drain. Add tomatoes, soup, paprika, cayenne pepper, bay leaf, chili powder and garlic. Simmer uncovered over low heat for 1 hour, stirring occasionally. Water may be added to achieve desired consistency. Add beans and salt. Heat thoroughly. Serves 6.

Meats

Spinach Meatballs

1 10-ounce package frozen chopped spinach
1 pound lean ground beef
1 onion, chopped
1 egg
1 teaspoon dried basil
¼ teaspoon garlic salt
1 teaspoon Worcestershire sauce
   Salt and pepper to taste
1 8-ounce can tomato sauce

Thaw and drain spinach. Mix all ingredients except tomato sauce. Mold into 9 large meatballs. Place in an ungreased 9-inch square pan and top with tomato sauce. Bake uncovered at 350 degrees for 45 minutes. Serves 4.

Sweet and Sour Meatballs

1½ pounds ground beef
⅓ cup finely chopped onion
   Garlic salt to taste
1 10¾-ounce can tomato soup
1½ tablespoons lemon juice
¼ cup sugar
   Cooked rice or noodles

Combine beef, onion and garlic salt and shape into balls. Brown on all sides in a large skillet and drain. Combine remaining ingredients except rice or noodles and pour over meatballs. Bring to a boil, cover and simmer for 1 hour. Serve meatballs with sauce over cooked rice or noodles. Serves 6 to 8.

Easy and delicious for a family meal.

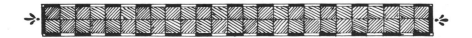

Meats

Roast Lamb with Lemon and Rosemary

1	leg of lamb		Fresh rosemary to taste
½	fresh lemon	2-3	cups water
	Salt and pepper to taste		Quince jelly
½	cup flour		

Remove leg of lamb from refrigerator at least ½ hour before cooking. Rub with cut lemon, season with salt and pepper, dredge with flour and insert fresh rosemary under skin using a pointed knife. Place fat side up on a meat rack. Roast uncovered at 300 degrees for 35 minutes per pound. Let roast rest 15 minutes before carving.

To make gravy, remove meat from pan and pour off most of liquid, leaving thicker drippings in pan. Add 2 to 3 cups water and stir with wire whisk to loosen drippings from pan. Simmer about 10 minutes. Serve lamb with gravy and quince jelly. Serves 10 to 12.

Cornelia's Leg of Lamb

1	leg of lamb, trimmed of fat	4	tablespoons prepared mustard
	Salt and pepper		
1-2	onions, sliced	4	teaspoons Worcestershire sauce
1	cup water		
1	tablespoon vinegar	1	tablespoon flour
½	teaspoon salt	1¼	cups water

Wipe lamb with damp cloth, season with salt and pepper and refrigerate overnight. About 4 hours before serving, salt and pepper again. Make 4 slashes in sides and put half of onion slices in slashes. Place lamb in roasting pan. Add water, vinegar, salt and remaining sliced onion. Cover and bake 1½ hours at 400 degrees. Add water as needed to prevent drying out. Combine mustard and Worcestershire; spread over lamb, cover and cook an additional 2 hours, basting with sauce.

To make gravy, mix flour and ¼ cup water until smooth. Add to pan drippings and mix well. Add 1 cup of water. Stir until well mixed; cook until desired thickness. Serves 8 to 10.

Use a meat thermometer to avoid over-cooking.

Meats

Lamb Provençale

1	pound lamb round steak	¼	cup chopped parsley
1	cup beef broth, divided		Salt and pepper to taste
1	clove garlic, halved		

Trim fat from lamb. Pour ½ cup broth into oven-proof casserole; rub meat with garlic and parsley. Season with salt and pepper. Bake 20 to 30 minutes at 350 degrees. Pour remaining broth over meat and bake an additional 5 to 10 minutes. Serve with mint jelly. Serves 2.

Pork Roast with Wine Sauce

½	cup flour	2-4	medium onions, thinly sliced
	Salt and pepper to taste	1	cup chicken bouillon
	Dried thyme to taste	¾	cup dry white wine
	Dried oregano to taste	1	clove garlic, finely chopped
1	6-pound pork loin	⅛	teaspoon ground nutmeg

Combine flour, salt, pepper, thyme and oregano and rub on all sides of roast. Cover roast with onion slices, securing with toothpicks. Wrap and refrigerate at least 12 hours. Unwrap, place in roasting pan and bake 30 minutes at 375 degrees. Lower heat to 325 degrees and cook 35 minutes per pound, basting often with mixture made from remaining ingredients. When roast is done, blend mixture into pan drippings over low heat stirring constantly until thickened. For easier carving, let roast sit covered, about 20 minutes before carving. Serve with thickened sauce. Serves 6 to 8.

For variation use pork loin chops and grill over charcoal.

Pork Chops Victoria

4-6	pork chops	1	cup beef broth
¼	cup vegetable oil	2	large tart apples, peeled, cored and quartered
2	medium onions, thinly sliced		Salt and pepper to taste
2	tablespoons flour	¼-½	teaspoon dried sage

Brown pork chops in oil and remove. In same pan, sauté onion until transparent. Mix in flour and broth; add chops, apples and seasonings. Simmer covered about 30 minutes until chops are done. Serves 4.

Meats

Pork Chops and Chestnuts

2	tablespoons oil	1	large onion, finely chopped
4	pork chops	1	cup sliced cooked chestnuts
	Salt and pepper to taste	1	cup beef broth or bouillon

Heat oil in heavy iron skillet. Season pork chops well with salt and pepper, brown both sides in oil and add onion and chestnuts. Continue cooking until all are browned. Remove from heat and pour beef broth over the chops. Cover skillet with a piece of well greased heavy brown paper. Continue cooking in oven at 350 degrees for 1 hour or until chops are tender. Serves 2.

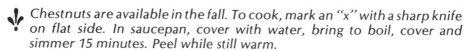 *Chestnuts are available in the fall. To cook, mark an "x" with a sharp knife on flat side. In saucepan, cover with water, bring to boil, cover and simmer 15 minutes. Peel while still warm.*

Richard's Pork Chops

4	pork loin chops	1	16-ounce can tomatoes, chopped and undrained
	Freshly ground pepper to taste		Coarse salt to taste
1½-2	tablespoons olive oil	1½	teaspoons cornstarch
1½	cups sliced fresh mushrooms	1	tablespoons water
½	cup dry white wine		Cooked rice

Trim fat from pork chops and pat dry. Sprinkle with pepper. Heat oil in skillet and brown chops, about 5 minutes on each side. Add mushrooms, cover tightly and cook 5 minutes. Add wine, tomatoes and salt. Cover and simmer 35 to 40 minutes. Remove chops to serving plate. Dissolve cornstarch in water and add to sauce. Cook briefly to thicken and serve sauce over chops or rice. Serves 4.

Meats

Pork Chow Mein

1	pound pork tenderloin	2	tablespoons cornstarch
	Vegetable oil	1	cup sliced fresh mushrooms
1	cup sliced celery	1	16-ounce can Chinese
1	medium onion, chopped		vegetables, drained
3	tablespoons soy sauce	1	16-ounce can bean sprouts,
2	beef bouillon cubes		rinsed and drained
2	cups water	½	teaspoon salt

Cut meat into ½-inch slices; then cut slices into ¼-inch strips. Brown meat in oil in a large skillet. Stir in celery, onion, soy sauce, bouillon and water. Cover and simmer 30 minutes. Mix cornstarch in small amount of water. Stir into meat mixture. Add mushrooms and Chinese vegetables. Cook, stirring constantly, until mixture thickens and boils. Boil and stir 1 minute. Simmer until mushrooms are tender. In separate pan, sprinkle bean sprouts with salt and heat, stirring occasionally. Serve meat mixture over bean sprouts. Serves 6.

Carolina Pork Barbeque

1	3-4 pound pork loin roast	2	cups cider vinegar
1	tablespoon salt	¼-½	cup ketchup
	Coarsely ground pepper	8	hamburger buns, split and
2	tablespoons sugar		toasted

Trim fat from roast and sprinkle all surfaces with salt and pepper. Place meat in a slow cooker. Sprinkle with sugar and add vinegar. Cook on low setting for 12 hours or until meat falls off bones. Place meat in bowl, removing bones and excess fat. Shred meat and stir in ketchup. Fill buns with meat and serve warm on buns. Serves 8.

For cooking on top of stove or in oven, cut pork into chunks if necessary and place in covered casserole with remaining ingredients except buns. Cook, adding water if necessary, over low heat or in 325 degree oven for 3 to 4 hours or until meat falls off bones.

Meats

Elegant Stuffed Veal Loin

1 5-pound boned loin of veal, well trimmed of fat	¼ cup olive oil
	Salt and pepper to taste
1 clove garlic, finely chopped	¼ cup mild wine vinegar
1 9-ounce can truffles, thickly sliced, liquid reserved or ¼ cup duxelles (Recipe follows)	1 cup chicken broth
	Herbed brandy sauce (Recipe follows)

Preheat oven to 500 degrees. Make a lengthwise pocket in meat. (Your butcher can do this.) Rub pocket with garlic. Stuff with truffles or duxelles. Roll meat lengthwise and tie at 1-inch intervals with string. Rub with olive oil and sprinkle with salt and pepper. Set on rack in shallow pan and roast uncovered until golden, about 15 to 20 minutes. Reduce oven temperature to 375 degrees. Sprinkle meat with vinegar and pour chicken broth and liquid from truffles (if used) in pan. Cover and continue roasting until done, about 1½ hours. Transfer to heated platter and serve with herbed brandy sauce. Serves 8 to 10.

Duxelles (Mushroom Concentrate):

½ cup unsalted butter	**Bouquet garni (1 bay leaf, ½**
3 tablespoons olive oil	**teaspoon dried thyme and**
2 pounds fresh mushrooms, finely chopped	**a few sprigs of parsley tied in cheesecloth bag)**
½ cup chopped shallot or green onion	½ cup Madeira wine or ¼ cup beef bouillon
	Salt and pepper to taste

Heat butter and olive oil in 10 or 12-inch skillet over low heat. Add mushrooms and shallots and stir well. Add garni and cook uncovered, stirring occasionally until most of moisture from mushrooms has evaporated, about 40 to 45 minutes. Add wine or stock and continue cooking until all liquid has evaporated and mushrooms are almost black, about 1½ hours. Remove garni and add salt and pepper to taste. Yields 2 cups.

Herbed Brandy Sauce:

½ cup cognac	4 cups whipping cream
2 tablespoons dried rosemary	Pan juices from veal roast
¼ cup unsalted butter	1 teaspoon salt
	¼ teaspoon pepper

Combine cognac and rosemary in small pan and let stand 15 minutes. Heat butter in heavy 4-quart saucepan over medium heat until bubbling. Heat cognac and ignite. Add to butter. Gradually add cream and stir constantly with wooden spoon until sauce has thickened and reduced by ⅔, about 20 minutes. Sauce can be made to this point several days in advance. Skim as much fat as possible from pan juices. If necessary, boil down until no more than ⅓ cup remains. Stir in cream mixture and whisk to combine thoroughly. Season with salt and pepper.

Meats

Ham and Cheese Quiche

½	cup chopped onion	1½	cups chopped cooked ham
⅓	cup chopped green pepper	1	9-inch deep-dish pie shell,
1	tablespoon butter		unbaked
1½	cups grated sharp Cheddar	2	eggs, beaten
	cheese	1	cup milk
1	tablespoon flour	½	teaspoon garlic salt
1	tablespoon finely chopped	¼	teaspoon pepper
	pimiento		

Sauté onion and green pepper in butter. Mix cheese and flour together. Add onion, green pepper, pimiento and ham to cheese and place in pie shell. Combine remaining ingredients and pour over all. Place pan on a baking sheet and bake 35 to 40 minutes at 375 degrees. Serves 6 to 8.

Sausage Egg Casserole

1	pound mildly seasoned pork	¼	teaspoon cayenne pepper
	sausage		(optional)
6	eggs	4	slices white bread, cubed
2	cups milk	1	cup grated sharp Cheddar
1	teaspoon salt		cheese
1	teaspoon dry mustard		

Sauté sausage and drain. Beat eggs with milk, salt, mustard and cayenne pepper. Layer bread, sausage and cheese in 9 x 13-inch baking dish. Pour egg mixture over ingredients in casserole. Chill overnight. Bake uncovered at 350 degrees for 45 minutes. Serves 6 to 8.

Beef Marinade

½	cup soy sauce	1	tablespoon ground ginger
½	cup dry sherry	1	teaspoon garlic salt
¼	cup peanut oil		

Combine all ingredients. Pour over beef and allow to marinate for at least 8 hours or overnight. Yields 1⅓ cups.

Wonderful for beef to be grilled; delicious flavor remains even when cooked meat is served cold. Especially good for chuck steak.

Meats

Chinese Sweet and Sour Sauce

½ cup vinegar
½ cup brown sugar
½ cup apricot preserves
½ cup peach preserves
1 8-ounce can applesauce

1 tablespoon grated fresh
   ginger root
1 clove garlic, finely chopped
⅛ teaspoon hot sauce

In a saucepan, combine all ingredients. Bring to a boil and cook for about 5 minutes, or until slightly thickened. Serve over pork or poultry, using as a glaze during the last few minutes of cooking. Yields 3 cups.

Keeps well in a jar in the refrigerator. For an appetizer, pour sauce over cream cheese and serve with crackers.

Mustard Sauce

4 tablespoons dry mustard
1 cup brown sugar
2 tablespoons flour

2 eggs
⅔ cup vinegar
½ cup water

Combine dry ingredients. Place liquid ingredients in a saucepan over low heat and mix well. Add dry ingredients. Whisk until well mixed and continue cooking until thickened. Store in refrigerator. Yields 2½ cups.

Excellent on ham or roast beef sandwiches or as dressing for chicken or tuna salad. For an appetizer, serve sauce with ham cubes for dipping.

Poultry

Poultry

*Other Poultry recipes may be found in **Southern Classics.**

Poultry

Crab Stuffed Chicken Breasts

8	chicken breast halves, skinned and boned	¼	cup chopped green pepper
¼	teaspoon salt	1	tablespoon lemon juice
1	egg, beaten	2	teaspoons Worcestershire sauce
1	cup herb seasoned stuffing	1	teaspoon prepared mustard
½	10¾-ounce can cream of mushroom soup		Melted butter
			Crispy rice cereal, crushed
1	6½-ounce can crabmeat, drained		Garlic powder (optional)

Sprinkle inside of chicken breasts with salt and flatten by pounding. Top with filling made of egg, stuffing, soup, crabmeat, green pepper, lemon juice, Worcestershire and mustard. Roll up chicken around stuffing; dip in melted butter and then cereal crumbs. Place seam side down in an ungreased shallow baking dish. Sprinkle lightly with garlic powder, if desired. Bake at 350 degrees for 1 to 1½ hours. Serves 6 to 8.

Avocado Chicken

4	chicken breast halves, skinned and boned	1	cup whipping cream
2	tablespoons lemon juice		Freshly grated nutmeg to taste
	Salt and pepper to taste	8	slices avocado
3	tablespoons unsalted butter	12	slices peeled tomato
¼	cup chicken broth	4	ounces grated Gruyère cheese
¼	cup dry white wine		

Lightly rub breasts with lemon juice and sprinkle with salt and pepper. Heat butter until foamy. Sauté chicken breasts, turning to keep coated. When cooked through, remove to a shallow baking dish. Add broth and wine to butter in pan. Reduce the liquid over high heat until it becomes syrupy. Add cream and continue cooking until mixture is thickened. Remove from heat and season with salt, pepper and nutmeg.

Arrange chicken, avocado and tomato slices alternately in an attractive pattern. Pour sauce over and top with cheese. Heat under broiler until glazed and bubbly. Serves 4.

This can be prepared up to the broiling stage and held for 1 hour. Bring to room temperature before broiling.

Poultry

Stuffed Chicken Breasts with Avocado Curry Sauce

6 chicken breast halves, skinned and boned
12 thin slices preserved ginger
12 whole mushrooms
Salt to taste
¼ cup flour

½ teaspoon paprika
3 tablespoons vegetable oil
½ cup chicken broth
¾ cup orange juice
2 teaspoons orange rind

Avocado Curry Sauce:
3 tablespoons butter
3 tablespoons finely chopped onion
½ cup finely chopped celery
⅓ cup flour
1 cup chicken broth

1 tablespoon lemon juice
Salt and pepper to taste
¼-½ teaspoon curry powder
1 cup half and half
1 small avocado

Flatten chicken breasts. Place 2 slices of ginger and 2 mushrooms cut in half in center of each breast. Fold meat over to enclose filling and tie or skewer. Sprinkle lightly with salt and roll in flour and paprika. In a skillet, heat oil and brown breasts slowly. Add broth, orange juice and rind and simmer covered until tender, about 40 minutes.

To make sauce, melt butter and sauté onion and celery. Whisk in flour. Stir in chicken broth, lemon juice and seasonings; cook until thickened. Add half and half and heat thoroughly. Before serving, peel and cube avocado; add to sauce. Serve chicken with a side dish such as white rice, topping both with sauce. Serves 6.

Mrs. Ronald Reagan's Baja California Chicken

8 chicken breast halves, boned
Seasoned salt to taste
Pepper to taste

2 cloves garlic, finely chopped
4 tablespoons olive oil
4 tablespoons tarragon vinegar
⅔ cup dry sherry

Sprinkle chicken with seasoned salt and pepper. Add garlic to oil and vinegar in a skillet. Sauté chicken pieces until golden brown, turning frequently. Remove from skillet; place in lightly greased 2-quart baking dish. Pour sherry over pieces and bake at 350 degrees for 10 minutes. Serves 8.

Ronald Reagan, fortieth President of the United States, took office January 1981.

Poultry

Chicken Elizabeth

4	chicken breast halves	1	tablespoon lemon juice
2	tablespoons butter	1	teaspoon salt
1	onion	1	teaspoon pepper
⅓	cup chopped green pepper		Dash dried tarragon
3	ounces dry vermouth		Dash paprika
1	cup sour cream	1	tablespoon cornstarch
¼	cup crumbled blue cheese	¼	cup water
	(1¼ ounces)		Cooked spinach noodles

Sauté chicken in butter until lightly browned. Place in 2-quart casserole, skin side up. Combine remaining ingredients except cornstarch, water and noodles in blender, blend well and pour over chicken. Bake covered at 350 degrees for 1 hour. Remove chicken to platter and keep warm. Combine cornstarch and water and pour half of mixture into sauce. Cook sauce in casserole or saucepan over medium heat, adding as much cornstarch mixture as needed to thicken sauce. Serve chicken with cooked spinach noodles and sauce. Serves 4.

For added color, garnish with pimiento strips or parsley or serve with a colorful vegetable.

Lynn's Special Chicken

6	chicken breast halves, skinned and boned	1	cup flour
		1	teaspoon salt
½	pound fresh mushrooms, sliced	½	teaspoon pepper
		½	teaspoon paprika
2	tablespoons butter	1	cup Italian bread crumbs
½	pound Swiss cheese, grated	¼	cup grated Swiss cheese
2	eggs, beaten		Butter

Pound chicken breasts to ¼-inch thickness. Sauté mushrooms in butter and mix with cheese. Place mixture on each chicken breast and fold in half. Secure with wooden toothpick. Place in freezer until firm, about 20 minutes. Dip in eggs, then in a mixture of flour, salt, pepper and paprika. Dip in a mixture of bread crumbs and Swiss cheese. Sauté in butter in a skillet until lightly browned on all sides. Place in a buttered shallow casserole dish and bake at 325 degrees for 20 to 30 minutes. Do not overcook. Serves 4 to 6.

Poultry

Chicken "Divine"

6	chicken breast halves	1	slice onion
	Salt and pepper to taste	¾	cup raw rice, cooked
1	pound fresh or frozen broccoli	2	tablespoons grated Parmesan cheese

Cheese Sauce:

¼	cup butter	1	cup grated sharp Cheddar cheese
1	teaspoon curry (optional)		
¼	cup flour	½	teaspoon salt
2	cups milk	⅛	teaspoon pepper
½	cup grated Parmesan cheese		

Sprinkle chicken with salt and pepper. Bake uncovered 1 hour at 350 degrees. Cool. Remove skin and bones and cut chicken into pieces. Cook broccoli with onion slice in salted water. Drain. Layer chicken, broccoli and rice in a buttered 2-quart casserole dish.

To make sauce, melt butter in a saucepan and stir in curry, if desired, and flour. Blend until smooth. Cook 2 minutes. Gradually add milk, stirring constantly until thickened. Add remaining ingredients. Continue stirring until cheeses have melted.

Pour cheese sauce over entire dish. Sprinkle Parmesan cheese on top. Bake uncovered 30 minutes at 350 degrees or until bubbly. Serves 6.

Tarragon Chicken

12	chicken breast halves, skinned and boned	½	cup butter
		½	cup dry white wine
½	cup flour for coating	½	cup flour
	Salt and pepper to taste	1	teaspoon dried tarragon
	Oil for browning	½	cup chicken broth
2	tablespoons chopped green onions	½	cup half and half

Shake chicken in a bag with flour, salt and pepper. In a skillet, sauté chicken in oil until done, about 8 to 10 minutes. Transfer chicken to a warmed dish. Pour off oil from skillet leaving the browned particles; sauté onions in butter. Add wine and whisk in flour to make a paste. Add tarragon and stir in chicken broth. Cook until thickened. Add half and half, heat and pour sauce over chicken. Serve with rice. Serves 12.

The chicken may be cooked and sauce made in advance. Before serving, pour sauce over chicken and warm in the oven.

Poultry

Chicken Sauté à la Russe

8	chicken breast halves, skinned and boned	¼	cup dry white wine
½	cup unsalted butter	3	tablespoons chopped fresh parsley
6	green onions, tops included, sliced	1	cup sour cream
3	medium tomatoes, peeled and chopped		

In a large skillet, sauté breasts in butter for 10 to 12 minutes. Add green onions and tomatoes. Cover and continue cooking until onions are tender and chicken is cooked through. Remove chicken to a platter and keep warm. Add wine and parsley to skillet, simmering 2 minutes. Add sour cream and stir until mixture is heated. Do not boil. To serve, pour sauce over chicken. Serves 6 to 8.

Crunchy Chicken Bake

8	chicken breast halves	¼	cup butter
1	cup water	1	10¾-ounce can cream of mushroom soup
1	cup vermouth	1	cup sour cream
1½	teaspoons salt		Pepper to taste
½	teaspoon curry	3	tablespoons mayonnaise
1	onion, sliced	1	cup Grape Nuts cereal
½	cup chopped celery	½	cup butter, melted
2	6-ounce boxes seasoned long grain and wild rice mix	½	3-ounce package slivered almonds
½	pound mushrooms, sliced		

Place chicken in a large pot. Add water, vermouth, salt, curry, onion and celery. Cover and cook chicken about 1½ hours. Cool, reserving liquid. Remove skin and bones and cut chicken into pieces. Return chicken to broth and marinate overnight in refrigerator.

The next day, strain and reserve broth and set chicken aside. Cook rice as directed, using chicken broth and water to make enough liquid. Sauté mushrooms in butter. Combine mushrooms, chicken, rice, soup, sour cream, pepper and mayonnaise. Pour into an ungreased 3-quart casserole dish. Mix cereal, butter and almonds and sprinkle on top of casserole. Bake 1 hour at 350 degrees. Serves 8.

Topping may be omitted if desired.

Poultry

Chinese Chicken with Cashews

12	chicken breast halves, skinned, boned and cut in ½-inch cubes	6	egg whites
		6	tablespoons cornstarch
		¾	teaspoon salt

Combine chicken with egg whites, cornstarch and salt; set aside.

Sauce:

½	cup dry sherry	4	tablespoons cornstarch
⅓	cup soy sauce	3	tablespoons white vinegar
6	tablespoons sugar	1	tablespoon sesame oil (optional)
6	tablespoons water		

Combine ingredients, mixing well; set aside.

To Finish:

2	cups vegetable oil	3	cloves garlic, finely chopped
1	large green pepper, cut in ½-inch pieces	1	tablespoon thinly sliced fresh ginger root
¾	cup dry-roasted cashew halves	1	8-ounce package frozen pea pods (optional)
6-8	green onions, thinly sliced		

Pour vegetable oil in wok or heavy 10-inch skillet. Place over medium heat until temperature reaches 375 degrees. Add chicken mixture, stirring constantly to separate chicken pieces. Cook 1 minute. Stir in green pepper and nuts. Remove from heat and drain mixture in a colander which has been set in another pan. Reserve 2 tablespoons of oil from pan. Put chicken mixture aside. Place wok or skillet with reserved oil over heat and add onion, garlic and ginger. Cook 1 minute. Add chicken mixture and stir in sauce. Add optional pea pods. Bring to a boil, stirring constantly and boil 1 minute. Serve over white rice. Serves 6.

If fresh ginger root is not available, whole dried ginger may be reconstituted.

Poultry

Quick Chicken Stroganoff

4	large chicken breast halves, skinned, boned and cut into bite-size pieces	1	chicken bouillon cube
¼-½	cup butter, divided	1¼	cups water
1	medium onion, chopped	1	cup sour cream
½	pound mushrooms, sliced	½	8-ounce package medium noodles, cooked
1	tablespoon flour	½	8-ounce package spinach noodles, cooked

In a skillet, sauté chicken using butter as needed. Remove from pan. Sauté onions and mushrooms in 2 tablespoons butter in same skillet. Stir in flour and bouillon; cook 1 minute. Gradually stir in water. Cook until thickened, stirring often to keep smooth. Stir in sour cream and chicken. Heat thoroughly but do not boil. Serve over hot cooked noodles. Serves 4.

Four quail may be substituted for chicken.

Chicken and Artichoke Casserole

1	whole chicken	1	clove garlic, minced
½	teaspoon salt	2	ounces mild Cheddar cheese, grated
¼	teaspoon pepper		
1	small onion, sliced	3	ounces Gruyère cheese, grated
2-3	celery stalks		
1	cup butter	2	3-ounce cans button mushrooms, drained
½	cup flour		
3½	cups milk	2	14-ounce cans artichoke hearts, drained and quartered
¼	teaspoon cayenne pepper		
1	tablespoon MSG (optional)		

In a large pot, barely cover chicken with water. Add salt, pepper, onion and celery. Simmer until done. Cool slightly; remove meat from bones and cut into bite-size pieces. In a saucepan, melt butter and blend in flour. Slowly add milk, stirring until thick. Add cayenne pepper, MSG, garlic and cheeses. Stir until cheese melts. Combine chicken, mushrooms, artichokes and sauce in a buttered 3-quart casserole. Bake uncovered 30 minutes at 350 degrees. Serves 8 to 10.

Lobster, shrimp or crab may be substituted for chicken.

Poultry

Chicken and Beef Spaghetti

4	large onions, chopped		Salt and pepper to taste
1	medium green pepper, chopped	2	teaspoons sugar
4-5	celery stalks, chopped	3	pounds chicken
	Olive oil	3	pounds ground beef
2	48-ounce jars spaghetti sauce with mushrooms	½	teaspoon garlic salt
		1	tablespoon Worcestershire sauce
1	28-ounce can tomatoes	1	8-ounce can sliced mushrooms, drained
1	16-ounce can tomato sauce or 1 6-ounce can tomato paste		Cooked thin spaghetti
1	bay leaf		Grated Cheddar or
½	teaspoon dried oregano		Parmesan cheese

In an 8 to 10-quart pot, sauté onion, green pepper and celery in enough oil to keep from burning. Stir in spaghetti sauce, tomatoes, tomato sauce, bay leaf, oregano, salt, pepper and sugar. Cook over medium heat, stirring occasionally. Wash chicken, skin and remove as much fat as possible. Add chicken to spaghetti sauce. Brown ground beef in skillet; season with garlic salt and Worcestershire. Drain and add to spaghetti sauce. Add salt and pepper to taste. Cook 45 minutes. Remove chicken and discard bones. Add chicken pieces and mushrooms to sauce and cook 1 hour. Serve over thin spaghetti and top with cheese. Serves 12 to 16.

Sherman's Spaghetti

3	pounds chicken	2	medium onions, chopped
½	teaspoon salt	¾	cup butter
¼	teaspoon pepper	1	1-pound package vermicelli
1	small onion, sliced	1	10-ounce can tomatoes and green chilies
2-3	celery stalks		
1	medium green pepper, chopped	1	2-pound box pasteurized process cheese spread, cubed

In a large pot, barely cover chicken with water. Add salt, pepper, onion and celery. Simmer about 1½ hours. Drain and reserve 6 cups broth. Remove chicken from bones and cut into bite-size pieces. Sauté green pepper and onion in butter. Cook vermicelli in reserved broth until tender. Do not drain. Combine with chicken, green pepper, onion, tomatoes and cheese. Place in 2 greased 2-quart casseroles. Bake uncovered 30 minutes at 350 degrees or until bubbly and cheese is melted. Yields 4 quarts.

Poultry

Chicken Curry

1	whole chicken	1	cup milk
2	tablespoons chopped green pepper	1	cup chicken broth
		¾	teaspoon salt
2	tablespoons chopped onion	1	cup sour cream
2	tablespoons chopped celery	¼	cup white wine
4	tablespoons butter		Cooked rice
1-2	tablespoons curry powder		Condiments
3	tablespoons flour		

Bake or stew chicken; skin and bone. Sauté green pepper, onion and celery in butter for 10 minutes. Stir in curry powder and flour. Gradually add milk and broth and cook, stirring, until sauce thickens. Stir in salt, sour cream, wine and chicken. Pour into buttered shallow 2-quart casserole and bake uncovered at 350 degrees for 30 minutes or until it bubbles. Serve over rice with condiments such as chutney, raisins and coconut. Serves 6 to 8.

Chicken Curry Olympia

1	3-pound chicken	2	tablespoons flour
½	teaspoon salt	1	tablespoon curry powder
¼	teaspoon pepper	1½	cups half and half
1	small onion	4	chicken bouillon cubes
2-3	celery stalks	2	cups chicken broth
1	cup butter	1	16-ounce can stewed tomatoes, drained and chopped
2	medium onions, grated		
1	clove garlic, finely chopped		

In a large pot, barely cover chicken with water. Add salt, pepper, onion and celery. Simmer about 1½ hours. Cool enough to handle; reserve broth. Remove meat from bones and cut into pieces. In butter, sauté onion and garlic. Stir in flour and curry. Add half and half and cook until thickened. Dissolve bouillon cubes in warm chicken broth and combine with sauce. Put chicken in sauce and add tomatoes. Cover and simmer for 1 hour. Serve over rice. Serves 6 to 8.

Suggested condiments include chopped hard-cooked eggs, toasted coconut, crumbled cooked bacon, green tomato pickle, chutney, raisins and chopped peanuts.

Poultry

Mexican Quiche

3	tablespoons finely chopped green chilies	1	cup whipping cream
1	9-inch pie shell, unbaked	1	teaspoon salt
1	cup cooked chicken	⅛	teaspoon pepper
½	pound grated Swiss cheese	1	ripe avocado, sliced
4	eggs, beaten		Sour cream
1	cup milk		Picante sauce (optional)

Spread chilies on bottom of pie shell; top with chicken and cheese. Combine eggs, milk, cream, salt and pepper until well mixed and pour over chilies, chicken and cheese. Bake for 40 minutes at 350 degrees or until done. Top with avocado slices arranged in pinwheel fashion and serve immediately to avoid discoloration of avocado. Serve with sour cream and Mexican picante sauce (a spicy tomato relish). Serves 4 to 6.

Chicken Rolls

2	cups chopped cooked chicken	2	8-ounce cans refrigerated crescent rolls
⅓	cup chopped fresh mushrooms	3	tablespoons butter, melted
1	4-ounce carton whipped cream cheese with chives	½	cup herb seasoned stuffing, finely crushed
¼-½	cup chopped water chestnuts	½	cup chopped pecans
1	teaspoon lemon pepper	1-2	cups Mushroom Sauce (See
2	tablespoons butter, softened		index for Chicken Loaf with Mushroom Sauce.)

Mix together chicken, mushrooms, cream cheese, water chestnuts, lemon pepper and softened butter. Unroll crescent roll dough and form 8 rectangles using 2 pieces of dough for each. Press center seam to seal. Put approximately ⅓ cup mixture on each rectangle of dough; fold to completely cover mixture and seal edges. Dip rolls in melted butter, next in stuffing and then in pecans. Place on an ungreased baking sheet and bake at 375 degrees for 15 to 20 minutes or until lightly browned. Serve topped with heated Mushroom Sauce. Yields 8 rolls, serving 8 for luncheon, 4 for dinner.

Filled rolls may be frozen before baking and removed from freezer for use as needed. For unexpected guests, remove from freezer, bake and top with a sauce made from a 10¾-ounce can cream of chicken soup, slightly diluted with milk.

Poultry

Chicken Loaf with Mushroom Sauce

1½ cups milk	1 cup long grain rice, cooked
1½ cups chicken broth	¾ cup finely chopped celery
4 eggs, beaten	1 teaspoon salt
2 cups firmly packed soft bread crumbs	Onion salt, garlic salt and pepper to taste
4 cups cooked chopped chicken	2 tablespoons chopped pimiento

Mushroom Sauce:

¼ cup butter	½ teaspoon paprika
6 tablespoons flour	1 teaspoon lemon juice
2 cups chicken broth	1 3-ounce can sliced mushrooms, drained
1 tablespoon chopped parsley	
1 teaspoon salt	1 cup half and half

The day before serving, combine milk and broth in large bowl. Blend in eggs and bread crumbs. Let mixture sit for several minutes. Add chicken, rice, celery, seasonings and pimiento. Spread evenly into greased 9 x 13-inch pan. Cover and place in refrigerator to season overnight. Bake uncovered at 350 degrees for 1 hour.

To prepare sauce, melt butter in saucepan. Add flour and blend well. Add chicken broth and cook over medium heat until thick. Add remaining ingredients, heat and serve over chicken. Serves 6.

Creamed Chicken and Shrimp

6-8 green onions, chopped	2 cups half and half
1 clove garlic, finely chopped	½ cup chopped fresh parsley
½ pound fresh mushrooms, sliced	2 cups cooked chicken, cut into bite-size pieces
1 cup butter	2 pounds shrimp, cooked and cleaned
8 tablespoons flour	
2 cups chicken broth	Salt and pepper to taste

Sauté onions, garlic and mushrooms in butter until tender. Stir in flour, mixing well; add chicken broth and half and half. Transfer to a double boiler and cook until mixture thickens. Add parsley, chicken, shrimp, salt and pepper. Heat thoroughly. Serve over rice, toast points or in pastry shells. Serves 12.

Poultry

Chicken Gertrude

1	5-pound chicken or hen	½	teaspoon MSG (optional)
3	tablespoons butter		Pepper to taste
3	tablespoons flour	1	4-ounce can sliced
1½	cups chicken broth		mushrooms, drained
1	cup half and half	2	cups cooked rice
2	cups grated sharp Cheddar	1	tablespoon finely chopped
	cheese		onion
1	teaspoon salt	1	cup slivered almonds

Stew and bone hen. In a saucepan, melt butter and stir in flour. Gradually add broth and half and half, stirring until sauce thickens. Add cheese, stirring constantly. Combine chicken, sauce, and remaining ingredients except almonds. Pour into a 2-quart casserole and top with almonds. Bake at 350 degrees for 40 minutes. Serves 6 to 8.

Honey Barbequed Chicken

¾	cup butter, melted	2	teaspoons salt
¼	cup wine vinegar	½	teaspoon dry mustard
¼	cup honey	1	chicken, cut in pieces
2	cloves garlic, finely chopped		

Combine all ingredients except chicken. Place chicken on grill, skin side up. Cook slowly, being sure rack is far enough from coals to prevent burning. Cook about 30 minutes or until tender, basting with sauce and turning frequently. Serves 4 to 6.

Partially cook chicken in oven or microwave before grilling; the reduced time on the grill results in less burning of the sauce.

Barbequed Chicken in Mustard Sauce

1	chicken, cut in pieces	4	tablespoons vinegar
	Salt and pepper to taste	3	tablespoons oil
½	cup prepared mustard	½-1	tablespoon brown sugar

Season chicken with salt and pepper. Combine remaining ingredients, stirring well. Pour sauce over chicken and bake uncovered 1 hour at 350 degrees. Serves 4 to 6.

Poultry

Barbequed Chicken

2	chicken fryers or 8-10 chicken breast halves	1	large onion, sliced
			Salt and pepper to taste

Sauce:

4½	tablespoons Worcestershire sauce	¼	teaspoon pepper
1	bay leaf	¾	cup vinegar
1½	cups tomato-vegetable juice	1	teaspoon sugar
¼	teaspoon cayenne pepper	3	cloves garlic, finely chopped
1	teaspoon salt	3	tablespoons butter

Place chicken in a roasting pan skin side up. Place sliced onions over chicken. Sprinkle with salt and pepper. Add water to cover bottom of pan and bake 30 minutes at 350 degrees. Turn chicken over and continue baking for 30 minutes. Meanwhile, combine sauce ingredients in a small saucepan. Cover and simmer for 20 minutes. Turn chicken skin side up and cover with sauce. Continue baking 1 hour, basting occasionally. Serves 8.

Barbeque Sauce

½	cup chopped onion	½	teaspoon pepper
1	tablespoon butter	2	tablespoons Worcestershire sauce
2	tablespoons honey		
2	tablespoons flour	1	cup fruit juice or sweet pickle juice
1	cup ketchup		
½	teaspoon ground cloves		

Sauté onion in butter. Add remaining ingredients and simmer 15 minutes. Yields 2½ cups.

Use as barbeque sauce for chicken, beef or pork.

Poultry

Lemon Chicken on the Grill

3 chickens, halved
2 cups salad oil
1 cup lemon juice
2 teaspons salt
2 teaspoons paprika

2 medium onions, chopped
4 teaspoons dried basil
3 teaspoons dried thyme
2 cloves garlic, finely chopped

Place chicken in a large mixing bowl. Combine remaining ingredients and pour over chicken. Marinate overnight in refrigerator. Cook chicken over medium heat on outdoor grill for 1 to 1½ hours. Baste with marinade every 15 minutes. Serves 6.

Mrs. Richard Riley's Chicken Liver Stroganoff

1 pound chicken livers
2 tablespoons butter
½ cup chopped onion
2 tablespoons flour
¼ teaspoon dried oregano
½ teaspoon Worcestershire
   sauce

½ teaspoon salt
   Dash pepper
1 6-ounce can sliced
   mushrooms, drained
¼ cup sour cream
   Cooked rice
8 slices bacon, crisply cooked

Remove veiny parts of liver with scissors. Brown livers in butter; set aside. Sauté onion until soft. Blend in flour and seasonings. Add mushrooms, sour cream and livers. Simmer 3 to 4 minutes; do not boil. Serve over rice and top with crumbled bacon. Serves 6.

Richard Riley became Governor of South Carolina on January 11, 1979.

Poultry

Stuffed Cornish Hens with Wine Sauce

1	6-ounce package seasoned long grain and wild rice mix	1	3-ounce can mushroom stems and pieces, drained
2½	cups chicken broth	6	tablespoons butter, melted
½	cup chopped celery	2	tablespoons soy sauce
½	cup sliced green onions	4	Cornish hens
⅔	cup sliced water chestnuts		Salt
			Melted butter

Wine Sauce:

½	pound fresh mushrooms, sliced	3	tablespoons dry white wine
¼	cup butter, melted	2	tablespoons sliced green onions
	Reserved pan drippings		

Prepare rice according to package directions, substituting broth for water. Cool and add celery, onion, water chestnuts, mushrooms, butter and soy sauce. Toss lightly to mix. Sprinkle inside of hens with salt and stuff with rice mixture. Bake at 375 degrees for 50 to 60 minutes or until done. Baste frequently with melted butter. Reserve pan drippings for wine sauce.

To prepare sauce, sauté mushrooms in butter and set aside. Combine pan drippings, wine and onions in small saucepan and cook over high heat until reduced by ½, about 10 minutes. Stir in mushrooms and serve over hens. Serves 4.

Smoked Turkey

1	13-16-pound whole turkey	1	cup butter, melted
4	tablespoons lemon juice	⅓	cup Worcestershire sauce
1	tablespoon celery salt	1	tablespoon dried oregano
1	tablespoon pepper	1	tablespoon dried basil or dill weed
¼	cup vegetable oil		

Wash and dry turkey. Rub with lemon juice, celery salt and pepper. Brush grill with a small amount of oil and place turkey on grate. Make a basting sauce of butter, Worcestershire and seasonings. Baste often. Cook in covered grill 4 to 6 hours. If using a smoker, cook 10 to 12 hours. Turkey is done when leg moves freely.

Poultry

Turkey Boudine

3	cups water	1	cup slivered almonds
1	5-pound turkey breast	1	8-ounce can sliced water
2	teaspoons onion salt		chestnuts, drained
1	teaspoon ground coriander	1	4-ounce can sliced
	Chives to taste		mushrooms, drained
	Parsley to taste	½	teaspoon cayenne pepper
3	10¾-ounce cans cream of	¾	cup sliced black olives
	chicken soup	¼-½	cup sherry
2	4-ounce jars chopped	2	cups grated Cheddar cheese
	pimientos, drained		

Place water in a stockpot. Add turkey breast, onion salt, coriander, chives and parsley and simmer until tender, about 2 hours. Remove meat from bone and cut into bite-size pieces. Reserve turkey stock. To the stock add soup, pimientos, almonds, water chestnuts, mushrooms, cayenne and olives. Cook until thickened. Add sherry. Place turkey in greased 3-quart casserole. Cover with sauce and top with cheese. Bake uncovered at 350 degrees until bubbly. Serves 6 to 8.

Serve with parsleyed rice.

Baked Turkey Breast

1	fresh or frozen 4-6 pound	2-3	tablespoons Worcestershire
	turkey breast		sauce
½	teaspoon salt	1	small onion, peeled
½	teaspoon pepper	2	tops celery

Thaw turkey if frozen; rinse and dry. Pat generously with salt, pepper and Worcestershire. Place onion and celery in cavity. Wrap tightly in double layers of foil and bake, breast-side down, for 4 hours at 325 degrees. Do not open door or foil. Remove from oven, cool, unwrap and slice. Serves 8 to 10.

This method of cooking results in turkey with a smoked flavor, perfect for party sandwiches or an easy meal at the lake or beach. It should be served sliced because it does not have a roasted appearance.

Game

Game

*Other Game recipes may be found in **Southern Classics.***

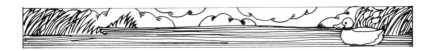

Game

Smothered Birds

12-18	dove or quail breasts	½	cup white wine
1	medium onion, chopped	½	teaspoon dried oregano
2	tablespoons butter, melted	½	teaspoon dried rosemary
2	tablespoons flour	¼	teaspoon pepper
1½	cups milk	½	teaspoon salt
½	cup mushrooms, sauteéd	1	teaspoon Kitchen Bouquet
½	cup finely chopped celery	1	cup sour cream

Arrange birds in large oven-proof dish. In a saucepan, sauté onion in butter. Add flour and milk to make a sauce, stirring until thickened. Add remaining ingredients except sour cream. Pour over birds. Cover dish loosely with foil. Bake at 350 degrees for 1 hour. Remove some of sauce from baking dish and combine with sour cream. Pour mixture over birds and return baking dish to oven to continue baking, uncovered, for 20 minutes. Serves 6 to 8.

Doves with Bacon

12	dove breasts	1	tablespoon cracked black pepper
	Salt		
	Flour	12	slices whole wheat bread
1	cup butter		Butter
2	10½-ounce cans beef consommé	4	cups chopped crisp-fried bacon
¾	cup water	½	cup sherry

Rinse doves, salt lightly and roll in flour. In a large skillet, melt butter and add doves, cooking until brown. Add consommé, water, pepper and additional salt to taste. Turn breast down, cover and cook over low heat for 1½ hours.

Toast and butter bread. Place dove on top and cover completely with bacon. Remove breasts to a warm platter. Add sherry to pan and heat. Serve dove breasts with sauce. Serves 4.

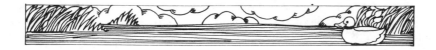

Game

Doves and Wild Rice

14-16 dove breasts
1 cup water
1 beef bouillon cube
1 teaspoon salt
1 cup golden sherry, divided
¾ cup chopped onion
½ cup chopped celery
2 6-ounce boxes brown and wild rice or seasoned long grain and wild rice
1 pound lean bulk sausage
1 clove garlic, finely chopped
½ pound fresh mushrooms, sliced
1 tablespoon Worcestershire sauce
1 tablespoon soy sauce
½ teaspoon dried basil
½ teaspoon pepper
⅛ teaspoon ground allspice
⅛ teaspoon ground cloves
1 10¾-ounce can cream of mushroom soup
1 cup sour cream

Boil in covered pot for 20 minutes dove breasts, water, bouillon, salt, ¾ cup sherry, onion and celery. Reserve broth. Remove dove meat from bone and cut into large bite-size chunks. Cook rice according to directions on box, using dove broth as part of liquid. Brown sausage in a large, heavy pot. Add dove meat and brown. Drain off fat. Add garlic, mushrooms, Worcestershire, soy sauce, basil, pepper, allspice and cloves. Simmer 10 minutes while stirring.

In a 9 x 13-inch casserole dish, combine dove and sausage mixture, rice, mushroom soup and sour cream. Bake covered at 350 degrees for 45 minutes. Pour ¼ cup sherry over mixture, cover and bake additional 15 minutes. Serves 8 to 10.

Wild Goose

4 slices bacon
1 wild goose
1 teaspoon dried rosemary
1 teaspoon dried tarragon
1 teaspoon salt
1 cup red wine
1½ cups chicken stock
1 cup dry white wine
1 cup orange juice
1 cup whipping cream

Spread bacon over breast of goose and place in roasting pan. Sprinkle with rosemary, tarragon and salt. Add red wine and stock. Bake uncovered at 475 degrees for 10 minutes. Reduce heat to 350 degrees and bake 2 hours. Add white wine and orange juice. Cook uncovered for 1 hour, basting often. To make gravy, add cream to liquids and drippings. Serves 2 to 4.

Game

Duckling in Grape Juice Marinade

1   clove garlic, finely chopped
2   teaspoons salt
1   teaspoon marjoram
1   tablespoon chopped parsley
½   teaspoon caraway seed
1   teaspoon Kitchen Bouquet
¾   cup grape juice
¼   cup madeira wine
1   4-pound duckling, cut into
        serving pieces

2   tablespoons butter
     Parsley for garnish
     Red and green grapes for
        garnish
1   3-ounce can sliced
        mushrooms, undrained
1   tablespoon cornstarch

In large bowl, combine garlic, salt, marjoram, parsley, caraway seed, Kitchen Bouquet, grape juice and wine. Marinate duck in mixture for 30 minutes. Melt butter in skillet over moderate heat. Remove meat from marinade and sauté until lightly brown on all sides; add marinade. Cover tightly and bake at 350 degrees for 2 hours. Remove duck and place in serving dish. Garnish with wreaths of parsley and alternate bunches of red and green grapes. Blend mushrooms and cornstarch and add to juices, stirring constantly until sauce thickens. Serve sauce in separate bowl. Serves 2 to 3.

Wild Rice and Duck

2   6-ounce packages seasoned
        long grain and wild rice
1   pound pork sausage
1   10¾-ounce can cream of
        mushroom soup

1   cup sour cream
4-5 ducks, cooked and deboned
½   pound fresh mushrooms,
        sliced
1½   cups herb seasoned stuffing

Cook rice according to package directions. Brown sausage in skillet and drain. Mix rice, sausage, mushroom soup and sour cream. Cut duck meat into large bite-size pieces and add to rice mixture. Place in 9 x 13-inch baking dish, top with mushrooms and sprinkle stuffing on top. Bake 45 minutes at 350 degrees. Serves 8.

Dove, chicken or turkey may be substituted for duck.

Game

Wild Duck

1	tablespoon flour	1	wild duck
1	oven cooking bag	¼	cup butter, melted
¼	cup dry white wine		Salt and pepper to taste
½	cup orange juice	½	fresh apple

Shake flour into cooking bag and put bag into 2-inch deep roasting pan. Pour wine and orange juice into bag; stir until blended. Brush duck with melted butter and sprinkle with salt and pepper. Place apple in duck's cavity and put duck into bag. Close bag. Make 6 small slits in top of bag. Bake at 350 degrees for 1 hour or until tender. Serves 2.

Sherried Quail Palmetto Bluff Lodge

4	whole quail	1	cup sherry
	Salt and freshly ground		Cooked wild rice
	pepper to taste		Sautéed mushrooms
½	cup butter		

Thoroughly clean and wash each bird. Sprinkle with salt and pepper. In a heavy skillet, melt butter and brown birds on all sides. Pour sherry over birds. Cover and simmer for 45 to 60 minutes or until tender. Serve with wild rice and sautéed mushrooms. Serves 2.

Grilled Venison Loin

Marinade:		½	cup wine vinegar
1	cup salad oil	1½	tablespoons chopped parsley
¾	cup soy sauce	2	cloves garlic, finely chopped
¼	cup Worcestershire sauce	½	cup lemon juice
2	tablespoons dry mustard		
2	tablespoons salt	1	venison loin

Mix marinade ingredients in blender or food processor. Pour over meat. Refrigerate several hours or overnight. Drain and grill over hot coals. Do not overcook; serve rare. Serves 4 to 6.

Restaurants

Restaurants

Restaurants

Shrimp Salad
A.J.'s of Columbia

1	pound cooked cleaned shrimp	⅓	cup finely chopped celery
¼	cup finely chopped green onion	2	tablespoons chopped pimiento
		½-⅔	cup mayonnaise

Coarsely chop shrimp. Combine with onion, celery and pimiento. Toss with one half cup of mayonnaise, adding more mayonnaise if desired. Use as spread for tea sandwiches or croissants. Serves 4.

Peach Melba
A. J.'s of Columbia

2	tablespoons cornstarch	Sliced peaches, fresh or canned
½	cup water	Vanilla ice cream
¼	cup currant jelly	Whipped cream
1	10-ounce package frozen raspberries, thawed	

To prepare melba sauce, dissolve cornstarch in water in a small saucepan over medium-high heat. Add jelly; continue cooking, stirring until sauce thickens. Stir in raspberries. Cool thoroughly and refrigerate.

To serve, place 3 or more peach slices in bottom of deep dessert bowl, wine glass or goblet. Top with 2 small scoops ice cream, 2 peach slices and 2 tablespoons melba sauce. Top with whipped cream. Serves 6 to 8.

Restaurants

Grilled Chicken Breasts
A. J.'s of Columbia

3	cups canned pineapple juice	8	boneless chicken breast
½	cup soy sauce		halves
½	cup dry sherry		

Combine ingredients for marinade. Place chicken in marinade in a plastic or glass container for at least 6 hours or up to 2 days. Cook on grill. Serves 8.

Fettuccine Carbonara
A. J.'s of Columbia

6	ounces fettuccine noodles	3	ounces chopped ham
6	tablespoons butter	4	slices bacon, cooked and
½	cup whipping cream		crumbled
⅔	cup frozen petite peas, cooked and drained	1	cup grated Parmesan cheese
			Salt and pepper to taste

Cook noodles according to directions on package. As noodles cook, melt butter in a saucepan. When noodles are almost al denté , add cream to butter and heat to very hot but not boiling temperature. Add peas, ham and bacon to butter mixture. Drain noodles well; toss with cream mixture and Parmesan cheese. Season with salt and pepper. Serve immediately. Serves 2 to 3.

Restaurants

Stuffed Crown Pork Flambé
Faculty House, University of South Carolina

1	14-rib pork crown roast	3	cups herb seasoned stuffing
	Salt and pepper	1	cup applesauce
3	green onions, tops included, sliced	½	cup plus 3 tablespoons brandy, divided
¼	cup butter	1	10-ounce jar apricot preserves
4	large mushrooms, sliced		
2	cooking apples, peeled, cored and chopped	1	9-ounce jar sweet pickled kumquats, drained

Sprinkle roast on all sides with salt and pepper; place, crown up, on a rack in a shallow roasting pan. Insert meat thermometer, making sure it does not touch fat or bone. Sauté onion in butter until tender but not browned. Add mushrooms; cook, stirring constantly until tender. Add apples; cook, stirring constantly 1 minute. Stir in stuffing, applesauce and 3 tablespoons brandy; spoon into center of roast. Cover stuffing and exposed ends of ribs with aluminum foil.

Combine and heat preserves and ¼ cup brandy; set ¼ cup mixture aside. Bake crown roast at 325 degrees for 35 to 40 minutes per pound or until meat thermometer registers 170, basting every 10 minutes after first hour with preserves mixture.

Remove roast from oven and let stand 15 minutes. Place on serving platter and garnish bone tips with kumquats. Heat reserved ¼ cup preserves mixture; pour ¼ cup brandy over heated mixture, ignite and pour over roast. Yields 10 servings.

Restaurants

Veal Piccata with Wild Rice
Chef Timpanaro, Fort Jackson Officers' Club

2	6-ounce packages long grain and wild rice mix	⅓	cup grated Parmesan cheese
12	4-ounce slices veal, thinly pounded	1	teaspoon chopped fresh parsley
⅔	cup flour	½	cup butter
	Salt, MSG, white pepper and garlic powder to taste		Butter
			Lemon juice to taste
3	eggs		Chopped fresh parsley

Cook rice according to package directions. While rice is cooking, begin preparation of veal. Lightly flour the cutlets. Season to taste with salt, MSG, white pepper and garlic powder. Beat eggs and add Parmesan cheese and parsley. Coat veal on both sides with egg mixture and sauté in butter in a skillet until lightly browned on both sides. Place veal on serving platter with wild rice. Combine desired amount butter, lemon juice and chopped parsley in same skillet; heat thoroughly and pour over veal. Serves 10 to 12.

Cherries Jubilee
Chef Timpanaro, Fort Jackson Officers' Club

1	16½-ounce can dark sweet pitted cherries	2	tablespoons brown sugar
	Juice of 2 oranges	3	tablespoons cornstarch
	Juice of 2 lemons	2	ounces Grand Marnier
3	whole cinnamon sticks	1	ounce Courvoisier

Drain cherries, reserving liquid. In a skillet, combine cherry, orange and lemon juices. Add cinnamon sticks and brown sugar. Simmer 3 minutes. Mix cornstarch with a little cold water and add to simmering juices and thicken. Add liqueurs and cherries. Ignite. Pour over cherry vanilla ice cream. Serves 6.

Swordfish Steaks
Richard J. Mackey, Manager of Griff's

½	cup mayonnaise	1	cup bread crumbs (from
4	8-ounce swordfish steaks		white or French bread)
2	tablespoons fresh lemon	1	cup chopped pecans
	juice	1	cup Béarnaise sauce

Spread mayonnaise on swordfish. Sprinkle with lemon juice and top with bread crumbs. Bake at 350 degrees for 30 minutes or until firm. Top one half of steak with chopped pecans and the other half with Béarnaise sauce before serving. Serves 4.

Béarnaise Sauce:

2	teaspoons dried tarragon	2	eggs
5	tablespoons white vinegar, divided	1	teaspoon salt
			Dash Tabasco sauce
¼	teaspoon dry mustard	½	teaspoon Worcestershire
3	green onions, finely chopped		sauce
		2	cups salad oil

Soak tarragon in 2 tablespoons vinegar for 5 minutes. Add mustard and green onions. Set aside. Blend eggs, 3 tablespoons vinegar, salt, Tabasco and Worcestershire together on low speed for 15 seconds. Turn speed control to high and slowly add salad oil until sauce is thick. Turn off blender and add tarragon mixture. Blend well for 15 seconds. Yields 2¾ cups.

Seafood Bisque
Richard J. Mackey, Manager of Griff's

½	cup flour	2	bay leaves
½	cup butter, melted	1	teaspoon paprika
4	cups milk	½	teaspoon white pepper
2	cups half and half	½	teaspoon salt
4	ounces crabmeat, drained	¼	cup dry white wine
4	ounces cleaned small shrimp		Butter

Combine flour with hot melted butter to make a roux. Roux should be cooked until bubbly, whisking constantly. Combine milk and half and half over medium heat. Add roux and remaining ingredients. Cook for 10 to 15 minutes over medium heat. Serve hot with a slice of butter on top. Serves 4 to 6.

This soup is very filling so may be served in small quantities.

Restaurants

Country Ham Strudel
Houston's Catering Service

1½	pounds puff pastry or strudel dough	1¼	pounds bean sprouts
1½	pounds country ham, very thinly sliced	3	hard-cooked eggs, chopped
2	pounds Gruyère or Swiss cheese, thinly sliced	1	ounce anchovy fillets, drained
		2	ounces capers, drained
		2	egg whites

Roll out puff pastry dough into a very thin rectangle (approximately 10 x 15-inches). Place thin layer of ham on top of pastry dough. Add thin layer of cheese, then bean sprouts. Add chopped eggs and anchovy fillets; sprinkle capers over top.

With a knife, trim rough edges of dough to form a rectangle. Brush outside edges with egg white. Begin to roll as with jelly roll. Roll tightly and seal edges. Turn onto buttered baking sheet. Brush egg white over top and sides. Bake at 350 degrees for 30 minutes or until golden brown. Let cool and slice in very thin slices for an excellent hors d'oeuvre. Serves 20.

Shrimp Houston
Houston's Catering Service

½	cup clarified butter	1	cup sliced mushrooms
1	clove garlic, crushed	3	pounds cleaned raw shrimp
½	cup chopped green onions	1	cup white wine
½	cup chopped green pepper		Salt and pepper to taste
¼	cup chopped celery		Cooked white rice

Heat butter in skillet. Add garlic and let simmer in butter a few seconds. Add green onions, green pepper and celery. Sauté 2 to 3 minutes and remove garlic. Add mushrooms and sauté 5 minutes. Add raw shrimp and sauté additional 5 minutes. Add wine and simmer 3 to 4 minutes. Serve over bed of rice. Serves 6.

Restaurants

Salmon Steak Papillote
Houston's Catering Service

4	tablespoons butter	¼	pound mushrooms, sliced
1½	ounces onions, cut in julienne strips		Salt, pepper and garlic powder to taste
2	ounces carrots, cut in julienne strips	4	salmon steaks
		3	tablespoons butter, melted
2½	ounces leeks, cut in julienne strips	1½	ounces white wine
		1½	ounces fish stock

Sauté onions in butter. Add carrots and leeks, cook for a few minutes, and then add fresh mushrooms. Simmer 3 minutes. Season with salt, pepper and garlic powder and set aside. Prepare 4 pieces of foil 3 times the size of each salmon steak. Divide vegetables among 4 pieces of foil and top with salmon. Fold and tightly seal three sides of foil around each salmon. Mix together butter, wine and fish stock and add to salmon packet. Seal foil to make an airtight container. Bake at 350 degrees for 15 minutes. Serves 4.

Lapin Moutarde
Lautrec Restaurant

1-2	rabbits, cut into pieces		Dijon-style mustard
1	cup flour	1-2	cups dry white wine
	Salt and pepper to taste	1	tablespoon rosemary leaves
	Butter and/or vegetable oil		

Dust pieces of rabbit with flour seasoned with salt and pepper. Sauté rabbit in butter or butter-oil mixture until lightly browned. Remove from pan and coat with mustard. Place in baking dish and add 1 to 2 cups wine and rosemary. Cover and seal dish with foil. Bake at 350 degrees for 30 minutes. Serves 4 to 8.

Rabbit is most often available frozen, precut into 8 pieces. Thaw before using.

Restaurants

Crème of Mushrooms
La Madeleine

1	pound mushrooms, sliced	3-4 tablespoons chicken broth
½	cup butter, melted	Salt to taste
2	cups flour	2 cups cream or half and half
2	quarts cold water	

Sauté mushrooms in butter. Add flour and mix until a paste is formed. Add cold water and whisk until lumps disappear. Bring to boil and add chicken broth. Add very small amount of salt (mixture already is salty). Mix again and cook over heat for five minutes. Add cream and warm thoroughly. Serves 4 to 6.

Other vegetables may be substituted for mushrooms.

Palmetto Club Crab Cakes
Palmetto Club

1	pound jumbo lump crabmeat	2 tablespoons butter, melted
2	eggs, slightly beaten	1 small green pepper, finely chopped
2	dashes lemon juice	1 small stalk celery, finely chopped
1	teaspoon baking powder	2 green onions, tops included, finely chopped
¼	teaspoon dry mustard or ½ teaspoon prepared Dijon-style mustard	Saltine cracker crumbs
1	tablespoon Worcestershire sauce	Pimiento for garnish
1	tablespoon seafood seasoning	Butter

Combine all ingredients except cracker crumbs, pimiento and butter; mix well. Form mixture into 6 balls and bread with cracker crumbs. Sauté in butter until light and golden brown. Yields 6 3-ounce cakes.

Restaurants

French Chocolate Mousse
Pandora's

2	cups milk	4	egg yolks, slightly beaten
¼	cup sugar	¾	cup whipping cream
3-4	ounces semi-sweet	1	tablespoon vanilla
	chocolate, melted	2	tablespoons brandy

In a saucepan, scald milk; add sugar and melted chocolate and stir over low heat. Pour a small amount of chocolate mixture into egg yolks, stirring to blend. Add egg yolk mixture to pan and stir constantly over low heat until custard thickens slightly; do not overcook. Strain if needed; cool pan by placing in cold water. Chill. Beat cream, vanilla and brandy in a bowl until stiff. Fold cold custard into whipped mixture until well blended. Spoon into dessert glasses and chill thoroughly before serving. Serves 6.

Moutarde Sauce
Le Petit Chateau

1	medium onion, finely chopped	1	teaspoon dried rosemary
½	cup butter	¼	teaspoon dried sage
¼	cup brandy	1	cup sour cream
3	6-8 ounce jars mustard (any combination of Dijon-style mustard and others)	½	teaspoon Beau Monde seasoning

Sauté onion in butter and brandy until onions are translucent. Add mustards, rosemary and sage. Remove from heat and blend in sour cream and Beau Monde. Process in a blender until smooth and creamy. Return to stove, reheat and serve over favorite cut of steak. Yields 3 to 4 cups.

Restaurants

Rouille Sauce
Pierre

6	cloves garlic, peeled	4	egg yolks
1	teaspoon salt	¼	teaspoon cayenne pepper
1	boiled medium potato, peeled	3	cups olive oil

Combine garlic and salt in blender. Add potato and mix well to make a paste. Add egg yolks and cayenne pepper. Continue blending and pour olive oil in a very thin stream over the mixture until it is completely absorbed. Yields 3½ to 4 cups.

Serve with fish, bouillabaise or vegetables. May be prepared up to two hours in advance.

Spinach Pancakes
Pierre

1	cup flour	2½	tablespoons melted butter
½	teaspoon salt	1	tablespoon finely chopped onion
2	teaspoons baking powder		
1	egg	1	cup cooked spinach
¾-1	cup milk		Vegetable oil

Sift flour, salt and baking powder together. Stir in unbeaten egg. Add enough milk to make a smooth batter. Add melted butter and stir. Add onion and spinach. Mix well. Heat a heavy frying pan and pour in enough oil to cover the bottom of the pan. Fry pancakes until well browned on both sides. Serves 2 to 3.

Romaine may be substituted for spinach. Serve with chicken, duck, fish or veal.

Cold Avocado Soup
Pierre

2	quarts milk	2	shallots
4	egg yolks	½	cup olive oil
4	avocados, peeled and seeded	1	teaspoon coriander
			Salt and pepper to taste

In a saucepan, boil milk and add egg yolks. Stir mixture over low heat for 5 minutes. Remove from heat and cool. Mix other ingredients in a food processor or blender until smooth. Add milk mixture and blend well. Serve chilled. Serves 12.

Avocado Tarragon Sauce for Fish
Pierre

1	cup sour cream	1	teaspoon coarsely chopped parsley
2	teaspoons tarragon vinegar		
2	teaspoons chopped green onion	1	avocado, peeled, seeded and mashed
¼	teaspoon seasoned salt		

Combine all of above ingredients. Serve cold on mild fish or cold salmon. Serves 6.

May be prepared up to 2 hours in advance.

Restaurants

Oysters à la Maison
Summit Club

1	stalk celery	1½	cups Cheddar cheese sauce
1	medium onion		(recipe below)
2½	pounds frozen leaf spinach,	75	oysters and half shells
	thawed and drained	½	pound lump crabmeat,
1	cup butter		finely chopped
½	cup anisette liqueur		Bacon bits for garnish

In a food grinder or processor, grind celery, onion and spinach. Melt butter in a large saucepan and add spinach mixture, anisette and cheese sauce. Warm mixture but do not cook. Spoon mixture in oyster shell halves and place oyster in center. Top with crabmeat and sprinkle bacon bits on top. Oysters can be frozen at this point for several weeks. To cook, run under broiler until bubbly and serve immediately. If frozen, slightly thaw before broiling. Yields 75 oysters.

Cheese Sauce:

2	tablespoons butter	½-1	cup grated Cheddar cheese
2	tablespoons flour		Dash cayenne pepper
1	cup milk		(optional)

Melt butter in a saucepan; add flour and stir. Remove from heat and gradually add milk, stirring with wire whisk. Return to heat and continue stirring until sauce thickens. Fold in cheese and stir until cheese melts and is well blended. Yields 1½ to 2 cups.

White Clam Sauce (Salsa alle Vongole)
Villa Tronco

¼	cup olive oil	¼	teaspoon dried oregano
1	clove garlic, thinly sliced	¼	teaspoon white pepper
¼	cup water	1	8-ounce can whole clams
½	teaspoon chopped parsley		with juice
½	teaspoon salt		

In a skillet, sauté garlic in olive oil until garlic is lightly browned. Slowly stir in water, parsley, salt, oregano and white pepper. Add clams and cook until clams are heated through. Serve hot over cooked spaghetti or homemade linguine noodles. Yields approximately 1½ cups.

Cakes & Pies

Cakes & Pies

*Other Cake and Pie recipes may be found in **Southern Classics.**

Cakes and Pies

Mahogany Cake

Cake:
1	cup butter, softened		Dash salt
1½	cups sugar	1	teaspoon baking soda
4	eggs, separated	1	cup buttermilk
2	cups cake flour	1	teaspoon vanilla
3	tablespoons cocoa		

Cream butter and gradually add sugar, beating well. Add egg yolks, one at a time, beating well after each addition. Sift together cake flour, cocoa and salt. Mix together baking soda and buttermilk. Add flour mixture alternately with buttermilk mixture, beginning and ending with flour. Add vanilla. In a separate bowl, beat egg whites until stiff peaks form. Gently fold egg whites into batter. Divide batter equally between 2 greased, floured and waxed paper-lined 9-inch cake pans. Bake 25 to 30 minutes at 350 degrees. Cool in pans 10 minutes before turning out onto wire rack to cool completely.

Mahogany Frosting:
1	egg	1	tablespoon brewed coffee
½	cup butter, softened	1	tablespoon milk
1	1-pound box powdered sugar	1	teaspoon vanilla
1	1-ounce square unsweetened chocolate, melted	½-1	cup chopped pecans Finely chopped pecans for garnish (optional)
1	tablespoon grated orange rind		

Cream egg, butter and sugar. Add melted chocolate, blending well. Add orange rind, coffee, milk and vanilla; cream well. If frosting is too thick, add milk by the teaspoon until it reaches spreading consistency. Stir in pecans. Spread frosting on cooled cake. Garnish with additional pecans sprinkled on top, if desired.

 When baking cakes and pies, all ingredients and utensils should be at room temperature. Unless otherwise stated, all-purpose flour should be used.

To ensure even baking, oven should be preheated to correct temperature.

Cakes and Pies

Best Fudge Cake

Cake:

3	1-ounce squares unsweetened chocolate
½	cup butter, softened
2¼	cups brown sugar
3	eggs
1½	teaspoons vanilla

2¼	cups sifted cake flour
2	teaspoons baking soda
½	teaspoon salt
1	cup sour cream
1	cup boiling water

Melt chocolate; set aside to cool. Cream butter and gradually add brown sugar, beating well. Add eggs, one at a time, beating well after each addition. Add cooled chocolate and vanilla, mixing well. Combine flour, baking soda and salt; add to creamed mixture alternately with sour cream, beginning and ending with flour mixture. Stir in boiling water. (Batter will be thin.) Pour batter into 2 greased and floured 8-inch cake pans. Bake 30 to 35 minutes at 350 degrees. Cool in pan 10 minutes before turning out onto wire rack to cool completely.

Filling:

1½	cups whipping cream	½	cup powdered sugar
1	teaspoon vanilla		

Beat cream and vanilla until foamy; gradually add sugar, beating until soft peaks form. Yields approximately 3 cups.

Mocha Frosting:

½	cup butter, softened	¼	cup strong coffee
5	cups powdered sugar	2	teaspoons vanilla
¼	cup cocoa	1-2	tablespoons whipping cream

Combine butter, sugar, cocoa, coffee and vanilla; beat until fluffy. Add whipping cream if frosting is too stiff, and beat well.

To assemble cake:

Split cake layers in half horizontally to make 4 layers. Place one layer on serving platter and top with ⅓ (approximately 1 cup) of filling. Top with second layer and another ⅓ of filling. Top with third layer and the remaining filling. Top with fourth layer. Spread frosting on top and sides of cake. Refrigerate until ready to serve. Garnish with chocolate curls, if desired. Serves 8 to 10.

 Freeze cakes and whipped cream topped pies before wrapping in plastic bag or freezer wrap.

Cakes and Pies

Sour Cream Chocolate Cake

4	1-ounce squares unsweetened chocolate	1	teaspoon vanilla
1	cup water, divided	2	cups flour
¾	cup sour cream	2	cups sugar
¼	cup butter, softened	1¼	teaspoons baking soda
2	eggs	½	teaspoon baking powder
		1	teaspoon salt

Melt chocolate in ½ cup water, stirring until smooth; cool. Combine ½ cup water, sour cream, butter, eggs and vanilla. Add cooled chocolate. Mix together flour, sugar, baking soda, baking powder and salt; add to chocolate mixture. Stir to combine and beat 3 minutes. Divide batter equally between 2 greased, floured, waxed paper-lined 8-inch cake pans. Bake 25 to 30 minutes at 350 degrees. Cool in pan for 10 minutes. Turn out onto wire rack to cool completely before frosting.

Chocolate Frosting:

3	1-ounce squares unsweetened chocolate	3	cups powdered sugar
¼	cup butter, softened	3	tablespoons milk
¼	cup sour cream	1	teaspoon vanilla
		¼	teaspoon salt

Melt chocolate; cool. Blend butter and sour cream; gradually add sugar. Add chocolate and blend; add milk, vanilla and salt. Beat until smooth. If too firm, add milk by teaspoon; if too soft, add powdered sugar.

Red Velvet Cake

1	cup butter, softened	1	cup buttermilk
3	cups sugar	1	teaspoon vanilla
6	eggs	½	teaspoon salt
1	ounce red food coloring	1	teaspoon baking soda
3	tablespoons cocoa	1	tablespoon vinegar or
3	cups flour		lemon juice

Cream butter and gradually add sugar. Add eggs, one at a time, beating well after each addition. Mix food coloring with cocoa and add to mixture. Add flour alternately with buttermilk. Add vanilla and salt. Mix baking soda with vinegar and gently stir into mixture; do not beat. Pour batter into 3 greased and floured 8-inch cake pans. Bake for 25 minutes at 325 degrees. Cool and frost with chocolate or cream cheese icing.

May also be baked in a large greased and floured tube pan at 325 degrees for 1½ hours or until done.

Cakes and Pies

Divine Chocolate Cheesecake

1½ cups graham cracker crumbs
¼ teaspoon ground cinnamon
4 tablespoons butter, melted
8 1-ounce squares semi-sweet chocolate
3 8-ounce packages cream cheese, softened
1 cup sugar
3 eggs
2 teaspoons cocoa
1 teaspoon vanilla
2 cups sour cream

Combine cracker crumbs, cinnamon and melted butter. Press mixture into bottom of an 8-inch spring-form pan. Chill.

Melt chocolate in the top of double boiler. In a large bowl, beat cream cheese until smooth and fluffy. Gradually add sugar. Add eggs, one at a time, beating well after each addition. Beat in chocolate, cocoa and vanilla, blending thoroughly. Beat in sour cream. Pour into prepared pan. Bake 1 hour and 10 minutes at 350 degrees. Cake will be runny but will firm as it chills. Cool to room temperature; refrigerate at least 5 hours before serving. Garnish with sweetened whipped cream and candied violets. Serve thinly sliced; serves 12.

Amaretto Cheesecake

1½ cups graham cracker crumbs
2 tablespoons sugar
1 teaspoon ground cinnamon
6 tablespoons butter, melted
3 8-ounce packages cream cheese, softened
1 cup sugar
4 eggs
⅓ cup Amaretto liqueur

Topping:
1 cup sour cream
4 teaspoons sugar
1 tablespoon Amaretto liqueur

To make crust, combine cracker crumbs, sugar, cinnamon and butter, mixing well. Press mixture onto bottom and ½ inch up the sides of a 9-inch spring-form pan. Chill.

To make filling, beat cream cheese until light and fluffy. Slowly add sugar, mixing well. Add eggs, one at a time, beating well after each addition. Stir in liqueur. Pour into prepared pan. Bake at 375 degrees for 45 to 50 minutes or until set.

To prepare topping, combine cream, sugar and liqueur, stirring well. Spoon over cheesecake. Bake 5 minutes at 500 degrees. Cool to room temperature; then refrigerate 24 to 48 hours. Serves 10 to 12.

Cakes and Pies

Sour Cream Pound Cake

1	cup butter, softened	1	cup sour cream
3	cups sugar	¼	teaspoon baking soda
6	eggs	1-2	teaspoons vanilla
3	cups flour		Powdered sugar

Cream butter and gradually add sugar. Add eggs, one at a time, beating well after each addition. Add flour. Fold in sour cream to which the baking soda has been added. Add desired flavoring, stirring well. Pour batter into a greased 12-cup tube pan. Bake 1½ hours at 300 degrees. Cool in pan 15 minutes before turning onto wire rack to cool completely. Dust with powdered sugar.

*The following flavorings may be substituted: 1 teaspoon vanilla and 2 teaspoons lemon extract **or** 1 teaspoon vanilla and 1 teaspoon almond extract **or** 1 teaspoon vanilla, 2 teaspoons lemon extract, 1 teaspoon almond extract and ¼ teaspoon mace*

Variation I: Whipping Cream Pound Cake
Substitute 1 cup whipping cream for 1 cup sour cream. Omit baking soda.

Variation II: Amaretto Pound Cake
Add ½ teaspoon salt. Substitute ½ cup Amaretto liqueur for vanilla.

After baking 1½ hours at 350 degrees, prick cake with a fork while still in pan; drizzle with half of glaze. Invert onto serving plate. Prick top with fork and top with remaining glaze. Serve with sweetened whipped cream, if desired.

Amaretto Glaze:

½	cup butter	1	cup sugar
¼	cup water	½	cup Amaretto liqueur

Combine all ingredients in saucepan and bring to a boil, stirring until sugar dissolves.

Any of the above cakes may be baked in a greased 9 x 13-inch pan. To decorate for the 4th of July, make a flag design using blueberries for stars, strawberries for red stripes and piped whipped cream for white stripes.

Cakes and Pies

Cream Cheese Pound Cake

1½	cups butter, softened		6	eggs
1	8-ounce package cream cheese, softened		3	cups cake flour
3	cups sugar		1-2	teaspoons vanilla
				Powdered sugar

Cream together butter and cream cheese; gradually add sugar. Add eggs, one at a time, beating well after each addition. On lowest speed, gradually add flour until fully mixed. Add vanilla. Pour batter into a greased and floured 12-cup tube pan. Bake 1½ to 2 hours at 325 degrees. Cool in pan 5 to 10 minutes before turning onto wire rack to cool completely. Dust with powdered sugar.

Chocolate Pound Cake

1	cup butter, softened		½	cup cocoa
½	cup vegetable shortening		½	teaspoon salt
3	cups sugar		½	teaspoon baking powder
5	eggs		1	cup milk
3	cups flour		1	tablespoon vanilla

Cream butter and shortening; gradually add sugar. Add eggs, one at a time, beating well after each addition. Sift together flour, cocoa, salt and baking powder; add alternately with milk, ending with dry ingredients. Add vanilla and mix well. Pour batter into a large greased and floured tube pan. Bake 1 hour and 20 minutes at 325 degrees. Frost with chocolate icing. Serves 15 to 20.

Chocolate Icing:

1	1-pound box powdered sugar		2	1-ounce squares unsweetened chocolate, melted
¼	cup butter, melted			
½	teaspoon vanilla		¼	cup milk, as needed

Combine sugar, butter, vanilla and chocolate, beating well. Gradually add milk, beating constantly, until spreading consistency is reached.

Cakes and Pies

Orange Glaze for Pound Cake

¼ cup orange juice   ¼ cup butter
¾ cup sugar

Combine ingredients in a saucepan. Heat until sugar dissolves; pour over cake while hot.

Chocolate Marzipan Cake

Cake:
1   8-ounce can almond paste   ¼   teaspoon almond extract
6   eggs, separated   ½   cup flour
½   cup sugar, divided   ¾   teaspoon baking powder
1½   tablespoons lemon juice   Dash salt
1   teaspoon grated lemon rind

Filling:
½   cup raspberry jam, strained
     and melted

Glaze:
7   1-ounce squares semi-sweet   ¼   cup unsalted butter
     chocolate

Garnish:
¼   cup sliced almonds, toasted

Break up almond paste and beat with egg yolks in a large bowl. Add ¼ cup sugar, lemon juice, lemon rind and almond extract, beating until mixture is completely smooth. In another bowl, beat egg whites until foamy. Gradually add ¼ cup sugar, beating until soft peaks form. Gently fold into egg yolk mixture. Sift flour, baking powder and salt together; fold into batter. Pour batter into 2 9-inch greased and floured cake pans. Bake 20 to 25 minutes at 350 degrees. Cool in pans for 5 minutes before turning out onto a wire rack to cool completely.

To assemble cake: Place one layer of cake on serving platter and spread with raspberry jam. Top with second layer of cake and refrigerate while glaze is prepared and cooled.

Glaze: Melt chocolate and butter in top of double boiler, stirring until smooth. Chill until thick enough to spread. Spread evenly over top and sides of cake. Decorate with almonds. Refrigerate until ready to serve. Serves 10 to 12.

Cakes and Pies

Macaroon Cake

6	eggs, separated	1	teaspoon vanilla
¾	cup vegetable shortening	3	cups sifted cake flour
½	cup butter, softened	1	cup milk
3	cups sugar	2	cups coconut
¾-1	teaspoon almond extract		Powdered sugar

Beat egg yolks with shortening and butter. Gradually add sugar, beating until light and fluffy. Add almond extract and vanilla, mixing well. Add flour alternately with milk, beginning and ending with flour. Add coconut, blending well. In a separate bowl, beat egg whites until stiff. Fold into batter. Pour into a large greased and floured tube pan. Bake for 2 hours at 300 degrees. Test for doneness with a wooden toothpick. Cool in pan for 20 minutes before turning out onto wire rack to cool completely. Sift powdered sugar on top. Serve with fresh or frozen strawberries, blueberries or other fruit or with chocolate sauce.

Must be prepared a day ahead, wrapped and stored in the refrigerator before serving.

Christmas Cake

1	cup butter, softened	½	pound pecans, chopped
1⅔	cups sugar	½	pound walnuts, chopped
5	eggs	2	cups sifted flour
½	pound red candied cherries	1	3½-ounce can coconut
½	pound green candied cherries		Sherry (optional)

Cream butter; gradually add sugar. Add eggs, one at a time, beating well after each addition. Coat fruit and nuts in small amount of measured flour; add flour, fruit, nuts and coconut to butter mixture. Combine well. Pour batter into a greased 10-inch tube pan lined on the bottom with greased waxed paper. Bake 3 hours at 250 degrees. Cool in pan 20 minutes before turning out onto a wire rack to cool completely. Sprinkle with sherry, if desired. Wrap or place in airtight container and store in a cool place.

This may be prepared several weeks before Christmas and stored until needed.

Cakes and Pies

Luscious Lemon Cake

Lemon Filling:
½ cup unsalted butter	1 cup sugar
½ cup fresh lemon juice	2 teaspoons grated lemon rind
5 egg yolks	

Mix all ingredients together in a saucepan. Cook over medium-high heat, stirring constantly with a whisk, until thickened and beginning to boil, about 5 minutes. Cool and refrigerate. Filling may be made 1 or 2 days prior to using with cake.

Cake:
¾ cup unsalted butter, softened	2 tablespoons fresh lemon juice
1¼ cups sugar	
3 eggs	1¾ cups cake flour
1 teaspoon grated lemon rind	2 teaspoons baking powder
¾ cup sour cream	¾ teaspoons baking soda
¼ cup orange juice	¾ teaspoon salt
1½ teaspoons lemon extract	

Cream butter and gradually add sugar. Add eggs, one at a time, beating well after each addition. Add lemon rind, sour cream, orange juice, lemon extract and lemon juice; mix until blended. Sift together flour, baking powder, baking soda and salt; fold into batter. Divide batter equally among 3 8-inch cake pans which have been greased, floured and lined with waxed paper. Bake approximately 20 minutes at 350 degrees. Cool in pans for 10 minutes; invert onto wire rack to cool completely.

Lemon Butter Frosting:
3 cups powdered sugar	5 tablespoons unsalted butter, softened
1 teaspoon grated lemon rind	
4 tablespoons sour cream	2 tablespoons Lemon Filling
¼ teaspoon lemon extract	

Combine all ingredients and beat well. Refrigerate 15 to 20 minutes or until firm enough to spread.

Garnish:
3 lemon slices, ¼-inch thick	Ivy leaves

To assemble cake, place one layer of cake on cake dish. Spread with ½ chilled lemon filling. Top with second layer of cake; spread with rest of lemon filling. Top with third layer of cake. Frost top and sides of assembled cake. Refrigerate until served. Garnish top of cake with twisted lemon slices in the center and surround the cake with washed ivy leaves.

Cakes and Pies

Fresh Apple Cake

3	cups flour	3	eggs
1	teaspoon salt	3	cups peeled, cored,
1	teaspoon baking soda		chopped apples
1	teaspoon baking powder	1	cup chopped pecans
2	cups sugar	1	teaspoon vanilla
1	cup vegetable oil		

Combine flour, salt, baking soda, baking powder and sugar. Add oil and eggs and beat to combine. Stir in apples, pecans and vanilla. Batter will be stiff. Put batter in an ungreased 10-inch tube pan. Bake 1 hour at 350 degrees. Cool in pan 20 minutes before turning out onto wire rack to cool completely.

Glaze:

¼	cup butter	3	tablespoons whipping cream
1	cup brown sugar	½	teaspoon vanilla (optional)
	Pinch salt		

In a saucepan, melt butter; add sugar, salt and cream, stirring to combine. Cook 2 minutes. Add vanilla if desired. Pour over cooled cake.

Golden Raisin Carrot Cake

2	cups sugar	1	teaspoon baking soda
1	cup vegetable oil	1	teaspoon salt
4	eggs	¼	teaspoon ground nutmeg
1	teaspoon vanilla	1	cup golden seedless raisins
2	cups flour	1	cup chopped pecans
2	teaspoons ground cinnamon	3	cups finely grated carrots

Cream Cheese Frosting:

¼	cup butter, softened	1	1-pound box powdered
1	8-ounce package cream		sugar, sifted
	cheese, softened	½	cup chopped pecans
1	teaspoon vanilla		

Cream sugar and oil. Add eggs and vanilla, mixing well. Combine flour, cinnamon, baking soda, salt and nutmeg. Stir into creamed mixture, mixing well. Fold in raisins, pecans and carrots. Pour batter into greased and floured 9 x 13-inch pan. Bake at 350 degrees for 45 to 50 minutes or until middle springs back when touched. Cool in pan.

For frosting, cream butter and cream cheese. Blend in vanilla. Gradually add sugar, beating until smooth and well blended. Stir in pecans. Spread over cooled cake. Serves 12.

Cakes and Pies

Emily's Bakery Frosting

1	cup vegetable shortening	1	teaspoon vanilla
1	cup butter, softened	½	teaspoon almond extract
4	cups sifted powdered sugar		Food coloring
1	egg white		

Blend shortening and butter; beat in sugar. Add egg white, vanilla and almond extract. Add food coloring as desired. Yields enough frosting to ice 2 cakes.

An excellent icing to use in a pastry bag for piping decorations on iced cake.

Never-Fail Caramel Icing

¾	cup butter	¾	teaspoon baking powder
1	1-pound box brown sugar	¾	teaspoon vanilla
½	cup half and half		

Melt butter; stir in brown sugar and half and half. Bring to a full boil, stirring constantly. Let boil exactly 2 minutes. Remove from heat and add baking powder. Beat mixture until satiny, about 10 minutes, adding vanilla toward the end of beating. Spread on cake. Yields enough icing for a 2-layer cake.

If baking powder is not fresh, the icing will fail. Fresh baking powder will bubble when a small amount is mixed with water.

Broiled Coconut Topping

½	cup butter, softened	1½	tablespoons milk
¾	cup brown sugar	¾	cup coconut

Cream butter and gradually add sugar. Add milk and beat until smooth. Add coconut and mix thoroughly. Spread over cooled cake in 9 x 13-inch cake pan. Place under broiler about 3 minutes or until top is bubbly and coconut is slightly toasted. Serve cake warm.

 A knife which has been placed in hot water will spread cake frosting more smoothly.

Cakes and Pies

Anita's Sour Cream Apple Pie

¾ cup sugar
2 tablespoons flour
1 cup sour cream
1 egg, beaten
½ teaspoon vanilla

⅛ teaspoon salt
2-3 cups peeled, finely chopped apples
1 9-inch deep-dish pie shell, unbaked

Topping:
⅓ cup sugar
1 teaspoon ground cinnamon

¼ cup flour
4 tablespoons butter

Mix sugar and flour in a bowl. Add remaining filling ingredients in order given, mixing well after each addition. Pour into unbaked pie shell. Bake 40 minutes at 350 degrees. To make topping, combine sugar, cinnamon and flour; cut in butter until crumbly. Sprinkle topping on hot pie and bake an additional 15 minutes at 250 degrees. Serve warm. Serves 6 to 8.

Grandmother's Coconut Cream Pie

¾ cup sugar
5 tablespoons cornstarch
¼ teaspoon salt
3 egg yolks
1½ cups water, divided
½ cup evaporated milk

1 tablespoon butter, softened
½ teaspoon vanilla
1¼ cups coconut
1 9-inch pie shell, baked and cooled

Meringue:
3 egg whites
Dash salt

6 tablespoons sugar

Combine sugar, cornstarch and salt. Beat egg yolks with 1 cup water. Add mixed dry ingredients. In a saucepan, scald milk and ½ cup water. Pour into egg mixture, stirring constantly. Cook in top of double boiler until thick. Add butter, vanilla and coconut. Cool. Pour into pie shell.

For meringue, beat egg whites; add salt, beating until foamy. Add sugar, 1 tablespoon at a time, beating constantly. Continue beating until meringue is stiff and glossy. Spread on pie, sealing filling. Bake at 400 degrees for 8 to 10 minutes or until light brown. Serves 8 to 10.

Cakes and Pies

Mrs. Ronald Reagan's Pumpkin Pecan Pie

4	eggs, slightly beaten	½	teaspoon ground cinnamon
2	cups canned pumpkin	¼	teaspoon salt
1	cup sugar	1	9-inch pie shell, unbaked
½	cup dark corn syrup	1	cup chopped pecans
1	teaspoon vanilla		

Combine all ingredients except pie shell and pecans. Pour into pie shell; top with pecans. Bake at 350 degrees for 40 minutes, or until set. Serves 6 to 8.

Ronald Reagan, fortieth President of the United States, took office January, 1981.

Peach Crisp

6	cups peeled, thinly sliced peaches	1	teaspoon ground cinnamon
⅓	cup sugar	2	tablespoons butter, melted

Topping:

¾	cup sugar	⅓	cup butter
½	cup flour		

Mix peaches, sugar, cinnamon and butter. Place in greased 8-inch square pan. In a bowl, combine sugar and flour; cut in butter until crumbly. Sprinkle topping over peaches. Bake 45 minutes at 375 degrees. Serve warm with sweetened whipped cream or ice cream. Serves 6 to 8.

Pawley's Island Derby Pie

1	9-inch deep-dish pie shell, unbaked	½	cup butter, melted
		1	teaspoon vanilla
2	eggs, beaten	1	cup chopped pecans
1	cup sugar	1	cup semi-sweet chocolate chips
½	cup flour		

Bake pie shell for 5 minutes at 350 degrees. Set aside to cool. Using a wooden spoon, blend together the remaining ingredients in order given. Pour filling into pie shell and bake at 350 degrees for 40 to 50 minutes or until firm. Serve warm, thinly sliced and topped with whipped cream or ice cream. Serves 8 to 10.

Cakes and Pies

Old-Fashioned Lemon Pie

1   9 or 10-inch pie shell

Filling:

1½	cups sugar	3	egg yolks, beaten
½	cup flour	6	tablespoons lemon juice
2	tablespoons cornstarch	2-3	teaspoons grated lemon rind
½	teaspoon salt	2	tablespoons butter, softened
2¼	cups boiling water		

Meringue:

3	egg whites	½	teaspoon vanilla
½	teaspoon cream of tartar	6½	tablespoons sugar, divided
	Dash salt		

Bake pie shell at 350 degrees until golden.

Combine sugar, flour, cornstarch and salt in top of double boiler. Add boiling water, stirring until smooth. Cook for 10 to 15 minutes, stirring constantly, until thick and smooth. Stir a little of hot mixture into beaten egg yolks. Add entire egg yolk mixture to hot mixture; cook 5 minutes, stirring. Blend in lemon juice and rind. Remove from heat. Add butter, stirring until melted. Cover filling tightly and let stand while preparing meringue.

For meringue, place egg whites in a bowl. Immediately before beating, add cream of tartar, salt and vanilla. Beat about 1 minute on high speed until ingredients form a soft meringue (one which will slide out of bowl). Add 6 tablespoons sugar, 1 teaspoon at a time, beating a few seconds after each addition. Beat until peaks are stiff. Pour filling into pie shell and spoon on the meringue, covering to the edge of pie crust. Sprinkle remaining ½ tablespoon sugar over entire surface of pie. Bake at 400 degrees for 10 to 20 minutes on lowest rack. Set on wire rack until pan is cool to touch and refrigerate 6 to 8 hours before serving. Serves 8 to 10.

Filling may be made 24 hours prior to baking. Keep filling refrigerated; bring to room temperature before baking.

Cakes and Pies

Wonderful Bourbon Pie

Crust:

1½ cups vanilla wafer crumbs	½ cup finely chopped pecans
1 tablespoon sugar	½ cup butter, melted

Filling:

1 cup butter, softened	6 eggs (See Note)
1 1-pound box powdered sugar	⅓ cup bourbon

For crust, blend dry ingredients; add melted butter. Press into 10-inch pie shell. Bake 5 minutes at 400 degrees. Cool completely.

For filling, cream butter; gradually add sugar, beating well. Add eggs, one at a time, beating well after each addition. Add bourbon in a very slow stream. The filling will look curdled at first but will become smooth and creamy. Pour into cooled crust. Freeze overnight. Serve frozen. Serves 8.

Flavor improves with age. Keeps well.

Note: If using a hand-held mixer, recipe works best with 5 eggs.

Lemon Chocolate Pie

1 16-ounce package semi-sweet chocolate chips	⅓ cup cornstarch
2 eggs	1 tablespoon grated lemon rind
½ cup sugar	¼ teaspoon salt
½ cup whipping cream	2 cups water
½ teaspoon vanilla	2 egg yolks
1 9-inch pie shell, baked	⅓ cup lemon juice
	1 cup sugar

Melt chocolate chips in top of a double boiler. Add eggs and sugar, blending thoroughly, and cool completely. Whip cream with vanilla until thick. Fold into chocolate and pour into baked pie shell; refrigerate. In a saucepan, combine cornstarch, lemon rind and salt. Gradually add water, mixing until smooth. In a separate bowl, beat egg yolks and lemon juice until ivory in color. Add sugar, beating well. Combine egg mixture with cornstarch mixture and cook over medium heat, stirring constantly, until thick; cool. Spoon over chocolate layer. Refrigerate 4 to 6 hours before serving. Serves 6 to 8.

Cakes and Pies

Chocoholics' Chocolate Chess Pie

2   1-ounce squares
     unsweetened chocolate
½   cup butter
1   cup sugar
1   tablespoon flour
     Dash salt
2   eggs, beaten

1   teaspoon vanilla or almond
     extract
⅓-½ cup chopped pecans or
     walnuts
1   9-inch pie shell, unbaked
     Sweetened whipped cream
     or ice cream

In a small saucepan, melt chocolate and butter over very low heat, stirring to blend; cool. Combine sugar, flour and salt; add eggs and vanilla or almond extract, mixing well. Blend in chocolate mixture. Stir in nuts. Pour into pie shell. Bake at 325 degrees for 35 minutes or until top cracks. Serve warm or cold with whipped cream or ice cream. May be refrigerated for easier cutting. Serves 6 to 8.

Lemon Chess Pie

4   eggs
1½   cups sugar
½   cup butter, softened
2   tablespoons yellow cornmeal
2   teaspoons vanilla
2   tablespoons half and half or
     milk

3-4 tablespoons fresh lemon
     juice
2   teaspoons grated lemon rind
     (optional)
     Dash salt
1   9-inch deep-dish pie shell,
     unbaked

Combine eggs, sugar and butter. Beat 5 minutes at high speed. Blend in remaining filling ingredients and pour into pie shell. Bake 1 hour at 325 degrees. Serve warm. Serves 6 to 8.

Other Desserts

ME7.
1984.

Other Desserts

*Other Dessert recipes may be found in **Southern Classics.**

Other Desserts

Jenny's Strawberry Torte

Batter:

½	cup vegetable shortening	½	teaspoon salt
1⅓	cups sugar	1	teaspoon vanilla
2	cups flour	1	cup pineapple juice
1	tablespoon baking powder	3	egg whites

Cream shortening and sugar. Sift together flour, baking powder and salt. Mix vanilla with pineapple juice. Add flour mixture alternately with pineapple mixture. In another bowl, beat egg whites until stiff; fold into batter. Divide batter equally between 2 9-inch cake pans which have been greased, floured and lined with waxed paper. Set aside.

Meringue:

3	egg whites	1	teaspoon vanilla
¼	teaspoon salt	¾	cup chopped pecans
⅔	cup sugar		

Beat egg whites with salt until stiff. Gradually add sugar. Fold in vanilla and pecans. Divide equally and spread over uncooked batter. Bake 35 to 40 minutes at 350 degrees. Cool in pans. Turn out on wire rack and remove waxed paper.

Frosting:

1	cup whipping cream	2	tablespoons powdered sugar

Beat cream until slightly thickened; add sugar and beat until soft peaks form.

To Assemble:

Sliced strawberries	Whole strawberries

Place one layer of cake, meringue side up, on serving platter. Spread with ½ of frosting. Layer with sliced strawberries. Top with second layer of cake, meringue side up; spread top with rest of frosting. Decorate top with whole strawberries. Store in refrigerator until ready to serve. Serves 8 to 10.

To retain crispness, torte should be made only two hours before serving.

Other Desserts

Italian Meringue Cake

Meringue:

4	egg whites	¾	teaspoon vanilla or almond
¼	teaspoon cream of tartar		extract
	Pinch salt	½	cup chopped pecans
1	cup sugar		

Filling:

8	1-ounce squares semi-sweet chocolate	2	tablespoons Grand Marnier or any brandy (optional)
4	tablespoons water	1½	pints fresh strawberries
2	cups whipping cream	½	cup sugar

Using an inverted 8-inch cake pan, trace and cut out 3 8-inch circles of waxed paper; place circles on baking sheets. Beat egg whites, add cream of tartar and salt and continue beating until stiff. Add sugar, 2 tablespoons at a time, and beat meringue until stiff and glossy. Fold in vanilla or almond extract and pecans. Spread meringue ¼-inch thick over the circles. Bake at 250 degrees for 50 to 60 minutes or until meringue is golden. Remove from oven, remove waxed paper and place meringue layers on wire rack to dry.

Melt chocolate with water in top of double boiler, stirring to combine. Whip cream, adding liqueur if desired, until stiff peaks form. Wash, hull and slice strawberries, reserving 8 to 10 whole ones for garnish. Sprinkle sliced strawberries with sugar.

To assemble cake, place a meringue layer on serving platter. Spread with a thin coat of melted chocolate. Top with ⅓ of the whipped cream. Top with ½ of the sliced strawberries. Repeat with second layer. Add third layer of meringue and spread with remaining ⅓ of whipped cream. Drizzle remaining chocolate over the top to make a design. Decorate edges of cake with whole strawberries. Refrigerate for 2 hours before serving. Serves 8 to 10.

Meringue layers may be made ahead and frozen.

Other Desserts

Chocolate Mousse Torte

Meringue:

5	egg whites	1¾	cup powdered sugar
	Pinch cream of tartar	⅓	cup cocoa
¾	cup sugar		

Mousse:

13	1-ounce squares semi-sweet chocolate	3	cups whipping cream
		1½	teaspoons vanilla
7	egg whites		Sweetened whipped cream
¼	teaspoon cream of tartar		for garnish (optional)

Using an inverted 8-inch square cake pan, trace 3 squares on parchment or waxed paper. Place squares on baking sheets and set aside.

To make meringue, beat egg whites and cream of tartar in a large bowl until whites hold soft peaks. Beat in sugar, 2 tablespoons at a time, beating until egg whites hold stiff peaks. Sift powdered sugar with cocoa and fold into egg whites. Divide meringue equally among the parchment paper squares, spreading it evenly to the edges. Bake 1 hour and 15 minutes at 300 degrees. If necessary for even baking, rearrange baking sheets on oven racks during baking time. Transfer meringues to wire racks to cool.

To make mousse, melt chocolate in top of double boiler; let cool to lukewarm. In a large bowl, beat egg whites with cream of tartar until they hold stiff peaks. In another bowl, beat whipping cream with vanilla until it holds stiff peaks. Carefully fold chocolate into egg whites; then fold in the cream.

To assemble torte, place 1 meringue square on serving platter. Spread with ⅓ of mousse. Repeat with other 2 layers. Chill, lightly covered, for 4 hours or overnight. Torte may be refrigerated up to 48 hours. Before serving, garnish with additional sweetened whipped cream piped in a decorative fashion, if desired. Serves 10 to 12.

Other Desserts

Lemon Torte

Meringue:

8	egg whites	3	teaspoons vinegar
1½	cups sugar	1	teaspoon vanilla

Filling:

4	tablespoons lemon juice	3	egg yolks, well beaten
2	teaspoons grated lemon rind	2	cups water
1	cup sugar	1½	teaspoons butter
4	tablespoons cornstarch		

Garnish:

1	cup whipping cream	1-2	tablespoons powdered sugar

To make meringue, beat egg whites until very stiff. Gradually add sugar, vinegar and vanilla. Pour into greased 9-inch spring-form pan. Bake at 350 degrees until the meringue rises to the top of the pan; reduce heat to 250 degrees and brown lightly, watching closely. Total baking time is 40 to 60 minutes. Cool meringue in pan for 20 minutes; remove to wire rack to cool completely. (Meringue will fall slightly in center while cooling.)

To make filling, mix lemon juice, rind, sugar and cornstarch well. Add beaten egg yolks, water and butter. Cook in top of double boiler for 20 minutes, or until thick enough to coat a metal spoon. Cool to room temperature; place in refrigerator to cool thoroughly.

For garnish, beat cream with powdered sugar until stiff peaks form.

To assemble torte, cover top of meringue with cold lemon filling. Garnish with sweetened whipped cream and refrigerate until served. Serves 10 to 12.

 When whipping cream, bowl, beaters and cream should be well chilled.

To ensure even baking, oven should be preheated to correct temperature.

Other Desserts

Lemon Charlotte

1	envelope unflavored gelatin	1½	teaspoons grated lemon rind
½	cup lemon juice	1	teaspoon vanilla
4	eggs, separated	3	3-ounce packages plain lady fingers
⅛	teaspoon salt		
1½	cups sugar, divided	1	cup whipping cream
3	tablespoons butter, softened		Whipped cream (optional)

Soften gelatin in lemon juice. Beat egg yolks, salt and gradually add 1 cup sugar, beating until thick. Place egg mixture, gelatin and butter in top of double boiler set over simmering water. Cook mixture 10 minutes or until thick enough to coat a spoon. Stir in lemon rind and vanilla. Remove from heat and cool completely. Line bottom and sides of a 9-inch spring-form pan with lady fingers. Whip cream until stiff. In another bowl, beat egg whites until peaks form and add remaining sugar, beating constantly. Fold egg whites and whipped cream gently into cooled mixture. Pour into spring-form pan. Chill several hours or overnight. To serve, unmold and garnish with additional whipped cream, if desired. Serves 10 to 12.

Holiday Trifle

2	cups whipping cream	3-4	3-ounce packages plain lady fingers
1	cup milk		
6	eggs	1	10-ounce jar raspberry preserves
½	cup sugar		
¼	teaspoon salt	½	cup cream sherry
1	teaspoon vanilla	1	cup whipping cream, whipped
½	teaspoon almond extract		Toasted sliced almonds

To make custard, scald cream and milk in a saucepan over low heat. In top of double boiler set over simmering water, beat eggs, sugar and salt. Gradually stir in scalded cream and milk. Cook over medium heat, stirring constantly with wire whisk, until mixture is thick enough to coat a metal spoon. Remove from heat; cool. Add vanilla and almond extract.

Spread lady fingers with raspberry preserves. Line bottom and sides of a 2-quart trifle bowl with lady fingers. Sprinkle with sherry and pour in a little custard. Repeat layers of lady fingers, sherry and custard, ending with custard. Cover and chill overnight. Before serving decorate with whipped cream and toasted almonds. Serves 12 to 14.

Other Desserts

Russian Cream with Strawberries Romanoff

Cream:

1	cup plus 3 tablespoons whipping cream	1	envelope unflavored gelatin
½	cup sugar	1	cup sour cream
		½	teaspoon vanilla

Strawberries:

4	cups fresh strawberries	1½	ounces Triple Sec
½	cup powdered sugar	1½	ounces rum
1½	ounces vodka		

For Russian Cream, blend cream, sugar and gelatin in a saucepan. Heat over very low heat until gelatin is completely dissolved. Cool until slightly thickened. Fold in sour cream and vanilla, whisking until smooth. Pour into a 3-cup mold or 6 individual half-cup molds. Cover and chill until set, at least 4 hours.

For Strawberries Romanoff, wash and hull strawberries. Toss with powdered sugar. Add vodka, Triple Sec and rum. Chill. Before serving, drain strawberries. Dip mold into warm water until edges just begin to liquify; invert onto serving platter and surround with strawberries. Serves 6.

Coconut Pistachio Mousse

2	cups half and half	3	ounces shelled chopped pistachio nuts
1	cup cream of coconut syrup		
3	egg yolks, slightly beaten	9	½-inch thick slices of pound cake
1½	tablespoons unflavored gelatin		Whipped cream, flavored with coconut syrup
	Pinch salt		Toasted coconut
3	egg whites		
1	tablespoon sugar		

Combine first five ingredients in large sauce pan. Cook over medium heat, stirring constantly, until gelatin is dissolved. Pour into a medium-size bowl and place in larger bowl or pan filled with ice. Chill until thick, about 20 to 30 minutes, stirring often. When thickened, beat egg whites until stiff peaks form. Gradually add sugar, beating until stiff. Carefully fold into gelatin mixture. Fold in nuts. Pour into 9 4-ounce molds. Place 1 slice cake atop each, trimming to fit. Chill at least 2 hours or overnight. To serve, unmold and garnish with whipped cream, flavored with coconut syrup, and toasted coconut. Serves 9.

Other Desserts

Hot Apricot Soufflé

Apricot Purée:
3½ cups water	⅛ teaspoon almond extract
2½ cups dried apricots	

Soufflé :
Sugar	⅛ teaspoon salt
8 egg whites	½ cup sugar
¼ teaspoon cream of tartar	2 cups apricot purée

Garnish:
1 cup whipping cream	⅛ teaspoon almond extract
2 tablespoons powdered sugar	

In a saucepan, bring water and apricots to a boil; reduce heat, cover and simmer for 30 minutes. Press apricots and cooking liquid through a sieve or purée in a blender or food processor. Measure 2 cups purée and add almond extract. Purée may be made 24 hours prior to making soufflé and stored in refrigerator. Bring to room temperature before proceeding.

One hour before serving, preheat oven to 325 degrees, butter a 2-quart casserole dish and sprinkle with a generous amount of sugar. In a large bowl, beat egg whites until foamy. Add cream of tartar and salt, beating until soft peaks form. Gradually add sugar, 2 tablespoons at a time, beating until stiff peaks form. Gently fold in apricot purée. Pour into prepared dish set in a larger pan of hot water. Bake 45 minutes.

For garnish, whip cream until slightly thickened, add sugar and almond extract. Continue beating until soft peaks form. Pour into a chilled serving bowl. Serve soufflé immediately with whipped cream. Serves 8.

Leftover purée is delicious on toast.

Other Desserts

Blueberries with Lemon Mousse

1	quart fresh blueberries	3	teaspoons grated lemon
1	cup sugar, divided		rind, divided
5	eggs, separated		Mint leaves, washed and
4	tablespoons lemon juice		dried
1	cup whipping cream		

After removing stems, wash and drain blueberries. Place in glass serving bowl, sprinkle with ¼ cup sugar, cover and refrigerate. In top of double boiler, beat egg yolks and gradually add remaining sugar, beating until lemon colored. Add lemon juice. Cook over simmering water, whisking constantly, until thick enough to coat a spoon. Do not boil. Remove from heat immediately and cool. Whip cream until stiff. In a separate bowl, beat egg whites until stiff. Fold egg whites gently into cooled lemon mixture. Fold in whipped cream and 2 teaspoons lemon rind, folding gently but thoroughly until mixture is smooth. Refrigerate until chilled. To serve, pour cold lemon mousse over blueberries. Garnish with remaining lemon rind and mint leaves. Serves 8.

Lemon Mousse may be made earlier in the day and poured over berries just before serving.

Leslie's Mocha Mousse

1	envelope unflavored gelatin	½	cup sugar
1	teaspoon instant coffee	¼	cup coffee liqueur
	granules	1	cup whipping cream
¾	cup cold water	1	pint strawberries, sliced and
1	8-ounce package cream		sweetened slightly
	cheese, softened		

Soften gelatin and coffee in water. Heat over low heat, stirring until dissolved. Cool. In a separate bowl, beat cream cheese, gradually adding sugar. Add liqueur, beating well. Add gelatin mixture, mixing well. Chill until partially set. Whip cream until stiff; fold into chilled mixture. Pour into a lightly oiled 4 to 5-cup ring mold. Chill. Unmold and place sliced, sweetened strawberries in center. Serves 8 to 10.

Mousse may be served in parfait glasses, garnished with strawberries.

Other Desserts

Chocolate Mousse

Crust:

1½ 8½-ounce boxes chocolate wafers, crushed

½ cup unsalted butter, melted

Filling:

16 1-ounce squares semi-sweet chocolate

2 eggs

4 eggs, separated

2 cups whipping cream

6 tablespoons powdered sugar

Garnish:

2 cups whipping cream, sweetened and whipped

Combine wafer crumbs and melted butter. Press onto the bottom and sides of 10-inch spring-form pan. Refrigerate for 30 minutes.

Melt chocolate in top of double boiler. Cool to lukewarm. Beat in 2 eggs, mixing well. Add 4 egg yolks, blending thoroughly. In a bowl, whip cream with powdered sugar until thick. In another bowl, beat egg whites until stiff peaks form. Stir a little of the whipped cream and egg whites into chocolate mixture. Fold in remaining whipped cream and egg whites gently and thoroughly. Pour batter into crust. Chill 6 hours or overnight. Several hours before serving, garnish with sweetened whipped cream spread or piped on top of pie. Serves 10.

Chocolate leaves may be used as additional garnish. To make leaves, melt 2 1-ounce squares semi-sweet chocolate and ½ teaspoon shortening in top of double boiler. Brush mixture on underside of 8 to 10 nonpoisonous leaves that have been washed and dried. Place on waxed paper-lined baking sheet and refrigerate until firm, about 20 minutes. Gently separate chocolate from leaf and decorate dessert. Yields 8 to 10 leaves. Store unused leaves in freezer.

Other Desserts

Cantaloupe Mousse

1   cantaloupe
2   tablespoons super-fine
      granulated sugar

¼   cup whipping cream
1   tablespoon apricot brandy

Cut melon in half; remove seeds. Scoop out balls from one half and refrigerate until later use. Purée pulp of other half in blender or food processor. Combine purée with sugar and cream; freeze for 30 minutes. Stir and freeze for additional 30 minutes. Transfer mousse to melon shells or stemmed glasses; freeze until ready to serve. To serve, remove mousse from freezer long enough to soften slightly; top with reserved melon balls and sprinkle with brandy. Serves 2.

Keeps well in freezer for several days.

Pots de Crème

6   ounces semi-sweet
      chocolate chips
1¼ cups half and half

2   egg yolks
      Dash salt

Stir chocolate and half and half in heavy pan over low heat until thick, but not boiling. In a bowl, beat yolks and salt until light and thick. Gradually fold into chocolate mixture. Spoon into pots de crème or ramekins. Refrigerate. Serves 4 to 5.

Other Desserts

Ice Cream Puff Fondue

Miniature Cream Puffs:
½   **cup water**
¼   **cup butter**
¼   **teaspoon salt**

½   **cup flour**
2   **eggs**

In a small saucepan, slowly bring to a boil water, butter and salt. Reduce heat to low and stir in flour all at once. Beat with wooden spoon until mixture leaves sides of pan and forms a small compact ball. Remove from heat and add eggs, one at a time, beating until smooth after each addition. Drop by teaspoon 2 inches apart on an ungreased baking sheet. Bake at 375 degrees for 25 to 30 minutes or until golden and puffed. Cool on wire rack. Yields 36 bite-size cream puffs.

Chocolate Fondue Sauce:
1   **14-ounce can sweetened condensed milk**
1   **12-ounce package semi-sweet chocolate chips**
½   **cup milk**

1   **7-ounce jar marshmallow cream or 1 6¼-ounce package miniature marshmallows**
1   **teaspoon vanilla**

Combine all ingredients in saucepan. Cook over medium heat, stirring until mixture is smooth and warmed. Sauce may be made ahead, refrigerated and reheated, adding a little milk if too thick. Yields 4 cups.

To Assemble:
36   **miniature cream puffs**
3   **pints favorite ice cream flavors**

4   **cups chocolate fondue sauce**

Cut tops off puffs; pull out centers to form hollow shells. Fill with ice cream, using melon baller to form small scoops. Replace tops and freeze.

To serve, heat sauce in chafing dish. Arrange filled puffs on serving platter. Dip filled puffs with fondue forks into sauce.

Crème Pâtissière may be substituted for ice cream.

Other Desserts

Crème Pâtissière

2	cups milk	1	tablespoon vanilla
6	egg yolks		Dash salt
½	cup sugar	2	tablespoons whipping
½	cup flour		cream, if needed
3	tablespoons butter		

Heat milk. Meanwhile, beat egg yolks in saucepan. Gradually add sugar, beating until mixture is thick and pale yellow. Add flour, mixing thoroughly. Gradually beat in 1⅓ cups of the hot milk and set aside remaining milk. Bring to a boil over moderately high heat, whisking often. As custard becomes lumpy, continue beating vigorously to smooth it. When it reaches a boil, custard should be very thick, like mayonnaise. If it becomes too thick, thin with small amounts of reserved milk throughout cooking. Lower heat to moderate and stir with a wooden spoon for 2 to 3 minutes to cook the flour. Remove from heat, beat in butter, one tablespoon at a time, and add vanilla and salt. Cover surface with plastic wrap. Chill. Serve as filling for pastry cups. Before serving, custard may be thinned with cream if needed; however, custard should be thick enough to hold its shape in a pastry shell. Yields 2½ cups.

Strawberries Chez Paul

1	quart strawberries, sliced or halved	2-4	ounces orange-flavored liqueur
1	cup powdered sugar	1	quart vanilla ice cream

Roll sliced or halved strawberries in powdered sugar. Pour liqueur over berries. Chill in refrigerator several hours. Before dinner, put ice cream out to soften. Place berries in individual bowls and top with softened ice cream. Serves 6 to 8.

Other Desserts

Peaches Almondine

1	29-ounce can peach halves, undrained	⅓	cup chopped almonds
½	teaspoon ground cinnamon	1	tablespoon butter
1	2-inch strip lemon rind	2	tablespoons brown sugar
2	tablespoons sherry		Vanilla ice cream

Combine peaches, cinnamon and lemon rind in a saucepan; cook over low heat for 10 to 15 minutes. Remove from heat and sprinkle with sherry. In a small saucepan, combine almonds, butter and brown sugar. Heat until bubbly; remove from heat and cool. Spoon warm peaches into parfait glasses, top with scoop of ice cream and crumble almond mixture on top. Serves 8.

Peach Ice Cream

4	cups milk, divided	4	eggs
2	tablespoons cornstarch	4	cups half and half
2	cups sugar	4	cups mashed peaches, sweetened
1¼	teaspoons salt		

Scald 3 cups milk in top of double boiler. Add cornstarch, sugar and salt. Cook, stirring, for 15 minutes. Beat eggs with remaining 1 cup milk. Stir into hot mixture. Cook 3 minutes or until custard coats a spoon. Cool; then add half and half and fruit. Freeze in ice cream maker according to manufacturer's directions. Yields 1 gallon.

Custard may be prepared ahead and refrigerated. Add half and half and fruit when ready to freeze.

Other Desserts

Pralines and Cream

½	cup oatmeal	2	12-ounce jars caramel ice
½	cup brown sugar		cream topping, divided
1	cup butter, softened	½	gallon vanilla ice cream,
1	cup chopped pecans		softened
2	cups sifted flour		

Mix together oatmeal, brown sugar, butter, pecans and flour. Spread in a 9 x 15-inch pan. Bake for 20 minutes at 350 degrees, stirring every 5 minutes to keep crumbled. Divide in half. Spread ½ mixture in an ungreased 9 x 15-inch pan. Pour one jar caramel topping over crumbs. Pack softened ice cream on top. Pour second jar caramel topping over ice cream. Sprinkle remaining crumbs on top. Freeze. When ready to serve, cut into squares. Store in freezer. Serves 15.

Whisper

2	scoops coffee ice cream	1	ounce brandy
1	ounce crème de cacao		Dash ground nutmeg

Place ingredients in blender and process until combined. Serve in wine or champagne glass with a shortbread cookie. Serves 1.

Other Desserts

Crème Fraîche

1 cup whipping cream	2½ tablespoons buttermilk

Combine ingredients in a jar. Cover tightly and shake for at least one minute. Let cream sit at room temperature for 8 hours or until thick. Store in refrigerator. Keeps 4 to 6 weeks. Serve on fresh fruit or as a garnish for borscht. Yields 1 cup.

Cannoli Cream for Fresh Fruit

4 cups ricotta cheese	2 tablespoons Marsala wine
1½ cups powdered sugar	1 cup whipping cream
1 tablespoon vanilla	Fresh fruit

Blend ricotta cheese until smooth in food processor or with mixer on highest speed. Add sugar and vanilla, mixing well. Add wine. Whip cream until it forms soft peaks. Fold into cheese mixture. Chill. Serve with fresh fruit, such as peaches or blueberries, sprinkled on top. Serves 8 to 10.

Grand Marnier Sauce

5 egg yolks	¼ cup Grand Marnier liqueur,
½ cup plus 2 tablespoons	divided
sugar, divided	1 cup whipping cream

In top of double boiler, beat yolks and ½ cup sugar over simmering water until thick and pale yellow. Remove from heat and add half of liqueur. Refrigerate until cooled. Beat cream with 2 tablespoons sugar until thick. Fold into cooled egg mixture; add remaining liqueur and refrigerate. Serves 8.

Delicious over fresh peaches, strawberries, blueberries or raspberries.

Other Desserts

Jane's Hot Fudge Sauce

2　cups sugar
1　12-ounce can evaporated
　　milk
4　1-ounce squares
　　unsweetened chocolate

¼　cup butter
1　teaspoon vanilla
⅛　teaspoon salt

Bring sugar and milk to a rolling boil, stirring constantly with wire whisk; boil for 1 minute. Reduce heat and add chocolate. Beat with whisk until blended well. Stir in butter, vanilla and salt. Cool; store in refrigerator. To serve, reheat in saucepan or microwave, but do not boil. Yields 3 cups.

Hot Caramel Sauce

1¼　cups brown sugar
⅔　cup light corn syrup
⅔　cup whipping cream

¼　cup unsalted butter
⅛　teaspoon salt

Combine all ingredients in a saucepan and cook over medium-high heat. Stir occasionally until mixture reaches soft ball stage, about 15 minutes. Let cool to lukewarm and serve over ice cream. Store in refrigerator, reheating before serving. Yields 2 cups.

Strawberry Sauce for Ice Cream

1　quart fresh strawberries
3　tablespoons orange-flavored
　　liqueur
1　teaspoon grated orange rind
½　teaspoon grated lemon rind
2　tablespoons orange juice

2　tablespoons sugar
2　teaspoons lemon juice
1　10-ounce package frozen
　　raspberries, thawed
　　Vanilla ice cream

Wash, hull and slice strawberries lengthwise, leaving small berries whole. Combine with liqueur, orange and lemon rind, orange juice, sugar and lemon juice. Cover and chill for 1 hour or more. Put raspberries through sieve to remove seeds; chill. Just before serving, combine raspberries with strawberry sauce. Spoon over firm vanilla ice cream in chilled individual dessert bowls. Serves 8 to 10.

Cookies
& Snacks

Cookies & Snacks

*Other Cookie and Snack recipes may be found in **Southern Classics.**

Cookies

Almond Cookie Sandwiches

1	cup butter, softened	1	6-ounce package semi-sweet chocolate chips
½	cup sugar		
1	5-ounce can unblanched almonds	1	cup whipping cream
		2	tablespoons instant coffee granules
2	teaspoons vanilla		
2	cups flour	1	1-pound box powdered sugar

Cream butter and gradually add sugar. Finely grate almonds in blender or food processor. Stir almonds, vanilla and flour into creamed mixture. Turn dough onto floured surface and knead a few times until smooth. Form dough into marble sized balls; place on ungreased baking sheets and flatten with fingers into 2-inch rounds. Bake at 350 degrees for 8 to 10 minutes or until lightly browned. While cookies are cooling, add chocolate chips to cream in a small saucepan. Stir over low heat until chocolate is melted and mixture is smooth. Add coffee granules; cool and add powdered sugar. Spread half the cookies with a thick layer of filling and top with remaining cookies. (It may be necessary to chill chocolate filling so that it does not run off cookies.) Refrigerate cookies. Sprinkle with powdered sugar just before serving. Makes 30 to 40 cookie sandwiches.

Apricot Florentine Cookies

⅔	cup chopped dried apricots	2	tablespoons honey
½	cup plus 2 tablespoons sugar	2	tablespoons whipping cream
1	cup sifted flour	1	tablespoon rum
1	cup finely chopped almonds	8	ounces semi-sweet chocolate, chopped
½	teaspoon grated orange rind		
7½	tablespoons butter, divided		

Toss apricots with 2 tablespoons sugar; add flour, almonds and orange rind. Over low heat, melt 6 tablespoons butter, ½ cup sugar, honey and cream; cook about 10 minutes until sugar is dissolved. Cool 5 minutes; add apricot mixture and rum. Drop onto ungreased non-stick baking sheet by ½ teaspoon about 2 inches apart. Flatten cookies and bake at 350 degrees for 8 to 10 minutes. Remove and cool. Heat chocolate and 1½ tablespoons butter over low heat until melted. Remove from heat and stir 3 minutes until glossy. Turn cookies upside down and spread with chocolate mixture. Store or freeze cookies separated by waxed paper. Yields 6 dozen.

Cookies

Praline Cookies

1   cup brown sugar
1   tablespoon flour
⅓   teaspoon salt
1   egg white

1   teaspoon vanilla
2   cups whole or chopped
     pecans

Sift together sugar, flour and salt. Beat egg white until stiff. Add vanilla. Fold in flour mixture. Fold in pecans. Drop by teaspoon onto baking sheets, which have been lined with greased aluminum foil. Bake for 30 to 35 minutes at 275 degrees. Cool. Peel cookies off foil. Yields 2 to 3 dozen.

Pecan Sandies

1   cup butter, softened
⅓   cup sugar
2   teaspoons water
2   teaspoons vanilla

2   cups flour
1   cup finely chopped pecans
     Powdered sugar

Cream butter; gradually add sugar. Add water and vanilla, mixing well. Blend in flour and pecans. Chill dough 4 hours. Shape into balls or fingers. Bake for about 20 minutes at 325 degrees on ungreased baking sheets. Remove from pan; cool slightly before rolling in powdered sugar. Yields 3 dozen.

Cookies

Sugar Cookies

1	cup sugar	4½	cups flour
1	cup powdered sugar	1	teaspoon salt
1	cup butter, softened	1	teaspoon baking soda
1	cup oil	1	teaspoon cream of tartar
2	eggs		Sugar
1	teaspoon vanilla		

Cream sugars, butter and oil. Add eggs and vanilla, combining well. Sift together flour, salt, baking soda and cream of tartar and add to creamed mixture, mixing until blended. Refrigerate 1 hour (or overnight). Make small balls and place on lightly greased baking sheet. Flatten dough with bottom of a glass dipped in sugar. Bake 7 to 8 minutes or until lightly browned at 350 degrees. Remove from sheet immediately and cool on wire rack. Yields 12 dozen.

Jane's Scotties

Batter:

½	cup butter	1	cup self-rising flour
½	cup brown sugar	1	egg, beaten
½	cup sugar	1	teaspoon vanilla

Glaze:

¼	cup brown sugar	2	tablespoons whipping cream

In a saucepan, combine butter and sugars, stirring over low heat until butter is melted. Remove from heat; add flour, egg and vanilla, mixing well. Pour batter into greased 8-inch square pan. Bake 30 to 35 minutes at 325 degrees. Cool completely. For glaze, boil together brown sugar and cream for 3 to 4 minutes; brush over top of cooled scotties. Cut into squares. Yields 25 squares.

Best made 24 hours before serving.

 To decorate sugar cookies, sprinkle before baking with a mixture of dry flavored gelatin and an equal amount of sugar.

Cookies

Chocolate Scotcheroos

1	cup sugar	1	cup semi-sweet chocolate chips
1	cup light corn syrup		
1	cup peanut butter	1	cup butterscotch chips
6	cups Rice Krispies		

Combine sugar and syrup in 3-quart saucepan. Cook over moderate heat, stirring frequently, until mixture begins to bubble. Remove from heat. Stir in peanut butter, mixing well. Add Rice Krispies, stirring until well blended. Press mixture into buttered 9 x 13-inch pan. Melt chocolate and butterscotch chips together over very low heat or in the top of a double boiler. Stir to blend well. Remove from heat and spread evenly over Rice Krispies mixture. Cool until firm. Cut into 1-inch squares. Yields approximately 100.

Carnival Cookies

6	eggs	1	cup butter, softened
1	1-pound box brown sugar	9	cups oatmeal
1½	teaspoons vanilla	1	12-ounce package chocolate chips
1½	teaspoons light corn syrup		
4	teaspoons baking soda	1	½-pound package M & M candy
1	28-ounce jar chunky peanut butter		

Mix ingredients in order given, combining each ingredient thoroughly before adding the next one. Shape dough into balls and flatten on ungreased baking sheets. Bake 10 to 12 minutes at 350 degrees. Makes 12 dozen.

 To ensure evenly baked cookies, oven should be preheated to correct temperature.

Toffee Cookies

1	cup butter, softened	6	1.45-ounce milk chocolate bars
1	cup brown sugar		
1	egg yolk	⅔	cup chopped pecans
1	cup flour		

Cream butter, sugar and egg yolk. Gradually add flour, stirring until well blended. Spread dough very thinly onto a lightly greased 10 x 15-inch jelly roll pan. Bake 15 to 20 minutes at 350 degrees or until medium brown. Remove from oven and lay chocolate bars on top. Spread evenly when melted. Sprinkle with pecans. Cool and cut into bars. Yields 5 to 6 dozen.

Bran Cookies

1	cup butter, softened	3	cups sifted flour
2	cups brown sugar	½	teaspoon salt
2	eggs	2	teaspoons baking powder
1	cup 40% bran cereal		Powdered sugar (optional)
1	teaspoon vanilla		

Cream butter; gradually add sugar, beating until creamy. Add eggs, one at a time, beating well after each addition. Add bran cereal and vanilla, mixing well. Sift together flour, salt and baking powder; add to creamed mixture, blending well. Refrigerate dough until firm enough to handle. Drop by scant teaspoonful onto a lightly greased baking sheet. Bake for 5 minutes at 400 degrees. Cool on sheet for 1 minute. Remove and cool completely. Cookies should be soft and chewy and may be sprinkled with powdered sugar if desired. Yields 5 to 6 dozen.

 Place cookie dough on sheets of aluminum foil cut to size of baking sheet. When cookies are done, slip foil off baking sheet and replace with foil sheet of unbaked cookies.

Cookies

Christmas Spice Cookies

2½	cups sifted flour	¾	cup butter, softened
2	teaspoons baking soda	1	cup sugar
½	teaspoon ground allspice	1	egg
½	teaspoon ground cinnamon	¼	cup light molasses
½	teaspoon ground cloves		Powdered sugar
¼	teaspoon ground ginger		

Sift flour, baking soda and spices into small bowl. Cream butter; gradually add sugar. Add egg and beat until light and fluffy. With spoon, beat in flour alternately with molasses. Cover dough and refrigerate 1 hour. Shape dough into ½-inch balls and roll in powdered sugar. Place on an ungreased baking sheet. Bake 8 to 10 minutes at 375 degrees. Cool. Sprinkle with powdered sugar. Yields 8½ dozen.

Mint Meringue Cookies

3	egg whites	1	6-ounce package semi-sweet chocolate chips
⅛	teaspoon salt		
½	teaspoon cream of tartar	½	teaspoon peppermint extract
¾	cup sugar	2-3	drops green food coloring
¾	cup coarsely chopped pecans		(optional)

In a large bowl, beat egg whites until foamy; add salt and cream of tartar and continue beating until stiff. Gradually beat in sugar. Fold in pecans chocolate chips, peppermint extract and food coloring. Drop from teaspoon onto baking sheet which has been lined with lightly greased waxed paper. Preheat oven to 200 degrees. Bake for 1 hour. Turn off oven and let cookies dry overnight. Do not open oven door. Yields 7 dozen.

Do not make on a humid or rainy day.

Cookies

Miniature Pecan Tarts

Pastry:

1	3-ounce package cream cheese, softened	½	cup butter, softened
		1	cup flour

Filling:

1	tablespoon butter, softened	¾	cup brown sugar
1	egg, slightly beaten	1	teaspoon vanilla
	Dash salt	⅔	cup chopped pecans

Cream together cream cheese and butter until well blended. Add flour, blending thoroughly. Refrigerate pastry 1 hour. Divide pastry into 24 balls. Press each ball into the bottom and sides of ungreased miniature muffin tins. For filling, mix ingredients in order given, mixing well after each addition. Pour into tart shells. Bake 20 to 25 minutes at 350 degrees. Cool slightly before removing tarts to a wire rack; cool completely. Yields 2 dozen.

Pecan Bars

Crust:

2	cups flour	⅔	cup brown sugar
1	teaspoon baking powder	½	cup butter, softened
⅛	teaspoon salt		

Filling:

4	eggs, beaten	1½	cups dark corn syrup
½	cup brown sugar	2	teaspoons vanilla
⅓	cup flour	¾	cup coarsely chopped pecans
1	teaspoon salt		

For crust, sift together flour, baking powder and salt. Stir in brown sugar. Cut in butter until well mixed. Press into an ungreased 9 x 13-inch pan. Bake for 12 minutes at 325 degrees.

For filling, combine eggs, brown sugar, flour and salt, mixing well. Blend in corn syrup and vanilla. Add pecans and pour over crust. Bake for 35 to 45 minutes at 325 degrees. Cut while warm. Yields 4 dozen.

Cookies

Chess Cakes

Crust:

2	cups sifted flour
½	cup powdered sugar

1	cup butter, softened

Batter:

4	eggs
1½	cups sugar
1	cup butter, softened
2	teaspoons vanilla

½	teaspoon almond extract
2	tablespoons whipping cream
	Dash salt

For crust, mix flour and sugar; cut in butter. Press into an ungreased 9 x 13-inch pan. Bake 15 minutes at 350 degrees. Cool completely.

For batter, beat together eggs, sugar and butter for 4 minutes. Add remaining ingredients, mixing well. Pour over crust and bake 1 hour at 325 degrees. Yields 20 squares.

Miniature Cheese Cakes

3	8-ounce packages cream cheese, softened
1¼	cups sugar, divided
5	eggs
1-1½	teaspoons vanilla

1	cup sour cream
¼	teaspoon vanilla
	Apricot, cherry or raspberry preserves

Beat cream cheese until smooth; gradually add 1 cup sugar. Add eggs, one at a time, beating well after each addition. Add vanilla, beating well. Divide among 24 paper-lined cupcake tins. Bake 45 minutes at 300 degrees. Meanwhile, combine sour cream, ¼ cup sugar and vanilla. Remove cheese cakes from oven, spoon on sour cream mixture and top with ¼-½ teaspoon of favorite preserves. Bake an additional 5 minutes. Cool to room temperature; refrigerate or freeze. Yields 24 cupcake-size cheese cakes.

Preserves may be omitted; top with strawberries or other fresh berries. For bite-size cheesecakes, fill miniature muffin tins ⅔ full and bake for 20 minutes at 300 degrees; continue preparation with same directions as for larger size. Yields 5 to 6 dozen.

Cookies

Better Than Brownies

½	cup butter	2	cups graham cracker crumbs or 1½ cups prepackaged graham cracker crumbs
5	tablespoons cocoa		
1	egg		
¼	cup sugar	1	cup coconut
1	teaspoon vanilla	½	cup chopped walnuts

Frosting:

¼	cup butter, softened	3	tablespoons milk
2	tablespoons instant vanilla pudding mix	2	cups powdered sugar
		½	teaspoon salt

Glaze:

4	1-ounce squares semi-sweet chocolate	1	1-ounce square unsweetened chocolate
1	tablespoon butter		

Place first 5 ingredients in top of double boiler. Cook, stirring, until melted and thick. Add crumbs, coconut and walnuts, mixing well. Press mixture into an ungreased 8-inch square pan. Set aside. Cream together frosting ingredients in order given. Spread on top of crust. Refrigerate 15 minutes.

Melt glaze ingredients in top of double boiler, stirring to blend. Spread over frosting. Refrigerate. Before serving, cut into bars with a sharp knife. Store in freezer. Yields 16.

Sophie's Bar Cookies

1	cup butter	3	eggs
1	16-ounce box dark brown sugar	1	tablespoon vanilla
2	cups flour	1	cup chopped pecans or walnuts
⅛	teaspoon salt		Powdered sugar (optional)
1	teaspoon baking powder		

In a warm oven, melt butter in a 9 x 13-inch baking pan. Pour butter into mixing bowl, add brown sugar and mix well. Combine flour, salt and baking powder; add to butter mixture alternately with eggs, beating well after each addition. Stir in vanilla and nuts. Pour into previously buttered pan and bake at 375 degrees for 25 to 30 minutes. Cool. Sprinkle with powdered sugar if desired and cut into bars. Yields 24.

Cookies should be very moist. Do not overbake.

Cookies

Chocolate Heaven

Cookie Layer:

½   cup butter, softened
1   cup sugar
4   eggs
1   cup flour

1   16-ounce can chocolate
    syrup
1   cup chopped pecans

Cream butter and gradually add sugar. Add eggs and beat well. Add flour and chocolate syrup and stir until well blended. Stir in pecans. Pour batter into an ungreased 10 x 15-inch jelly roll pan. Bake for 25 minutes at 325 degrees. Cool in pan while preparing frosting.

Frosting:

½   cup butter
⅓   cup milk
½   cup sugar

½   cup semi-sweet chocolate
    chips

Bring butter, milk, and sugar to a boil; boil 1 minute. Remove from heat and add chocolate chips, stirring until smooth. Pour hot icing over cake. Cover with foil and refrigerate until ready to serve. Serves 16.

These are best stored in the freezer and cut more easily when frozen.

Chocolate Iced Brownies

2   1-ounce squares
    unsweetened chocolate
½   cup butter
3   eggs, beaten

1   cup sugar
4   tablespoons flour
1   teaspoon vanilla
½   cup chopped pecans

Icing:

1   1-ounce square
    unsweetened chocolate
¼   cup butter

1   cup sifted powdered sugar
½   egg, beaten

In top of a double boiler, melt chocolate and butter, stirring to blend. In a bowl, mix eggs, sugar, flour and vanilla; add to chocolate mixture, mixing until well combined. Stir in pecans. Pour batter into a greased, waxed paper-lined 8 x 8-inch or 7 x 11-inch pan. Bake 25 minutes at 350 degrees. Cool in pan.

For icing, in top of a double boiler, melt chocolate and butter, stirring to blend. Add powdered sugar and ½ beaten egg. Beat until smooth and slightly thickened. Spread on cake. Refrigerate or place in freezer for a few minutes to make cutting easier. Yields 1 dozen.

Cookies

Grandma Bea's Apricot Squares

Filling:

1	4-ounce package dried apricots
⅔	cup water
2	tablespoons sugar

Crust:

1¼	cups flour
¼	teaspoon salt
1	cup dark brown sugar
¾	cup butter, chilled, cut into ½-inch pieces
½	cup coconut
¾	cup oatmeal
½	cup finely chopped walnuts

Place apricots and water in a saucepan. Bring to a boil over high heat; reduce heat, cover and simmer 30 minutes or until very tender, adding water if necessary. Drain. Mash apricots and stir in sugar. Cool to room temperature.

Combine flour, salt and brown sugar in bowl. Cut in butter until mixture resembles coarse meal. Stir in coconut, oatmeal and nuts. Press 3 cups of mixture into an ungreased 8-inch square pan. Spread filling to edges over crust. Firmly press remaining crust mixture evenly over top. Bake 60 to 70 minutes at 325 degrees. Top should be semi-firm to touch. Cool and cut into squares. Yields 16.

Delicious Date Bars

2	eggs	1	cup chopped dates
¾	cup sugar	1	cup chopped pecans
½	cup flour		Whipped cream flavored
1	teaspoon baking powder		with sherry (optional)

Beat eggs; gradually add sugar. Sift together flour and baking powder; add to egg mixture, stirring until blended. Fold in dates and pecans. Pour batter into greased and floured 8-inch square pan. Bake 30 to 40 minutes at 325 degrees. Cool. To serve, cut into squares. Garnish with sherry-flavored whipped cream, if desired. Serves 6 to 8.

Cookies

Lemon Squares

Crust:

1	cup butter, softened	½	cup powdered sugar
2	cups flour		

Filling:

4	eggs, slightly beaten	4	tablespoons flour
2	cups sugar	2	teaspoons baking powder
4	tablespoons lemon juice	½	teaspoon salt
2	tablespoons finely grated lemon rind		Powdered sugar for topping

Blend butter with flour and powdered sugar. Press pastry into an ungreased 9 x 13-inch pan. Bake at 375 degrees for 20 minutes or until brown around the edges. While crust is baking, mix filling ingredients in order given, mixing well after each addition. Pour over baked crust and continue baking for 25 to 30 minutes at 350 degrees. Cool in pan. Sift powdered sugar on top. Yields 36 small squares.

Pecan Graham Bars

1	cup butter	18	graham cracker squares
½	cup brown sugar	½	cup chopped pecans

Combine butter and sugar in a saucepan. Bring to a boil and boil 2 or 3 minutes. Place graham crackers in a single layer on a foil-lined baking sheet. Pour sugar mixture over crackers. Sprinkle top with pecans. Bake 6 to 8 minutes at 350 degrees, watching carefully as they burn easily. Cool completely before removing from foil. Yields 3 dozen.

Cookies

Raspberry Squares

1	cup butter, softened	2½	cups flour
2	tablespoons sour cream	1	12-ounce jar raspberry
3	eggs, separated		preserves
1	cup plus 2 tablespoons sugar, divided	1½	cups chopped pecans

Combine butter, sour cream and 3 egg yolks. Add 2 tablespoons sugar and flour to form pastry. Press into the bottom and slightly up the sides of an ungreased 10 x 15-inch pan. Spread raspberry preserves evenly over the pastry. Sprinkle with pecans. To form meringue topping, beat egg whites and gradually add remaining sugar, beating until thick and foamy. Spread meringue over nuts. Bake on the lowest rack at 325 degrees for 25 to 30 minutes or until meringue is lightly browned. Cut into small squares while still warm. Yields 3 dozen.

Chocolate Fruit Balls

1	cup butter, softened	1	6-ounce jar maraschino
1	1-pound box powdered sugar		cherries, drained and chopped
2	cups graham cracker crumbs	1	12-ounce package semi-sweet chocolate chips
1	8-ounce can coconut	2	ounces paraffin
2	cups chopped golden raisins		
2	cups ground pecans		

Cream butter; gradually add sugar and beat until smooth. Add cracker crumbs, coconut, raisins, pecans and cherries, mixing well. Chill for at least 1 hour. Melt chocolate and paraffin in top of double boiler. Roll chilled mixture into balls and, using fondue fork or toothpick, dip into chocolate mixture. Place on waxed paper. Store in airtight container. Yields 8 dozen.

Recipe may be halved. Great for Christmas giving.

 If substituting prepackaged graham cracker crumbs for homemade, use a smaller amount. Prepackaged crumbs are more finely crushed.

Snacks

Orange Balls

½ cup frozen orange juice
concentrate
2¾ cups crushed vanilla wafers
1 cup powdered sugar

½ cup butter, melted and
cooled
1 cup chopped pecans

Mix ingredients in order given. Shape into small balls and roll in additional powdered sugar to coat. Store in freezer; remove as needed. Yields 3 dozen.

Fudge

2 1-ounce squares
unsweetened chocolate,
grated
2 cups sugar
⅔ cup milk

2 tablespoons light corn syrup
2 tablespoons butter
1 teaspoon vanilla
1 cup chopped pecans

Combine chocolate, sugar, milk and corn syrup in a heavy saucepan over medium heat. Bring mixture to a slow boil and boil for 18 minutes or to the soft ball stage. Do not stir. Remove from heat and place saucepan in a pan of cool water. Add butter, vanilla and nuts. Cool for 20 minutes. Beat by hand until fudge begins to lose gloss and pour on a buttered 9-inch dinner plate or 8-inch square pan. Cut into pieces after completely hardened.

Do not make on a humid day!

Buttermilk Candy

2 cups sugar
½ cup buttermilk
1 teaspoon butter

1 teaspoon vanilla
1 cup chopped pecans

In a medium-size saucepan, combine sugar and buttermilk. Bring to a slow boil and cook until the soft ball stage. Do not stir or scrape the sides of saucepan as candy will turn brittle. Remove from heat and set pan in a container of cold water. Add butter, vanilla and pecans and allow to cool to 110 degrees on candy thermometer. Beat by hand until candy begins to lose its gloss. Pour onto a buttered 9-inch dinner plate or 8-inch square pan. Cut into squares.

290

Snacks

Russian Mint Patties

1	cup butter, softened	1	teaspoon peppermint extract
2	cups sifted powdered sugar	1	teaspoon vanilla
4	1-ounce squares	1	cup whipping cream
	unsweetened chocolate,	18	vanilla wafers
	melted and cooled	¼	cup chopped pecans
4	eggs	18	maraschino cherries

Cream butter and gradually add sugar, beating well. Stir in chocolate. Add eggs, one at a time, beating well after each addition. Blend in peppermint and vanilla. In another bowl, whip cream until firm peaks are formed. Place cupcake liners in 18 muffin tins. Place a vanilla wafer in each liner. Fill ¾ full with chocolate mixture; top with whipped cream. Sprinkle each with pecans and top with a cherry. Freeze. Once frozen, store in plastic freezer bag. Remove from freezer about 30 minutes prior to serving. Serves 18.

Keeps well in freezer for unexpected company.

Tiny Gingerbread Houses

Houses:

Graham crackers	Sugar

Frosting:

1½	cups sifted powdered sugar	Food coloring
1	egg white	Assorted candies, gumdrops,
	Dash salt	sprinkles
1	teaspoon lemon juice	

Break graham crackers in half very gently. In a heavy skillet, melt ½-inch layer of sugar over low heat. Carefully dip cracker ends in syrup and assemble 4 crackers to form walls of house. Cut 2 triangles and place on ends for gables. Place 2 more crackers at an angle to form peaked roof.

For frosting, combine sugar, egg white, salt and lemon juice in a bowl and beat until stiff peaks form. Cover with a damp cloth until ready to use. Divide frosting into several bowls. Reserving 1 bowl for use as snow, add food coloring to remaining bowls. Use a separate spreader for each color. Decorate as desired, using icing to glue candy. Yields 2 houses.

Houses may be assembled for children to decorate. Multiply icing recipe by 4 and use 1 box of graham crackers to make 8 houses.

Snacks

Leck's Granola Snack

1½ cups almonds, raw or toasted
1 4-ounce package banana chips
½ cup unsalted sunflower seeds
½ cup unsalted pumpkin seeds
¾ cup unsalted roasted peanuts
¾ cup unsalted cashews
½ cup chopped dried apricots
1 cup raisins
1 cup semi-sweet chocolate or carob chips
1 15-ounce box granola-type cereal

Mix all ingredients thoroughly. Store in air-tight container. Serve as a snack or as a topping for fresh fruit. Serves 30.

Above ingredients are available at health food stores.

Sweet Cereal Mix

1 cup crunchy peanut butter
½ cup butter
1 12-ounce package semi-sweet chocolate chips
1 12-ounce box Rice Chex cereal
1 1-pound box powdered sugar

Slowly melt peanut butter, butter and chocolate chips. Put cereal in roaster pan and pour warmed mixture over it, stirring gently to cover all the cereal. Put in a large plastic bag, add sugar and shake. Store in airtight container.

Children love to help make and eat this snack.

Harvest Popcorn

⅓ cup butter
1 teaspoon dried dill weed
1 teaspoon soy sauce
1 teaspoon Worcestershire sauce
1 teaspoon lemon pepper
½ teaspoon garlic salt
3 quarts popped popcorn
2 cups shoestring potato sticks
1 cup mixed nuts

Melt butter and add dill, soy sauce, Worcestershire, lemon pepper and garlic salt. Stir to blend. Mix popcorn, potato sticks, and nuts in large roaster pan and cover with warm mixture. Bake 6 to 8 minutes at 350 degrees. Serve warm or keep fresh in an airtight container. Yields 4 quarts.

Index

Index

Index

Index

Index

Index

Index

Index

Index

Index

Index

Index

Index

Index

Index

Index

Index

Index

Index

Index

Index

Index

We would like to thank our members and friends who contributed their recipes to **Putting On The Grits**, including:

Sara Rebecca Airheart
Patricia Anne Albertson
Pam Holloman Allison
Sally Harper Ames
Sara Mazyck Anderson
Susan Ellenblast Anderson
Nina Nelson Andrews
Katherine Simons Armato
Peggy Herndon Ashley
Susie Haltiwanger Ashley
Katherine Thorne Austin
Char Wogens Backman
Mary Simpson Bailey
Elizabeth Owings Ball
Tommy Pizzuti Barkley
Jane Thompson Barnes
Sallie Burgess Barnes
Lynn Smith Barron
Susan Robertson Barron
Ann Baughn
Ross Barham Beale
Virginia McLannahan Beale
Sherry Jinks Beck
Nora Kizer Bell
Gale Johnson Belser
Mary Rainey Belser
Susan McClanan Boatwright
Kevin Warwick Bockman
Donnell Miller Bouknight
Caroline Stroman Bowen
Mary Wells W. Bowers
Ethel Tobias Bowman
Cary Bryan Boyd
Patricia Williams Boykin
Mary Lorick Boyle
Ruth Hill Boyle
Gene Clarkson Brabham
Nan Berry Bracy
Varian Crews Brandon
Georgia Taylor Brenneke
Katherine Mullins Bristow
Julia Barnes Brooker
Bonnie Truesdale Bruner
Diane Clement Bruner
JoAnn Taylor Brunson
Jean Davis Bruton
Blanche Jines Bryan
Helen Sehorn Bryan
Beverley Cappleman Buchanan
Anne Brantley Clare Bull
Gail Lafaye Bunch
Jean Parks Bunch
Nancy Burch Bunch
Rebecca Ann Bunch
Donna Taylor Bundrick
Fran Hotinger Burnett
Nola Covington Burnette
Frances Wendt Burns
Martha Flemming Burton
Margaret Pope Cain
Mary Mac Hancock Cain
Elizabeth Dial Caldwell
Elizabeth Walz Campbell
Louisa Tobias Campbell

Marjorie Smith Campbell
Lucille Sligh Cantey
Nancy Townsend Carpenter
Christina Ann Carson
Helen Pride Craig Carson
Louise Campbell Carter
Margaret Kelley Carter
Sara Harmon Caughman
Sarah Exum Cauthen
Bebie Linn Chambers
Coleman McPherson Chambliss
Betsy Heath Champion
Mary Boyd Brown Chaplin
Nell Stevenson Chastain
Mary Emelyn Childs
Mary Ruffin Childs
Hattee Zeigler Christain
Carole Cooper Clark
Jane Bowen Clarke
Sarah Bull Clarkson
Anne Walker Cleveland
Anne Springs Close
Mildred Cody
Jan Benkwith Cohn
Sisi Sims Coker
Leita Trammell Coleman
Lucy McLain Coleman
Tinka Reich Coleman
Blair Blackwell Cooper
Norrie Nicholson Cooper
Cynthia Simmons Corley
Elizabeth Exum Courson
James P. Covington
Susan McClain Craig
Bonnie Boineau Crawford
Mopsy Weaver Crawford
Elizabeth Wyman Crews
Mary Lamoreaux Cribb
Cassandra Cox Crooks
Pinny Morgan Crouch
Margaret Rubel Cullum
Verd Craig Cunningham
Susan Breeden Cutler
Sophia Milling Dana
Angela McIntosh Daniel
Bea Johnson Daves
Mahalie Brown Davies
Jane Sheriff Davis
Susan Parker DePass
Fay Allen DesPortes
Margaret Thompson DesPortes
Susan Brabham DesPortes
Ginny Newell Dibble
Lolly Weston Dickson
Pat Johnson Dodson
Ann Record Dolin
Jane Ballenger Dorn
May Belser Douglass
Annette McManeus Dozier
Ellen Seastrunk Dozier
Robert Fenton Dozier
Anne Chamblin Draffin
Julia McLain DuRant
Nancy Fersner Dukes

Macky Dana Dunbar
Susan Maxwell Durst
Anna Corrie Edgerton
Molly Rembert Edmunds
Bettie Fort Edwards
Janie Dickerson Edwards
Helen Zeigler Ellerbe
Kathy Long Ellis
Winna Kerr Ellis
Barbara Brasington Ellison
Cis Kibler Ellison
Pat Gardner Ellison
Ellen Finley Emerson
Lucy Kiser Emerson
Margaret McFaddin England
Corky Erwin
Elise Mullins Evans
Elizabeth Russell Exum
Mary Boykin Exum
Harriet Gage Fairey
Marie Johnson Fairey
Jane Patterson Fancher
Ada Bryant Feagle
Barbara Wall Fensterle
Mary Fleming Willis Finlay
Christie Anderson Fisher
Elizabeth Bates Fisher
Elaine Finklea Folline
Jamie Forrester
Ann Haselden Foster
Ginger Archer Foster
Marshall Lipscomb Foster
Catherine Heyward Fouche'
Rebecca Talbert Fouche'
Al Jay Fowler
Isabel Singleton Fowler
Caroline Hodges Freeman
Patricia Slate Freeman
Mary Palmer Gaddy
John Thomas Gandy
Connor Hill Gantt
Cutie Smythe Gantt
Libby Lee Gantt
Elizabeth Thompson Gettys
Alison Aldridge Gibbes
Ethel Graeber Gibbes
Nancy Corson Gibbes
Sarah Davies Gibbes
Cornelia Danforth Gibbons
E. David Gibbons
Virginia Tompkins Gignilliat
Eleanor Anne Gillespie
Melinda Summers Gillespie
Ann Bailey Gilpin
Elizabeth Brooker Glazebrook
Louise Owens Glenn
Ginny Craver Good
Sarah Spencer Gramling
Susan McElveen Graybill
Lucille Noyce Green
Anne Johnston Gregg
Lee Mason Gregory
Judy West Grier
Anne Belser Grimball

Caroline Gordon Grimball
Mary Weston Grimball
Cain Calmes Haley
Anna Andrews Haltiwanger
Cheryl St. John Haltiwanger
Maxie McDuffie Haltiwanger
Sallie Bailey Haltiwanger
Katrina Pardue Hammond
Plum Josey Hammond
Sara Williamson Harmon
Roberta Munger Harris
Bettie Whitmire Hart
Georgia Herbert Hart
Milly McLaurin Hart
John Roland Harvin
Katharine Kinloch Harvin
Margaret Barnwell Harvin
Maria Grimball Harvin
Dale Wilson Hatchell
Anne Sullivan Haynie
Connie Walpole Haynie
Mary Ann Simmons Heath
Kelsey Bistline Heiner
Cary Allen Henderson
Lyn Howell Hensel
Ann Scott Herndon
Annabelle Carroll Heyward
Church Carroll Heyward
Cynthia Brown Heyward
Susan Burnett Heyward
Mona Harvey Hiatt
Edith Holler Hines
Lady Nicholson Hodges
Susan Graybill Hodges
Sallie King Hollis
Jan Greiner Holloway
Anne Searson Holmes
Happy Price Holmes
Lucille Overstreet Holmes
Melissa Farmer Holmes
Jane E. Honaker
Barbara Powell Honig
Laura Hooker
Laura Dixon Hooten
Alline Garrison Hope
Katherine May Hopkins
Laurie Boyle Hopkins
Elizabeth Morris Howell
Polly Tarwater Howser
Kappy McNulty Hubbard
Harriet Boatwright Huiet
Reba Sims Hull
Jean Milroy Humphrey
Opal Harmes Humphrey
Cecil Griggs Hunnicutt
Dee Hunter
Jill F. Huntley
Mackey Johnston Irick
Jeannie Mitchell Irvin
Caroline Dial Jenkins
Ann Richmond Jennings
Ann McCracken John
Frances Padgett John
Becky Woodrin Johnson

Bunny Hicklin Johnson
Dorothy C. Johnson
Beth Kincaid Johnston
Carol Blackman Johnston
Mary Elizabeth Jones
Robin Timmerman Josey
Ann McDonald Juk
Fain Ravenel Kapeluck
Mary Price Beckman Kapp
Lisa Crawford Kean
Marty Kennedy Keels
Adair Floyd Keenan
Suzanne Lear Keenan
Martha Chandler Kennedy
Anna Belle Heyward Kibler
Elizabeth Fristoe Kibler
Anne Morrisette Kight
Ellen Heath Kinard
Catherine Snyder King
Dacia Lewis King
Louise Gilland King
Frances Judy Kitchens
Rita Hughes Kittredge
Harriet Brunson Kneece
Sarah Easterling Kummer
Paula Speight LaMotte
Sue Rheutan Lacy
Peggy Kilgore Lafaye
Martha Wyant Laird
Patricia Dobson Lamar
Susalee Eggleston Lamb
Mary Lee Blakeney Lang
Alice Thomas Lashley
Lillian Bollin Lawrence
Martha Councill Leake
Salley McCrady Lesley
Ann Boykin Ligon
Mary Roberts Lindsey
Lucy Holmes Little
Marie Hart Little
Sally Kite Lowery
Alice Brown Lucas
Carol Yandle Lumpkin
Caroline Dalton Lumpkin
Betsy Macdonald
Cindy Dalton Macdonald
Sarah Payne Maddox
Boo Major
Madge Graydon Major
Janet Lawrence Mani
Bottsie Holliday Manning
Chappy McLain Manning
Caroline Melton Marchant
Elizabeth Gilmore Marchant
Lisa-Anne Grime Marley
Joy Koester Marshall
Sally Watkins Marshall
Jill Clark Martin
Nancy Chisolm Martin
Sophie Ellison Martin
Leck Paschal Mason
Mary Louise Gaillard Mason
Melanie Logan Mauldin
Ann Skipper McAden

Mary Lide McArthur
Pamela Margaret McCain
Ashley Clemmons McCall
Patricia Bultman McCallum
Beverly McClure
Rody Doane McClure
Judy Watson McCoy
Suzanne Heath McCoy
Jo Ann McCracken
Jean Flinn McCrady
Becky Bynum McCutchen
Elise Scoville McCutchen
Grace Perry McCutchen
Jane Perry McCutchen
Beverly Walker McDonald
Sylvia Buck McDonald
Pamela Benson McDowell
Barbara Watson McElveen
Harriet Felder McElveen
Harriet Felder McElveen
Julie Johnson McGowan
Lilly Brannen McGregor
Pat McLaughlin McKay
Sandra Stephens McLain
Robin Boyle McLeod
Yancy Alford McLeod
Fenton Brown McManeus
Beth Laffitte McMaster
John Gregg McMaster
Judy Cooke McMaster
Sally Anne McMaster
Jessie Coleman McPherson
Sally Bates McWilliams
Susan Pedrick McWilliams
Edith Blackard Meadows
Toby Seabrook Meetze
Susan Milliken Merry
Virginia Gurley Meynard
Deborah Haston Mickler
Caroline Hammond Miley
Kathryn F. Miller
Retta Sanders Miller
Ronald E. Miller
Anne Walker Milliken
Helen Nicholson Milliken
Margaret Starr Milroy
Marianne Cole Miot
Cabell C. Mitchell
Jane McLaurin Mood
Rosemary Cooper Moody
Elizabeth Darby Moore
Julia Seabrook Moore
Patricia Craig Moore
Totsie Smith Moore
Ann Sharp Moorman
Mary Bacon Morawetz
Corine Lafaye Morgan
Betsy Wall Morris
Kay Lind Morris
Elizabeth Wherry Moss
Jane Watkins Mudd
Malinda Waites Murchison
Betty Crayton Murdaugh
Helen Whaley Murdaugh

Rebecca Adams Murphy
Sarah Sturdevant Murphy
Margaret Osborne Myers
Patricia Pearce Myers
LeGrand Moorer Nelson
Christy Johnston Nexsen
Norris Wright Nicholson
Amy Brewer Norris
Mackey Sadler Norris
Robin Harmon O'Neil
Julia Keenan Oliphant
Sharron Brown Osborne
Nancy Crowther Otis
Rachel Rowell Otis
Rhoda Jones Paschal
Joyce Baker Patterson
Martha Louis Patterson
Katherine A. Patton
Lynn McLeod Pavey
Alice Barron Pearce
Johnnie Chapman Pearce
Carroll Rooney Peters
Judy Stewart Pitts
Grace Zimmerman Plowden
Eleanor Cain Pope
Margaret Christian Pope
Alice Dillard Potter
Linda Kimble Powell
Elizabeth Duncan Powers
Peggy Rorison Powers
Lindsay Burnside Pressley
Jane Eleazer Prevost
Lynn Bugg Pritchard
Eleanor Craig Pulliam
Sally Means Quantz
Barbara Pearson Ransford
Mary Dana Reading
Nancy Davis Reagan
Virginia McGee Reynolds
Carol Cheever Ridenhour
Fred L. Ridenhour
Ann Yarborough Riley
Ester Jane Rinehart
Susan Gibbes Robinson
Elizabeth Jenkins Roddey
Freddie Strickland Rodgers
Mary Dickerson Rodgers
Kay Hunnicutt Roman
Nora DuVal Roman
Charles B. Roman
Nancy Robinson Ruff
Mary Ellen Rheutan Rush

Ray Wannamaker Sabalis
Catherine McFarland Sadler
Ken Salley
Minerva Wylie Sanner
Gail Fowler Sapp
Ursula's Cooking School
Nancy Okerson Schulhoff
Bette DuRant Seastrunk
Elizabeth Parrott Seastrunk
Eloise DuBose Seegars
Isabel Dillon Sherrill
Sabie Moorer Simmons
Anne Burriss Sims
Anne Taylor Sims
Amelia Wilson Smith
Anne Allston Smith
Dorothy Brown Smith
Jane Bruce Smith
Johnie Bolt Smith
Mardi Graham Smith
Mary Adams Smith
Nina Nelson Smith
Sallie Clark Smith
Mary Gregg Chisolm Smythe
Troy McLaughlin Snyder
Elizabeth Hardy Spence
Charlotte Moore Sponar
Louise Brunson Spong
Elsie Taylor Stanley
Ernest Howard Stanley
Beverly Johnston Stidham
Margaret Bennett Stover
Mary Phelan Strasburger
Margaret Charles Stubbs
Kay Catheral Stursberg
Anne Macdonald Sumwalt
Joyce Mills Sumwalt
Barbara Bundy Sweet
Raven Graydon Tarpley
Gina Johnson Taylor
Grace Rauton Taylor
Alix Robinson Tew
Nancy Dana Theus
Harriet Ferguson Thogersen
Ann Marshall Thornton
Nancy Moore Thurmond
Janet Russell Timmerman
Jill Wieland Tobias
Elizabeth Clarke Todd
Jennifer Johnson Todd
Susan Chandler Todd
Marion King Tompkins

Sally Pride Tompkins
Christina Rood Traylor
Margaret Thomas Trotter
Carolyn Shuford Tupper
Philip Urso
Amelia Watson Usry
Sharon Singletary Vanzant
Eileen McGuire Vaughan
Ann Thomas Waites
Bryan Lawrence Walker
Claudia Moore Walker
Elizabeth Cranford Walker
Joann Cason Walker
Tracie Owens Walker
Virginia Cleveland Walker
Jeanne Frost Wardlaw
Martha Moore Warner
Linda Hild Warren
Suzanne Bruce Warthen
Beth Gayden Watkins
Margaret Talbert Watson
Carey Judy Weathers
Harry Dallon Weathers '
Margaret Woodliff Webb
Suzanne Bech Webster
Mary Prioleau Wesley
Anne Thornhill Weston
Barbara Badcock Weston
Polly Hanckel Weston
Sandra Loyd Weston
Katherine Asbill Whatley
Carolyn Gibbes White
Elizabeth A. White
Marilyn C. White
Kelly Miller Whitmer
Eliza Maass Wilkins
Elizabeth McCutchen Williams
Elizabeth Middleton Williams
Emma Howell Williams
Laura Manning Williams
Mason Keith Williams
Nancy Kerr Williams
Sharon Childers Williams
Dorothy Reber Williamson
Elisabeth Mays Williamson
Beth Johnson Wilson
Charles A. Wilson
Loula McGlasson Wilson
Mary Dale Wilson
Mary Rudisill Wingfield
Elizabeth D. Wooten
Anne Ayers Yarbrough

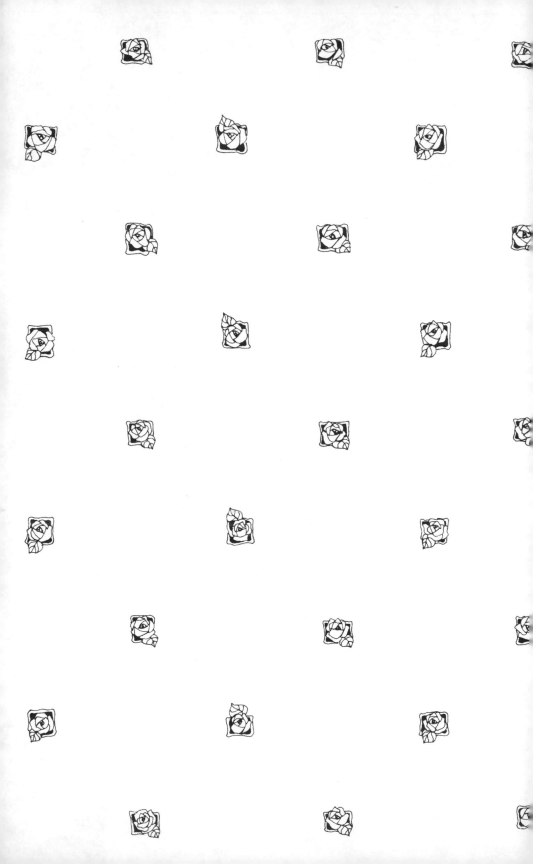

JLC COOKBOOK
3612 Landmark Drive, Suite A
Columbia, South Carolina 29204

Please send me ___ copies of **PUTTING ON THE GRITS** @ $13.95 each $ _____

add postage and handling @ $2.75 each $ _____

Total $ _____

Name _____
PLEASE PRINT

Address _____

City _____ State _____ Zip _____

Please make checks payable to JLC Cookbook. Proceeds will benefit the community through the Junior League of Columbia, Inc.

JLC COOKBOOK
3612 Landmark Drive, Suite A
Columbia, South Carolina 29204

Please send me ___ copies of **PUTTING ON THE GRITS** @ $13.95 each $ _____

add postage and handling @ $2.75 each $ _____

Total $ _____

Name _____
PLEASE PRINT

Address _____

City _____ State _____ Zip _____

Please make checks payable to JLC Cookbook. Proceeds will benefit the community through the Junior League of Columbia, Inc.

JLC COOKBOOK
3612 Landmark Drive, Suite A
Columbia, South Carolina 29204

Please send me ___ copies of **PUTTING ON THE GRITS** @ $13.95 each $ _____

add postage and handling @ $2.75 each $ _____

Total $ _____

Name _____
PLEASE PRINT

Address _____

City _____ State _____ Zip _____

Please make checks payable to JLC Cookbook. Proceeds will benefit the community through the Junior League of Columbia, Inc.

Please list book stores or gift shops in your area that you would like to handle this book.

_____

_____

_____

_____

_____

_____

_____

- -

Please list book stores or gift shops in your area that you would like to handle this book.

_____

_____

_____

_____

_____

_____

_____

- -

Please list book stores or gift shops in your area that you would like to handle this book.

_____

_____

_____

_____

_____

_____